Paolo Segneri, James Ford

The Quaresimale of Paolo Segneri

Translated from the original Italian

Paolo Segneri, James Ford

The Quaresimale of Paolo Segneri
Translated from the original Italian

ISBN/EAN: 9783741189265

Manufactured in Europe, USA, Canada, Australia, Japa

Cover: Foto ©Lupo / pixelio.de

Manufactured and distributed by brebook publishing software (www.brebook.com)

Paolo Segneri, James Ford

The Quaresimale of Paolo Segneri

ivz
QUARESIMALE

OF

P. PAOLO SEGNERI

TRANSLATED FROM THE ORIGINAL ITALIAN

BY

JAMES FORD, A.M.,
Prebendary of Exeter Cathedral.

WITH A PREFACE RELATING TO THE AUTHOR.

FIRST SERIES.
Fourth Edition.

LONDON:
JOSEPH MASTERS, ALDERSGATE STREET,
AND NEW BOND STREET.
OXFORD: PARKER. CAMBRIDGE: MACMILLAN.
EXETER: CLIFFORD; W. ROBERTS. BATH: SIMMS.
MDCCCLXIX.

LONDON:
PRINTED BY JOSEPH MASTERS AND SON,
ALDERSGATE STREET.

TRANSLATOR'S PREFACE.

WHEN a foreign Author has for the first time to be introduced to the public by means of a translation, some unusual length of preface may be allowed. But is it not strange, that Paolo Segneri, the reputed founder of Italian eloquence in the seventeenth century, should require any introduction to us at all? To the great poets and historians of Italy we have not failed to award all the praise, to which they are so justly entitled. Her theologians we seem in the meantime to have passed by. This neglect might be ascribed to some Protestant distrust and jealousy on our part, did not the fact of our having so highly appreciated many Roman Catholic writers of the Gallican Church at once check the supposition. We are happily familiar with Massillon, Pascal, and Bossuet: from whence therefore is it, that we know little or nothing of Venini, Valsecchi, and Segneri? The distinguished grammarian Corticelli, in the list of the authors, whom he quotes in his *Regole ed osservazioni della lingua Toscana*,[1] goes out of his way to affix an epithet to the name of Segneri. That epithet is *il famoso:* and yet, it appears, his great fame has not reached our shores. It may not therefore be amiss to pay off, at least by a small first instalment, some of the arrears we owe to Italian Theology; even though, in doing this, we should be carried beyond the nearer and safer shores of the Gallican Church to the immediate vicinity of Rome itself, the last scene of our Author's ministry.

[1] Bassano, 1802. Dall' ottava edizione Veneta.

No danger truly need be apprehended from such an approximation, so far as these Sermons are concerned: for not only are they free, beyond what might have been expected, from any statements of doctrine, against which we must decidedly *protest*, and which would therefore "gender strife;" but in their very subject—that of Repentance—and in the very time, when they were preached—the season of Lent—we have some security that matters of "doubtful disputation" are here excluded, and the chief stress laid on those duties of an amended life, in the importance and necessity of which we are all of us, it is hoped, still cordially agreed. *Sono questi un tal genere di volumi, che non contengono altro, fuor che rimproveri, reprensioni, minacce.* Such is the Author's own account of the *Quaresimale* in his dedication of it to Cosmo the third, Grand Duke of Tuscany. And who among us does not admit that "reproofs, rebukes, and threatenings" are a necessary part of God's message to sinful men? Yea, who among us does not feel them to be a necessary message from Heaven to his own soul?

Paolo Segneri was born in the year 1624 at Nettuno, a maritime town in the *Campagna di Roma*, of pious parents, and of a good family. He was placed, when young, in the College of "the Society of Jesus" at Rome, where young men of the first families in Italy were wont to receive a general and a religious education. Here he first displayed his remarkable powers of mind and application, and profited above his equals, and above, in many other respects, his superiors. It was then that his parents, encouraged by the marked success attending his studies and the promise he gave of future distinction, wished him much to get himself a name by engaging in some secular profession. But the young Segneri looked far beyond all this world could offer: he aspired to the Ministry of saving souls, and was anxious to devote himself to the most laborious and self-denying, and, in the world's eye, the least honoured part of it, that of a simple Missionary. His particular wish and the highest object of his holy ambition was to follow the steps of Xavier and other great preachers into the Indies: but in this his Ecclesiastical superiors thwarted him: no doubt from a desire to reserve so great ministerial gifts for the benefit of his own countrymen. So bitter was his disappointment on this occasion, that he once expressed a hope that he might some day, in one of his sea-missions along the coast, fall into the hands of pirates, and by them be carried into distant lands, where he might evangelize and convert the heathen, and even die, GOD's will being so, in his dear Master's cause. Nor, in this preference of a work among strangers and foreigners, has he been entirely frustrated: for, although his personal Ministry was confined to his native land, yet by his excellent writings and exhortations, translated, as they have been, into other tongues, his "sound is gone out" into many other lands; and we trust has now at length reached our own, if not for our conversion, yet for our "instruction in righteousness."

In 1640 Segneri completed his Noviciate among the Jesuits; and having passed through the introductory stages in the Ministry, according to the usages of his Church, he was in 1653 ordained Priest. It was not, however, till the year 1655 that he entered upon his career, destined to be so brilliant before Angels and men, as a Home Missionary to the Italians; in which he afterwards laboured uninterruptedly for no less a period than twenty-seven years. During all this time, he seems to have acted on a regular plan. One half of each year he devoted to the laborious task of traversing on foot the principal parts of Italy, preaching in its cities, towns, and villages; the remaining half he gave to the more tranquil and meditative life of the recluse, chiefly in the College of his Order at Florence, where in 1679 he published this *Quaresimale* or Lent Sermons, forty in number, containing, as he tells us, the substance of his oral discourses. From this judicious distribution of his time and wise employment of his talents he was in the year 1692 called away by Pope Innocent XII., who, in testimony to his worth and to his eminent success, as a preacher, raised him to the same holy office in the Apostolic College at Rome, where the principal Dignitaries of the Church are wont to attend. This very distinguished position he held only two years; death translating him in 1694 both to his rest and to his reward.

It is recorded that he accepted this preferment with great

reluctance, and that afterwards, when he was thus set on "a pinnacle of the temple," he would often sigh for a return to his former simple Missionary life, and to his calm studious retirement: no small proof of his blessed humility and of the saintly devotedness of his heart to GOD. For his sudden rise in the Church was attended with no change for the worse in the character of his Ministry. His godly zeal was not relaxed by the warm sunshine of courtly distinction and favour. He was the same man of GOD and the same preacher of the truth in the high places of the Vatican, as he had been in the lowly vales of the Apennine. The very text of the first of his printed sermons, preached before the Cardinals and Bishops, if not before the very Pope himself, seems to bear some witness to this—"*Then gathered the chief Priests and the Pharisees a council,*" &c., S. John xi. 47. In this remarkable sermon he insists upon the loftiness and the purity of those motives, which should direct the counsels of Ecclesiastical Rulers. His voice gives no smooth, not yet "uncertain sound," when speaking of the sins, which so easily beset any rich powerful Hierarchy, whether at Rome, or elsewhere. How true, how noble, how undaunted are his words!—*Signori miei, se il servizio di questa Santa Sede non sempre vien promosso da tutti, come si converrebbe, eccone la cagione principalissima: perchè dalle passioni private ci lasciamo tirare, chi quà, chi là; onde, se quei Cherubini, quali sono posti a guidare il cocchio della Gloria Divina, non sempre tutti tengono fissi gli occhi all' istesso termine, che è Dio solo, qual maraviglia, se il cocchio non vada innanzi, e se tal volta crolli, chini, si truovi poco men che a pericolo di cadere, o almeno d'interrompere i suoi trionfi?*

Though we are chiefly concerned with our Author in his public capacity of a religious teacher, one or two particulars, recorded[1] of his private life, may be mentioned with advantage. He was wont, as a special exercise of devotion, to "look unto JESUS" on each day of the week under one or other of His Mediatorial offices. On Monday, he contemplated Him, as a Judge; on Tuesday, as a King; on Wednesday, as a Physician; on Thursday, as a Husband; on Friday, as a Redeemer; on Saturday, as a Brother; on Sun-

---

[1] See his life by *P. Giuseppe Massei.* (Sect. li., vii., iv.)

day, as a Glorifier; while he viewed himself at the same time, in his several corresponding relations to the LORD, as being a sinner, or a subject, or a patient, as the case might be. Again, that he might have constantly before him his "vow in Heaven," he inscribed on the walls of his chamber these five letters, P R O P E: and nothing but the importunity of a confidential friend wrested from him the secret of this ingenious memento—" Povertà, Ritiramento, Orazione, Penitenza, Esame." Incidents, such as these, combine with others, that might be adduced, in showing with what propriety his friend and patron Cardinal Palavicini, the celebrated historian of the Council of Trent, turned the name of *Paulus Segnerus* into this beautiful anagram—" *Purus Angelus es.*"

His published Theological works are comprised in four goodly quarto volumes. They have passed, either in their complete form or in separate portions, through many editions;[1] those, which proceeded from the Baglioni press at Venice in such rapid succession to each other from A.D. 1701—1775, being probably the best. They have also been translated, in whole or in part, into many foreign languages; not only into Latin, German, French, and Spanish, as might have been expected, but into Turkish, Arabic, and Illyrian; a fact, which attests their value and the wide-spread fame of their Author. A considerable body of Divinity might indeed be extracted from them. The truth of Christianity is proved in the *Incredulo senza scusa:* the sinner is called to repentance in the *Quaresimale:* the believer is taught to pray and to meditate daily on a given text of Scripture in the *Manna dell' anima:* the LAW of CHRIST is explained to him in the *Cristiano istruito:* and then by means of the *Parroco istruito* the Minister of GOD, set over him "in the LORD," is fitted to render him the best spiritual service. The peculiarities of the Author's creed are indeed to be met with in all these writings, so as to demand caution in the reader; but their general purport is highly instructive and edifying.

[1] For a complete list of these Editions, see the learned work of the De Backers, now in course of publication, in series, at Liege, and entitled *Bibliothèque des écrivains de la compagnie de Jésus, &c.*

a 2

TRANSLATOR'S PREFACE.

Once only does Segneri appear before us, as a Controversialist. The mystic theories of the Quietists were troubling many minds at that time; and he was applied to by a perplexed friend for his opinion. He published four tracts on this disputed subject: they contain a clear exposure of the errors in question, accompanied, however, with a fair and judicious arbitration between the conflicting claims of active and passive devotion, in other words, of Meditation and Contemplation; its proper place and importance being assigned to each, as a means of grace, in the guidance of souls and in the exercise of communion with GOD. We know not what influence these controversial tracts of Segneri might have had in producing the Papal brief of 1699, which condemned the *Explication des maximes des Saints sur la vie intérieure*. Certainly Innocent XII., the author of that brief, must have been well acquainted with his writings, as he certainly was with his preaching.

There were other devotional and pastoral treatises, the fruits of his unwearied zeal; but his *Quaresimale*, his *Manna dell' anima* and his *Cristiano istruito*, are particularly to be observed, on account of the pure and beautiful Italian, in which they are written. The famous standard dictionary *della Crusca*, the work of an Academy, expressly established for the refining and perfecting of that language, frequently refers for its authorities to these writings; which indeed rank high among the literary productions of that most classical land. Still, it was in his character of *Missionarius et Concionator*, that he reached the noblest distinction; one, which the wisest and the best judges in the matter have not hesitated to award to him.[1] Professor Meneghelli styles him "the

---

[1] *La fama non si arrestò nel magnificare il suo merito; e le medaglie ne eternarono il nome: ma il più saldo bronzo sta nel onorevole iscrizione dettata dal vero, non tocca dal tempo—Il Segneri Ristauratore della eloquenza Italiana.* Meneghelli (Elogio di P. Segneri.)

E del Segneri chi più squisitamente ti ammaestra? Chi più caldo ti move? Chi più abbondante, concitato, magnifico? Purgalo di poche metaphore ardite, quanto concedevalo, o più tosto chiedevolo, l'età sua, e poi vedi in tutte l'altre parti il solo Oratore degno di parlare ad uomini Italiani, agli eredi, cioè, di quel popolo, a cui parlò Marco Tullio. Conte Giulio Perticari. (Degli Scrittori del Trecento e de' loro imitatori. Ch. xiv.)

Mi stancherei a numerare le virtù del Cicerone moderno, dico, del Segneri; le cui vestigie pajono oggi abbandonate da tutti onde seguire i Francesi, che non

Restorer of Italian eloquence;" Perticari speaks of him, as being "the modern Cicero," the only orator (alluding to the preference then generally shown to the French divines) fit to address the descendants of a people, who had listened to the eloquence of Marcus Tullius. Praise so exalted seems to place Segneri on a pedestal by himself, such as he alone was capable of occupying at the critical period of the fortunes of Italian literature, when he lived. The glory, which the first revival of letters in the fourteenth century had shed upon his country, had suffered a temporary eclipse in the century, that immediately followed: but then it was destined to shine forth again in the sixteenth and seventeenth centuries, which were times of a second literary revival in the many learned and excellent writers they produced. These were the *autori moderni ed approvati*, in distinction from their glorious predecessors, the *autori del buon secolo* (the fourteenth,) with whom they shared the proud honour of being the restorers and refiners of the Tuscan idiom; and among them, as regards Theology, Segneri stood conspicuous among his brethren.[1]

But, rightly to estimate his high claims, as a pulpit Reformer, we must consider what was the ordinary character of the sermons preached at the time, when he engaged in his preparatory studies for the Ministry. It bare upon it the degenerate mark of the learning and literature of the day. It is described by a competent judge, as strongly savouring *del capriccio o della barbarie, del falso o del gigantesco, del bizarro o del ridicolo*.[2] It was a reproach to the Truth of GOD, being either narrowed into the subtleties of the Schoolmen;[3] or inflated with specu-

potranno insegnare eloquenza agl' Italiani giammai. Perticari. (Della necessità d'instituire in Roma una cathedra di letteratura Classica Italiana. S. xvi.)

[1] Fabroni tells us that Segneri assisted in the *Vocabolario degli Academici della Crusca*, edited in his day, and particularly mentions his contributions under the letter E. *Fabronius* (Vitæ Italorum, &c., Vol. XV.)

[2] Elogio di P. Segneri, dall' abate Ant. Meneghelli, P. O. nella I. R. Università di Padova.

[3] The famous Cardinal Bembo gives us his opinion of the character of preaching in Italy in the 16th century. He once defended his absence during Lent from Sermon (in that country, be it remembered, a separate Service) in these words: "*Che vi debbo io fare? Perciochè mai altro non si ode, che garrire il Dottor Sottile contro il Dottor Angelico; e poi venirsene Aristotole per terzo a terminare la quistione proposta.*" *Ortensio Landi* (Paradossi, Lib. ii. Pa-

lations and fabulous legends; or gaudily decorated after a
heathen fashion (as our Author himself tells us in his preface
to the *Quaresimale;*) or stuffed with an ill-assorted farrago,
to which arts and sciences, astrology, anatomy, and even
alchemy, were made to contribute. The preachers, many of
them knowing better, adapted their style to the perverted
popular taste, seeking their own glory; while their sermons were not only defective in plain Scriptural statements
of the Truth, but they failed in that close appeal to men's
understandings, hearts, and lives, which is far the most eloquent, as it is the only effective, preaching. Not that there
had not been from time to time in Italy able and eminent
divines, whose light shone the brighter from the surrounding
darkness. There was Fra Giordano di Rivalta in the 14th
century; Bernardino da Sienna, Altavanti, Barletta, and Savonarola in the 15th; Ochino, Badoardo, Panigarola, Mazza-
rini, and Fiamma in the 16th. But these and other like men,
however useful in their several generations, seem never by
their united influence to have given a definite, consistent, and
much less Scriptural character to the national pulpit: so that,
when our reformer girded himself to the work, there were no
approved models for his imitation. He saw many beacons to
warn him against error; but he found few, if any, to show him
a "more excellent way." He had recourse, therefore, to the
best precedents and models of antiquity. For the formation
of a correct style he applied himself to the study of the old
classics, and particularly to the orations of Cicero, some of
which he translated into Italian. He chose S. Chrysostom
for his guide among the Fathers of the Church. He calls
him (Pred. xxv. s. 5,) "his eloquent master," to whom he
was under the greatest obligations. *Non voglio io la gloria
per me di si bel pensiero: la cedo a quello, al quale io debbo, sopra
d'ogni altro de' Padri, tutto quel poco, ch' io vaglio nel predicare, se
nulla vaglio: la cedo a San Giovanni Crisostomo,* (Pred. xxiv. s. 2.)
One may indeed occasionally trace in these sermons the acute
mind, and even the forensic manner, of that Master in Israel.
Among the School divines, Thomas Aquinas, "the greatest

rad. 29.) For a specimen of hyperboles, used in their preaching, see *Maffei; Storia della Letteratura Italiana* (Lib. iv. c. 6.)

of them,"[1] was his special favourite. And then, with a view to perfect himself in the knowledge and command of his native language, he fixed on Boccaccio for his pattern. In following him, however, he was anything but a mere copyist. He retained all his nice exactness and idiomatic power of expression, but free from his long words, long sentences, and rather pompous monotony of style. He invariably adopted the *conciossiache* in marked preference to the *conciossiacosache*, its unwieldy precursor; and introduced a greater variety and conciseness, and far more natural easy flow into the construction of his periods, adapting his style to the thought, which he wished to express. Though a reformer, he was not overfond of his own notions; nor did he introduce a single innovation without adequate cause. He disclaims everything of the kind. *Quanto alla lingua, ho riputato certamente mio debito il sottopormi con rigoro non piccolo a quelle leggi, che sono in esse le reverite generalmente e le rette, per non violarla, qual Italiano ingiurioso. Contuttociò chi non vede, che, salvo il mio intendimento, io non ho potuto, nell' abbigliarla di voci splendide e scelte, servire al lusso, proporzionato più a prediche da barriera, che da battaglia, ma servire al solo decoro, con amare a ciò quelle voci, che godano in uno il credito di sincere in quella città, che fatica tanto per coglierne ad uso publico il più bel fiore, e che nelle altre non abbian uopo di chi le divolgarizzi.* So far was he from needlessly departing from conventional modes of speech, that he is thought to have retained some things, of which his judgment disapproved, solely in deference to established opinion, and to avoid giving offence. To this we may probably trace the tone of exaggeration, and some overcolouring for effect in the narrations of facts, with a few offences against good taste, which occasionally appear in his *Quaresimale*. At a later period of his Ministry he learnt to correct himself, more or less, in these particulars.[2]

[1] Hooker, Eccl. Pol. iii. § 9.
[2] *E vero che qualche avanzo dell' infelice gusto del secolo vedesi in P. Segneri; e forse egli non ardì di fare una intera riforma dell' eloquenza, temendo che non si potesse ciò eseguire tutt' a un colpo, e che convenisse dar qualche cosa all' universale entusiasmo, cogliendo la briglia per non perdersi dietro alla metafora ed ai controposti. ...... lettera del Card. Nori, scritta al Magliabecchi da Pisa nel 16.. mentre era in ..... Università Pr......, e vi predicava il P.*

But his wisdom was chiefly shown in that particular, which of all others is most requisite to the success of the Christian Ministry. It was shown in the choice of his subject, and in his method of treating it. *Mi son proposto ogni volta una verità, non solamente Cristiana, ma pratica, e di provarla davvero.* In laying down this rule, always to select a Christian truth, a practical Christian truth, and to demonstrate it on solid rational grounds, so as really to bring it home to men's convictions, he struck a decisive blow at the most prevailing and the most dangerous abuses of the pulpit. He gave, moreover, a proof that what he sought in his Ministry was not the praise of men, but the praise of GOD; not the display of his own ingenuity, but the manifestation of the Truth; not the passing gratification of his hearers, but their chiefest Eternal good. And well indeed has he redeemed his pledge in the Sermons before us. His text, it is true, as is generally the case with Italian sermons, is rather a motto, than a source of exposition; but the subject is invariably one of great practical importance in the faith of CHRIST; it is kept constantly in view throughout the discourse; and, while the inspired Scriptures occupy the front ground, their holy lessons are illustrated and enforced in many varied ways; the Fathers, Church History, Christian biography, the passing events of the day, Pagan antiquity, and the phenomena of the natural world, all contributing their several shares to this particular purpose. By thus bringing forth out of the treasures of his well-stored mind "things new and old," he keeps up the interest of the sermon. The hearer's attention is not allowed to flag: it is rather led onwards step by step to an increasing conviction of the truth under consideration, each new argument, not weakening (as it sometimes happens) what has preceded, but adding to the force and momentum of the whole.[1] And all this

---

Segneri, si raccoglie che questi ne' primi anni erasi mostrato anche più indulgente a visi del suo tempo, e che poi erasene egli stesso emendato. Tiraboschi. (Storia &c., Modena, 1787, Tomo viii. Lib. iii. c. v. § xi.)

[1] This is well expressed in the short life of Segneri, prefixed to the Como edition of 1828. *Nel primo accignersi alla tessitura delle sue orazioni intendea studiosamente a porsi in pieno possesso del suo soggetto, a misurarne col pensier la estensione, a calcolarne i vantaggi, a digradarne i sentimenti e le idee, e per ultimo a disporne gli argomenti per modo, che crescendo di mano in mano ed af-*

versatility in the handling of his subject well accords with sermons for *Lent*, designed to be so many " calls to the unconverted," in which every allowable method must be used by the preacher, so as to gain and fix the attention of the careless and worldly-distracted, if "by any means" he may "save some." In Segneri's untiring zeal and importunity, his colloquial hand-to-hand combats with the mistakes, the prejudices, the excuses, the contradictions of sinful men, and, above all, in his loving way of speaking the Truth,[1] we trace the character of a man, who is taught of GOD to win souls to CHRIST. We are reminded of the peculiar gifts in this respect of our Baxter, Horneck, and Skelton; we are led even to a far higher contemplation, that of the great Apostle, who "*with many other words* did *testify* and *exhort*, saying, Save yourselves from this untoward generation." (Acts ii. 40.)

And truly, that seventeenth century, with the sins of which Segneri had to grapple, was an "untoward generation." It is quite painful to dwell on the licentiousness of public morals in Italy at this period, as they here lie exposed to our view in the unsparing denunciations of this great preacher of Repentance. The picture, which almost every sermon places before us, of wide-spread national depravity, growing up by the side of high intellectual culture and singular refinement in the arts and sciences, is really appalling. Such advanced civilization, as it is called, is seen to be quite compatible (never may it be so seen among ourselves!) with the debasement of political and social principles, and with a life, nothing short of practical infidelity.

At a later period in the same century, *le père Bourdaloue* arose to correct the faults and abuses of the pulpit in the Church of France, which were like in kind, though not in extent, to those prevailing in the Church of Rome. He also had to contend against the bad taste, as well as the bad

forzandosi vicendevolmente incalzassero sempre più l'uditore; così che in fine non vedesse nè verso nè via di svincolarsi da quella irresistibile convinzione, in cui trovavasi annodato. Abbellì poi la sostanza e la solidità delle ragioni con una imaginazione feconda e vivissima nelle descrizioni e ne' racconti, i quali tuttora stampano un orma profonda nell' animo di chi li legge.

[1] Witness his most endearing and untranslateable expression, *Amatissimi peccatori, Dilettissimi peccatori*. (Serm. i. § 2, 6.)

habits of the age. A considerable resemblance has been traced between their respective styles. Though he may be Segneri's equal in powers of argumentation and in command of the Scriptures and of the Fathers, yet he seems to fall short of him in that fertile invention, charming naturalness, and warm glowing animation, which are the happy national characteristics of the Italian. Both deserve the high praise of having sought to convince the understanding of their hearers by the solid deductions of reason, and of having restored to the degraded ordinance of preaching its proper aim and Divine efficacy. Both " by manifestation of *the Truth*" commended themselves " to every man's *conscience* in the *sight of God.*" (2 Cor. iv. 2.)

Having said thus much of his Author,—not more, it is hoped, than was necessary, as we premised, to the first introduction of a stranger—the translator must now say a few words on his own performance. While writing the above eulogy, he has felt, that, the more he advanced in Segneri's favour, the more he risked the success of his own translation, should it fail in satisfying the justly raised expectations of the reader. He hopes that many will have recourse to the Italian text; and that others, who are not able to drink at the fountain-head, will kindly *stoop down* to the waters, here drawn off, not expecting to find in them all the purity and medicinal strength of the parent spring. For, when was a translation ever known to give the complete vigour and soul of the original? He has laboured and done his best,

"If answerable style I can obtain."

Still, in distrust of his undertaking, or, to say the least, as a matter of prudence, he thinks it best at first to publish *Twelve Sermons* only of this *Quaresimale*, leaving it to his readers to decide for him by their verdict, whether he is to proceed with the remainder.

It may be right, in conclusion, to notice, that in a few places he has condensed the matter, and that he has omitted all passages of a decided Roman Catholic, as well as others of a questionable character, after the most serious and candid consideration on his part given to each. These omissions are noted, where they occur. In the quotations from Holy Scripture, he has substituted our Authorized Version for the Vulgate; excepting where the retention of the very words of the Vulgate was rendered necessary by the argument, or the accompanying remarks, of the preacher. The references to authorities are not given, as they encumber the page, and do not seem required in a work of this practical character. Each sermon has its Italian division into sections (a wise and convenient arrangement;) but the sections have in some places been subdivided into paragraphs.

These alterations, it is hoped, will be, more or less, for the advantage of the English reader, whose edification the translator has felt himself chiefly bound to consult: and he trusts that he has succeeded in this, without doing any wrong to the good Padre, whose kind allowance—(it may be, approval)—he would not quite despair of obtaining, if the souls departed be at all conscious of the treatment we bestow on their works, which they left behind them. For, as Dean Stanhope wisely observes, in the Preface to his translation of "The Christian Directory" of Parsons, (a writer of the same Church and of the same religious Order, as Segneri,) "We are mightily mis-
"taken, if we imagine that the points, for which men of dif-
"ferent opinions contend so eagerly here below, are of that
"concern to the Blessed above, which they seem to us. In
"those happy regions, where perfect peace and concord, holi-
"ness, and zeal for GOD's Glory reign, there is more joy at
"the conversion of one sinner, more praise for the pious
"labour of one little tract, which makes men good livers,
"than for the winning proselytes to this or that Communion
"(as distinct from the rest, that disagree with it in less sub-
"stantial niceties,) than for vast volumes of subtle disputants,
"which make for the interest of any of those factions, into
"which Christendom is so unfortunately divided."

CONTENTS.

SERMON I.
THE DANGER OF SIN FROM THE NEARNESS OF DEATH . **PAGE** 1

SERMON II.
GOD THE ONLY TRUE FRIEND 19

SERMON III.
A DISSUASIVE FROM TAKING REVENGE . . 38

SERMON IV.
HUNGER AFTER THE FOOD OF GOD'S WORD . 57

SERMON V.
THE SINNER PUT TO SHAME AT THE LAST DAY . 73

SERMON VI.
THE FEAR OF GOD FROM A SENSE OF HIS POWER . . 93

SERMON VII.
THE UNDERVALUATION OF THE SOUL 114

SERMON VIII.
A DISSUASIVE FROM THE FEAR OF MAN 131

CONTENTS.

SERMON X.[1]

The Soul's Journey to Heaven 151

SERMON XI.

Inability to Repent the Effect of Deferring Repentance . 172

SERMON XII.

On Shamelessness in Sinning 191

SERMON XIII.

The Curse Entailed on Ill-gotten Wealth . . 210

[1] Sermon IX. (being on Purgatory) is omitted.

SERMON I.

THE DANGER OF SIN FROM THE NEARNESS OF DEATH.

"REMEMBER, O MAN, THAT THOU ART DUST, AND THAT UNTO DUST THOU SHALT RETURN."—*Office of the Church.*

1. I COME before you, my respected hearers, to deliver a most mournful message. I must confess that I have undertaken this office with extreme reluctance, being sore grieved at having to distress you so much on this first morning of our becoming mutually acquainted with each other. The thought only of what I have to tell you strikes a cold chill at my heart through intense horror. And yet what good can come of my silence? or, what would concealment avail? I will at once declare my message. All here present, whether young or old, masters or servants, nobles or commoners, all of you must at last Die! *It is appointed unto all men once to die.* (Heb. ix. 27.) Alas! what do I behold? On hearing so tremendous an announcement, not one among you is moved: not one of you changes colour: not one of you looks altered. So far from it, I cannot but perceive that you are secretly inclined rather to regard me under a ludicrous aspect, as a person coming here to pass off, as something new, a story, that has been told you over and over again. And where is the man, you ask me, who at this time of day does not know that we must all die? *What man is he that liveth, and shall not see death?* (Ps. lxxxix. 47.) This is what we are continually hearing from so many pulpits: this is what we are

continually reading on so many tombs: this is what so many corpses, though silent, are continually sounding in our ears. In short, this is something we know already.—Do you know this? How is it possible you should? Why, tell me; are you not the very same persons, who only yesterday were running about the city in all the gaiety of your Carnival, some representing the lover, some the maniac, some the parasite? Are you not the same persons, who joined with such eagerness in the dance, who allowed yourselves in the excess of dissipation, who acted, like so many senseless heathens, in giving yourselves over to licentiousness? Was it you then, who were sitting with such evident delight at the theatres? Was it you, who were speaking so rapturously in the boxes? Answer me. I ask you, did you not pass this night, the night before Ash-Wednesday, in riotous self-indulgence and in all the common amusements of worldly life and society—would to heaven, that it may not have been even in pleasures, still less suited to your characters? And, while you behave in this manner, do you still pretend to know for a certainty that you must die? Oh, what blindness! Oh, what insensibility! Oh, what madness! Oh, what wickedness!... However, for the sake of argument, I will suppose that you do in some sense know this: I will even give you credit for freely confessing it. *Remember, O man, remember that thou art dust!* Here then I have the very thing I desire of you: for it will now be my business to prove how daring is the presumption of those, who, while they acknowledge this truth, live one single moment in deadly sin. . . .

2. Most men, when in any great danger, are more naturally inclined to show fear than courage. Thus you observe that in the ship of Jonah, that untractable prophet, one person alone was found, who slept soundly, while the thunder, the storm, and the tempest were raging around. The rest were all of them either shouting, or lamenting; or they were consulting and working hard together, how to escape the impending shipwreck. "For man," as I find it concluded by T. Aquinas, "is more disposed to that fear, by which he avoids evil, than he is to that boldness, with which he meets it." But this truth holds good only in regard to temporal

dangers, which are the ones less formidable and destructive; it does not apply to the concerns of Eternity, where the danger is so much more irremediable and appalling. In this latter case (who would believe it?) mortal man is usually self-confident: he not only does not fear it, he despises it; he not only does not avoid it, he rushes forward to meet it. What then, ye sinners, whom I most dearly love in the LORD, do you think of your condition? You well know that the dreadful sentence of everlasting condemnation was fulminated against you at that very instant of time, when in thought, or in word, or in deed, you sinned against GOD. Nothing whatever, in giving effect to this sentence, is further required. Those quenchless flames are even now blazing, which are doomed to be your couch for ever. *A fire is kindled in My anger,* so speaks the LORD, *which shall burn upon you.* (Jer. xv. 14.) Already are the torments prepared and the executioners in waiting. What then is wanting? Only the rupture of that slight and scanty thread, by which you hang suspended over the mouth of *the bottomless pit.* (Rev. ix. 2.) And, in spite of all this, you are free from any alarm. You can spend your evening in the pleasures of the table, or in frivolous conversation and company; and then calmly close your eyes to sleep. If this be not the height of rashness, pray, inform me, what is? I allow that your thread of life, as it now sustains you, may yet last for a time and retain its hold: but it may also prove weak and worn out. If so, and the probability on each side be equal, how can you possibly cling to that view of your position, which emboldens you to be confident at so great a peril, in preference to that, which warns you to fear at so great a profit?

3. But I have made a grievous mistake by saying that the probability was equal. What in all the world can certify you of the duration of your life for a single moment? Not the bezoar antidotes of the east, nor the pulverized pearls, nor the liquid potable gold, nor the sweet compound of gems; those appliances, which man's ambition has invented, so that not even death itself should be without its luxury. On the other hand, how many things may in an instant deprive you of your life! In ancient times people were wont to flatter

themselves with the belief that the Fates were only three in number. Seneca however did not so flatter himself: he declared they rather seemed to him to be innumerable. "There is nothing, that has not power to destroy human life." View the entire aggregate of all the creatures. They are, every one of them, it may be said, like so many Fates, with their weapons about them; that is, all are waiting and quite able to put us to death. Even were it not so, have we yet to learn that there is no necessity for us to seek death from any external cause? In our own selves we have quite enough for this purpose. Man, though he little thinks it, carries about within him the seeds of decay in his own constitution; just as iron generates its rust, and wood its worm, and cloth its moth. . . . But how, in a state of such fearful uncertainty, can you venture to live one single moment in deadly sin? Is this then the care you take of your souls? Is this the regard you pay to your latter end? Is this the anxiety you feel about your happiness—to know that you are compassed about with such formidable danger, and yet not to bestir yourselves?

Some persons are astonished at the conduct of Elijah, how, when persecuted by a powerful Queen, he could so calmly lie down to rest in an open field: *He lay and slept under a juniper tree.* (1 Kings xix. 5.) But this in no wise surprises me. Is it not quite agreed among us that Elijah was a holy man of GOD? He had then a right to take his rest. I am rather astonished to see a Saul asleep, a Holofernes asleep, a Sisera asleep, though they lay not in an open field, but under the security of a tent. And what will become of them, if captured in this state by their vigilant pursuers? Would to heaven, that we saw not their examples imitated daily by Christians! Multitudes retire to rest at night with the guilt of some deadly sin on their souls, yet utterly regardless of the many frightful dangers, which might at any time overtake them; whether from the rupture of a blood-vessel, or from suffocation in the throat, or from a stoppage of the heart, or from the simple bite of some venomous insect. And can these persons venture to close their eyes—say only for a single moment? Oh, monstrous insensibility! Oh, immeasurable folly! There are found in Africa certain extremely fierce animals, called oryxes, and resembling wild bulls: they possess such a degree of self-confidence as to sleep even within the nets of the huntsmen; nor do they make the least stir to escape, when the neighing of horses and the barking of dogs is sounding all around. Now is not their rashness something most surprising? But sinners seem to me to act just the same part. Why do I say, seem? It actually is so. *They lie at the head of all the streets, as a wild bull in a net; they are full of the fury of the Lord, of the rebuke of thy God.* (Isa. li. 20.) Could their state have been better described? They, who, laden with iniquity—*full of the fury of the Lord*—cleave habitually to their improper connections; they, who restore not that stolen property; they, who repair not that injured reputation; they, who hide that secret malice in their hearts, know full well that, in consequence of these sins, they lie caught in the innermost snares of hell. And yet how do they behave there? Do they forsooth make one single vigorous effort at once to escape? "They sleep as the oryx in a net." Oh, what a dreadful thing! "They sleep as the oryx in a net." And is it possible that they can have ever sunk into such profound self-security? What is your assurance, ye wretched men, that a general hue and cry of all the creatures may not even now be proclaimed against you? that the horses may not be loosened and the dogs let free against your souls? And all this while, are you lying fast asleep? sleeping wholly unconcerned in any place, *at the head of all the streets?* Are you asleep (can worse be said of you?) like Samson, even in the harlot's bosom? *They lie upon beds of ivory and stretch themselves upon their couches.* (Amos vi. 4.)

4. And here, my brethren, you ought to consider that, if not one among us can assure himself of a single moment (with such jealous care has God, among His other prerogatives, reserved to Himself His command over time,) least of all can that man do so, who is living in sin. Sin has brought death into the world. This we all know. *Death came by sin;* (Rom. v. 12;) and because of this, sin has always possessed a most tremendous power to accelerate the approach of death, and to bring it about, long before it otherwise would have

come. Very numerous are the passages in Scripture, which confirm this truth. *Be not wicked over much* (Eccl. vii. 17:) so it is expressly said in Ecclesiastes—Give not up yourselves, as a prey to wickedness. Don't consent to go on living, as you do, at this heedless and licentious rate. Don't collect your burden, as the common saying goes, from every grass and weed in your path—*Be not wicked over much*. And for what reason? Lest thou *shouldest die before thy time*. The *life of the wicked man shall be accomplished before his time* (Job xv. 32:) so Job asserts; and he repeats it, *The wicked were cut down out of time* (xxii. 16.) And Solomon openly declared that *the years of the wicked shall be shortened*, (Prov. x. 27;) they, for the most part, fall to the earth, like wild grapes, rotting, before they come to maturity, or like tares, withered before their full age. . . . . . Put away, then, my hearers, put far away from you all vain confidence. It is quite true that Death was seen in the deserts of Patmos, mounted on a feeble, lean, jaded horse; and you may be contemplating death under this same aspect: but, let me tell you, that, when death wears his spur, he makes his horse go fast. And know you not what is the spur? *The sting of death is sin* (1 Cor. xv. 56:) so Paul exclaims, *The sting of death is sin*. Some have, Alas! been so woefully deceived, as to cherish the notion that, quite on the other hand, penitential exercises are this spur; and hence no sooner do they see one of their associates becoming serious, courting retirement, and entering upon a spiritual life, than they feign a kind of pity for him. "Oh, how foolishly you are acting," they say. "Don't you perceive that you are killing yourself? What a simpleton! what a simpleton!" Excuse me, if I upbraid you in return. You are the far greatest simpletons, who have yet to learn that the *sting of death is sin*. It is not fasting, that so hastens on death. I rather find in Ecclesiasticus a promise to this effect: "He that is abstinent prolongeth his life," (xxxvii. 31, Vulg.) The austerities of a religious life are not then here to blame. But the blame lies with those horrid blasphemies, which people, as a habit, and with such excessive insolence, allow to escape from their lips: those robberies, those frauds, those oppressions of the poor, those acts of hypocrisy and profaneness, in regard to the Sacred Ordinances of religion, and no less monstrous acts of ingratitude towards the very Author of our existence—*these* are the spur of death. And this accords with what we observe in all righteous human laws, where the freehold and the temporary use and enjoyment of property is taken away from the man, who refuses to yield due homage and submission to his Sovereign.

5. Did time permit, I should have a pleasure in showing you, from the uniform testimony of all ages, how death has frequently seized upon the wicked, not only at times, when it might have been expected, but also unawares, which, least of all, it could ever be anticipated. But, to confine ourselves to the Divine Scriptures, search and examine them all throughout; you will find that none of those holy men, of whose salvation we feel sure, none of them, if I mistake not, was known to have died by any evil accident; save only the sons of patient Job, who were at once crushed to death by the fall of that palace, destined so suddenly to be their grave. And even in this case what were the particular circumstances? It happened, when they were feasting together; the very time itself breeding a misgiving in their wise father's mind, lest they should then contract some defilement, the innocency of youth being always endangered on such occasions. With this exception, if we take the case of men of the most distinguished piety, if we look to an Abraham, an Aaron, an Isaac, a Jacob, a Joseph, a Samuel, a Moses, a Mattathias, a Tobias, and persons like these, we shall observe that they all died in peace, bequeathing to their survivors wise counsels, some to their children, some to their people. On the other hand, glance but hastily at the case of wicked men, and what a sad spectacle you have before you; some carried off by the water, others by the fire, others by wild beasts, others by many divers and strange kinds of death—all of them the more hideous, as being the less expected. Shuddering at such a spectacle, the Psalmist exclaimed, *Oh, how suddenly do they consume, perish, and come to a fearful end!* (Ps. lxxiii. 18.) Suddenly expired the proud Pharaoh with all his host, engulphed in the depths of the Red Sea. Suddenly expired

those greedy wretches, who lusted after the flesh-pots of Egypt. Suddenly expired those rebels, who murmured against the promised land. And just so, suddenly expired many many others, recorded in Scripture: they all brought upon themselves a like miserable end: *Suddenly did they perish!* You will find all of them to have been guilty in the same manner of some kindred offence.

Now what would I have you infer from this fact? That what we call "a sudden death" falls exclusively to the lot of the wicked? By no means. Certainly not. This clearly would be a mistake. For it is the will of GOD that good men in this world should sometimes share in the judgments, peculiar to the wicked. GOD orders this for their purification, or for their special trial; or to prevent people believing that the only reward for goodness lies beyond the grave. If, however, we are to rely on an induction, plainly drawn from Scripture, I maintain that these sudden departures out of this world are far more frequently the portion of sinners, than of righteous men. Listen to those astounding words of Solomon; *He that being often reproved hardeneth his neck shall suddenly be destroyed, and that without remedy.* (Prov. xxix. 1.) Reasons, drawn from natural causes, will help to confirm this truth. How often do sinners bring on themselves such a death by the gluttonous excesses, with which they overload their stomachs; by the unbridled licentiousness, by which they impair their vital energy; by freedom in evil speaking, by which they make themselves enemies; by their quarrels at play, by their rivalries in love, by their rash acceptance of liabilities, by the repinings of envy, by the cares of ambition, and by other such irregularities. From all these bad practices a good man stands aloof. Of him we may justly say with the Apostle, that *all things work together for good* (Rom. viii. 28,) while his strict and self-denying life often serves to keep death at a distance from him. Be this as it may, know you how GOD in this matter deals with mankind? Exactly as we do with timber in a forest. Having to cut down wood, for the purpose of forming some useful article of taste or furniture, we proceed with care and caution. We consider whether it is sound, well seasoned, and particularly whether it is the proper time for felling it; which is at the wane of the moon. But, having to cut down wood merely for the fireside, merely to burn, we then go to work quite differently. Any time will then answer our purpose. Hardened sinners—pray, what kind of wood are they? Why, wood to cast into the fire. Are any so ignorant, as not to know this? *They are hewn down and cast into the fire.* (S. Luke iii. 9.) Hence they may be cut down indifferently, at any time. Why so much thought? why so much caution about them? *There is no regard paid to their death.* (Ps. lxxiii. 4, Vulg.) No one cares about it.

6. Now if, in your case, ye sinners, whom I most dearly love in the LORD, there be so much more likelihood of your meeting a miserable end—one, that may overtake you, when you least think of it, either when you are sunk in the deepest sleep, or at the very height of your amusements, or at any of your pleasant pastimes—Oh, I implore you, tell me candidly, is it not rash, and stupid in you to the extreme, to live one single moment in deadly sin? Where is your pledge and assurance, that the same fate, which has befallen so many others, may not also be yours? *They spend their days in wealth, and in a moment go down to the grave.* (Job xxi. 13.) They aggravate their guilt by despising it; and so the heavy burden, that presses them down, brings them to a more speedy end. Has GOD, then, shown you a special favour by revealing to you the hour of your death? Or, has He, at least, promised that He will send it, not like the thief, who treads softly, lest he should awaken you; but like the courier, who sounds his horn from a distance, that you may be in readiness to receive him? What, what is it, that makes you so bold and head-strong? S. Gregory asks, "What confidence can a man entertain, so long as he lies under a constant apprehension of being punished."

When the people of Nineveh heard that before forty days their city was to be destroyed, they instantly repented with fear and trembling. Straightway they put on sackcloth; immediately they covered themselves with ashes; never did it occur to them to delay all this, until such time, as they had the king's order for so doing. For the king, as it often happens, was probably the last person to hear these appalling tidings; either because he discouraged people's talking of such matters in his presence, or was generally inaccessible, or because, at such an awful crisis, every person was providing for his own safety. Now, why, in this case, was all this mighty hurry? Did they not for a certainty know that they had yet full forty days left them? *Yet forty days!* (Jonah iii. 4.) Why then did they not say, "Let us wait a little. It requires not many hours to pacify the Almighty: a moment will suffice: an act of repentance just before the dawn of the fortieth day will save us?" Assuredly they might have said this: and accordingly, if at dinner, there was no need they should rise from table; or, if at any amusement, they might have finished their game. But only suppose they had done so. What would be your opinion of them? Would you not regard them, as a most rash, presumptuous, and head-strong set of people, quite undeserving of the pardon, they received in virtue of their immediate obedience? But how far more aggravated, my hearers, is our case. The Ninevites could reckon upon full forty days, granted them, as a set time for repentance: and therefore the greater their security was, the less would have been their rashness, had they continued an hour or so longer in their sins. But your security does not extend even thus far: no: CHRIST declares, *Ye know not when the time is.* (S. Mark xiii. 33.) The destruction of your mortal body may not only be very near, but close and imminent: it may take place this very week, which is now passing, this morning, this moment. For death goes about always armed with two weapons, a sword and a bow. *He will whet his sword, he hath bent his bow.* (Ps. vii. 13.) With his *sword* he strikes the aged, who can no longer escape for refuge; with it he strikes the sickly, he strikes the feeble. And with his *bow* he strikes the young, who trust in their pride to save themselves by flight. And how then will you be able to defend yourselves from the charge of rashness, if you refuse to improve the least time you have yet remaining? What say you to this? What answer do you make? Never could the sportsman carry the falcon on his fist with such perfect ease, unless he had first bandaged its eyes. So has the devil dealt with you. He has closed your eyes, my hearers; and now he has you quite under his command.

7. I can only see one way left for you for evading my argument. You may say that, although you have no certainty of a longer life, yet at least you have a fair hope of it; that, notwithstanding the many great dangers, we described, as besetting sinners, still many sinners escape, enjoy health, live to old age, and die at last in the calm possession of their faculties; and that hence you sooner hope to share in their good fortune, than have any fear of the reverse. But not so quick, I pray you; or you will make me suspect you have forgotten altogether the main purport of my discourse. We are speaking of the Soul? Are we not? the Soul, which is your true self and being; the Soul, whose nature is immortal; the Soul, whose loss is irreparable? And of this Soul within you can you speak with so little reflection? "Ah remember, remember," let me say with S. Chrysostom, " remember that you are speaking of the Soul!" And have you formed so mean an estimate of its value, as to expose it to a chance? It might peradventure turn out well; 1 grant it; but, if it did not, my hearers—what then? I do not object to your risking your property, or staking your reputation, or that you should even expose your health: for these are all like those goods, which, being on the hasty spur of an emergency thrown overboard into the sea, may, when the shipwreck is over, be recovered. But the Soul! Alas! this is no such easy matter: for who does not understand that, when we venture to risk the loss of what is irrecoverable, not to act with the utmost caution is tantamount to acting with the utmost temerity?

8. And yet, egregious folly! do we not show far greater prudence in any concern of mere worldly advantage, than in things affecting Eternity? The Emperor Adrian knew from the declaration of an oracle that the transit of the Euphrates would be fatal to the Governors of Rome. He therefore of his own accord surrendered all Armenia to the Persians, all Assyria, all Mesopotamia, the countries, that had been subdued by Trajan. His object in this was to preclude every necessity of having ever to cross that ill-omened river. He

fixed on its banks the limits of his empire. Yet why need I borrow famous examples from history? Are you not yourselves aware what prudent rules you are careful to lay down, and to be guided by, in all your family matters, howsoever trivial? Are you taken seriously ill? You do not say, "There is no need of my calling in the physician; perhaps I may get well without the help of medicine." Are you setting out on a foreign war? You do not say, "There is no need of my making my will; perhaps I may return home in safety." Have you to lend a considerable sum of money to your friend? You do not straightway place yourself in his power : no; you act, as Tobias did. He well knew that Gabael was an honest, religious, trustworthy man : but this did not prevent his requiring of him a written bond of security for the sum of money he advanced him. "He left in trust with Gabael ten talents of silver under his handwriting." (Tobit i. 14; ix. 5.) When you sow your seed, you choose a fine day. When you go to law, you find out the cleverest advocate. When you engage in commerce, you employ the most accredited agents. To be brief, in every business of life, where you have it in your power to use means and precaution, you never trust the event to accident. Why then in a business, like that of Eternity, so far surpassing everything else in importance, do you behave so unwisely? Why, having it in your power to repent to-day, do you say, "No; perhaps I shall have time to repent to-morrow?" Oh, Christians, believe me, I cannot account for such inconsistency, and I am constrained to cry aloud with S. Chrysostom, in an ecstasy of astonishment, "What! Do you deliver yourself up to a contingency?" Do you trust to a mere accident? You decline doing this in the case of a lawsuit, or of a loan of money, or in the smallest and most trifling matter, relating to your property : and yet you leave your Soul to chance. Be astounded, O ye Heavens! Be terror-struck, ye Celestial beings, at the mention of an audacity, like this, so far outstripping all the experience of the world! *Who hath heard such things? The Virgin of Israel hath done a very horrible thing!* (Jer. xviii. 13.)

9. And yet, is it not clear that even audacity such as this would be more tolerable, did people run the risk for the sake

of some considerable advantage? That rule of Appian was accepted on all hands, in its general application to human affairs; "It is the height of madness for the sake of mere trifles to incur serious danger." This is nothing else than fishing with a hook, made of gold; so that no success in our sport could ever repay us for its loss. If a farmer at seed-time risks a large quantity of grain, if a banker at the exchange ventures a vast sum of money, and if a client in giving fees spends half his fortune, each of these persons does so in the full hope that his expected gains will far exceed his outgoings: nor, if you search the pages of ancient history, will you ever read of any pilot so rash, as to face the combined furies of wind and storm on a voyage to the distant Indies, with the view of lading his vessel there, not with a golden fleece, but with a cargo of sand and dung. But what, Christians, are you doing? With a view to what gain do you consent to live in such imminent risk of endless perdition? For what gain, I say? Seemeth it unto you that the good you get by living in sin will, when tried in the balance, outweigh the evil, that you must suffer by dying in sin? We will suppose you not to die in your present condition, as sinners: so far, I allow, you have the enjoyment of your sin; whether it be of some carnal gratification, or of a certain sum of money, or of a certain worldly honour, or of a certain revenge. But, if you die?—Why, if you die, it is a matter with you of going down quick into Hell, there to pay off the pleasure of a mere moment with an anguish lasting as Eternity. And does the advantage you enjoy in this life seem to you any equivalent whatever to the mischief you would thereby inflict on yourselves at your death? Oh! the deceitfulness, the infatuation of men! *The children of men are deceitful upon the weights.* (Ps. lxii. 9.) How is it possible that any temporal, transitory, frivolous, empty advantage should, under any circumstances, weigh more with you, than an endless evil? Never in the house of any counterfeiter of money will you find a set of scales to utter such palpable falsehood, unless mechanically contrived for that very purpose. It is not so much that the weights are deceitful among the children of men, as *the children of men are deceitful upon the weights.* It is you, who unfairly bias your own judgments, even as your lusts would have it, when you thus rebel against every, the clearest, light of your reason. *They are of those that rebel against the light.* (Job xxiv. 13.)

10. By the tender mercies of JESUS, be no longer your own deceivers. *Deceive not yourselves.* (Jer. xxxvii. 9.) Awake, and repent of your sins. Delay not a moment to examine your hearts, and to reflect upon what you gain by your present manner of life.. If you find your gain to exceed your risk, then consider all I have said to you, as nothing : but, if your gain should come infinitely short, then, have pity, I intreat you, on your own souls! Do you wish to treasure up sorrow for the future, and to have to complain with the afflicted Jeremiah, *Mine enemies chased me sore like a bird without cause.* (Lam. iii. 52.) Oh, the bitterness this would cause you! and how sore would be your heart-rending lamentation! The prophet is speaking in the person of a sinner; he grieves to be carried away, just like a bird, that foolishly allows itself to be decoyed by its pursuers: and for what?— *without cause;* for a mere nothing, a paltry grain of seed! "Mine enemies chased me like a bird *without cause.*"

And is it then your wish to be of this number? Ah, Christians, what are all the good things of this world, when contrasted, I say not with the less, but with the very least, of those never-ending miseries, in the teeth of which you are casting yourselves by your sins? A grain of seed! no; not even so much, as this! And yet for so mere a trifle you are determined on your heedless career, sporting yourself in the midst of your terrible seducers, at the most awful risk of being made their captives for ever, of ruining your souls, of perishing! "Oh, most criminal presumption, from whence dost thou spring?" (Ecclus. xxxvii. 8, Vulg.) I have no power adequately to express my abhorrence of such monstrous temerity. I stand aghast at it; I am constrained to be silent.

THE SECOND PART.

11. If then, as I have shown, it is for man, a mere creature of the dust, liable to be scattered by every breath of wind,

such exceeding rashness, to live one single moment in deadly sin, what will you who live in this sin, not for a single moment, but for days, for months, for whole years—*days without number*, (Jer. ii. 32)—be able to answer me in self-defence? Are you acting prudently? Are you behaving wisely? Have you any chance of escaping condemnation? Seneca tells us that "no person can with safety expose himself to very frequent perils." Why? "An evil accident often passes by, but it finds him out at last." We may walk over a pitfall for once, and not tumble in; we may touch birdlime for once, and not be defiled; we may swallow poison for once, and not die. There is nothing to surprise us in this: whether it arise from the protection of heaven, or some particular destiny, men do sometimes escape. But where will you find me the man, who could drink in poison, like water, and yet not die? or make free with bird-lime, as with a bed of flowers, and yet not be defiled? or dance over a pitfall, as over a marble pavement, and yet not tumble in? If therefore to expose oneself but for once, and then only a single moment, to the peril of damnation, be so rash a proceeding, what must it be to continue in such a state for so long a period, that, at the year's end, the days, in which you have been evidently exposed to this peril, will be found far to outnumber those, in which in all probability you have been secured from it?

12. There is a very common curiosity among Christians in asking, whether in the Church the number of those is greatest, who die in a state of salvation, or of those, who fall headlong into perdition? It is no business of mine to act as arbitrator in this great controversy. Were it however, I should gladly lean to the favourable side, and pronounce that among Catholics the number of the elect exceeded that of the damned. But, though in this decision I should have many on my side, I nevertheless doubt, whether you would find, among ancients or moderns, one single theologian, who would tell you that the majority of habitual sinners are saved. Alas! it is not so. S. Gregory, S. Augustine, S. Ambrose, S. Jerome, who are the four principal Doctors of the Church, unanimously hold the contrary opinion. S. Jerome expresses

himself here in a very emphatic manner: "Out of a hundred thousand men, whose lives were invariably bad, scarcely one finds favour with God." Nor let any of you feel surprise at this: for, as men have lived, so for the most part they die. When a tree is cut down, on what side does it fall? It falls on the side, to which it leans. Leaning to the right, it then falls to the right: leaning to the left, it then falls to the left. These evil livers always incline to the left; and yet, when they are to be cut down, they put in a claim to fall to the right, as good men fall. No measure truly of Grace would be enough to accomplish this for them, short of one, acting like a violent hurricane, such as with a miraculous force should shove them to the opposite side. But who has ever been a worthy subject to receive such Grace? "Scarcely one out of a hundred thousand!" Knowing therefore from your present state that you belong in every probability to the condemned, rather than to the elect, are you not cherishing a presumption, akin to madness, while you still persist in following the same evil courses? Even supposing that in the case of sinners, like yourselves, the majority were saved and the minority only lost, you ought to be in perpetual fear, lest your lot should be found among the latter. How then will you fare, if the majority are lost, and the minority saved?

Arnolphus, Count of Flanders, was once bowed down under the excruciating pain of the stone. His medical men proposed a surgical operation: but he wished the experiment first to be made on some other subject. A search therefore was made for all persons in his dominions, who were suffering from the same complaint. They found twenty such; these were all operated upon by the same surgeons, and then so successfully treated that, out of the whole number of twenty, only one of them died. The medical men now all returned in high spirits to Arnolphus, and recommended him to submit to the operation. But he, on hearing that it had failed in one single instance, instead of taking heart, turned suddenly pale. "Who among you," he asked, "will insure me against the fate of this unhappy man?" And then, more intimidated by the death of one, than encouraged by the recovery of the nineteen, he would on no account consent to undergo so great a risk. Now let us suppose, out of these twenty patients, that were operated upon, instead of nineteen being cured and one only dying, the reverse had happened; that the nineteen had died, and one only been cured. What, under these circumstances, would this prudent prince have said? Would he not have immediately driven from his presence those rash and inconsiderate medical advisers? Could anything have induced him to hazard the operation, under the hope that himself must needs be that one eminently fortunate man? Ah, my dear Christians, that rashness, which seems so unaccountable in matters affecting the body, is precisely that, of which you yourselves stand guilty in the care you take of your souls. S. Jerome asserts that not out of twenty, or out of thirty, but that "out of a hundred thousand habitual sinners scarcely one is saved:" and can you then possibly be more emboldened by the happy escape of the one, than put to fear by the sad end of the ninety-nine thousand nine hundred and ninety-nine? Ten was the number of those brethren, who went down to buy food in Egypt: yet, when they heard that one of their company must remain there, as a prisoner, a feeling of anxiety pervaded them all. Twelve was the number of those disciples, who sat down to supper with our LORD the night before His death: yet, when they heard that one of their company should prove a traitor, all of them without exception turned pale. But is no misgiving of this sort raised in your minds, when you know that the majority of persons, who, like yourselves, are living in sin, must finally perish? In you is confirmed what Job spake of the ungodly; *God gave him a space for repentance, but he abuses it to the furtherance of his pride* (xxiv. 23, Vulg.) Oh, pride indeed! That you in the midst of a wholesale slaughter should be the one singularly fortunate person to escape! to be thus wonderfully privileged and protected! destined hereafter to be pointed out in Paradise, as a prodigy; "as if he were escaped out of a battle!" the very words of Ecclesiasticus (xl. 6)—out of a battle; yea, rather, out of a most entire and universal overthrow!

13. Oh, let me prostrate myself at the feet of the LORD

and vent my sorrow in His presence,[1] Beloved JESUS! whence arises this excess of audacity in the hearts of men? What has so besotted them? What has thus driven them mad? Can it be that they find such delight in offending Thee, that, provided they can only do so, they care not for the harm they are inflicting on themselves? Oh, that I knew the best method, during this Lent, to humble them, to humanize them, and to win them over to my LORD! Is it Thy wish that I should intreat them with all long-suffering? So will I intreat them. Is it Thy wish that I should admonish them and put them in fear? So, so will I do. Shall I cry aloud in their ears, and rebuke them sharply? I will do it. I am here on Thy business. Command me; all shall be done. *All that Thou commandest me I will speak unto them.* (Jer. i. 17.) I seek not their favour and applause. I seek only to please Thee. Who can tell whether this present Lent may not be my last? Behold then now, how with ashes on my head I desire to go forth among you, crying aloud, "Repent, O! my people, Repent! No longer delay to cleanse yourselves from all your filthiness. No longer delay to root out your bad passions. No longer delay to mourn over every sinful habit of your lives. Do you still refuse me? Then I address my appeal to those very ashes we bear upon our heads. Here they are; uncover them; exhibit them. Do I not see them as well on the auburn locks of the young, as on the grey hairs of the aged? To these ashes of our Lent-season I make my appeal. Let them speak. Let them decide the question between us, whether any rashness can compare with this—to acknowledge oneself to be every moment liable to death, and yet to venture for a single moment to live in deadly sin?

[1] In the original the address is here made, as in some other places, directly to the Crucifix. By transferring it to the LORD Himself, every occasion of offence to certain minds is taken away, while all, that was intended by the Preacher, is fully retained.

SERMON II.

GOD THE ONLY TRUE FRIEND.

S. MATTH. VIII. 10.

"WHEN JESUS HEARD IT HE MARVELLED, AND SAID UNTO THEM THAT FOLLOWED, VERILY I SAY UNTO YOU, I HAVE NOT FOUND SO GREAT FAITH, NO, NOT IN ISRAEL."

1. HE, who does not feel astonished in the extreme, when he hears this morning of CHRIST's being astonished, betrays his own stupidity. He clearly shows his total want of understanding, as to the nature of wonder, when expressed by a Being of Infinite Wisdom. Give me your attention. What signal act of virtue was it, that gained this exalted praise for the centurion? Was it because he reverently paraded his soldiers in the presence of CHRIST, honouring Him, as the mighty LORD of Hosts, with spears reversed, colours lowered to the ground, while he lauded Him to the skies with all the thrilling strains of martial music? Did he erect to Him any altars? Did he dedicate to Him any images? Did he offer to Him any sacrifices? Perhaps he tore from his own brows the laurel crown, to cast it at His feet? Perhaps he surrendered his spoils and trophies, and consecrated them to Him as votive offerings, in acknowledgment that He was the LORD and the giver of victory? What did he do? Why, simply this. He declared his full confidence in CHRIST: he believed Him perfectly able, even from a distance, to restore his sick servant to health, were He only to pledge one single word to that

effect; *Only speak the word, and my servant shall be whole!* And was it for this, CHRIST broke out in such a transport of astonishment, so very unlike Him? Was it for this, He praised the centurion so highly? Was it for this, He paid the centurion such honour? Did He for this go so far (what more can be said?) as to swear, *Verily I say unto you, I have not found so great faith, no, not in Israel!* Such was indeed the fact. Now-a-days unbelief is everywhere so common, that it is a matter of astonishment to find a single person, who places an entire trust in GOD, even in the less considerable operations of His hand. . . . But the matter of astonishment really should be, not, as CHRIST said to this centurion, to fall in with one, who believes; but rather to find one, who does not. Attend therefore; and I will prove what I say.

2. It cannot be denied that our worldly friends are vastly liberal in their kind words. Only hear them talk. Oh, in what fine set terms do they devote themselves to your interests, offer you all they possess, and entreat your commands![1] The only way, they tell you, in which you can possibly offend them is by declining their services. But, should you too credulously listen to all their magnificent offers, how soon will you discover your error! Laban, who promised you his beautiful Rachel, presents you with a Leah. Saul, who promised you his first-born Merab, presents you with a Michal. Nothing indeed is now more common than to promise much and to perform little. Such conduct reminds us of the clouds on a fine summer's day, coming after a long season of drought: they appear to promise an abundance of rain: but, after all, to the infinite disappointment of the poor expecting villagers, who come out to catch the welcome supply, they end in nothing beyond a few sprinkling drops, and so pass away. GOD however does not treat us in this manner. He can say with perfect truth, *My covenant will I not break, nor alter the thing that is gone out of My lips.* (Ps. lxxxix. 34.) You will find that, contrary to the custom of men, who pro-

---

[1] Such spontaneous proffers of boundless liberality and devotedness to you are still the conventional terms of polite good breeding in Italy, and still more in Spain. They came from the East, where perhaps we may trace an instance of them at a very early period. Gen. xxiii. 10—12, 15.

mise much and perform little, GOD far exceeds His promise in His performance. He had promised Hezekiah that the terrible army of haughty Sennacherib should not enter Jerusalem, that it should not so much as *shoot an arrow there, nor come before it with shield, nor cast a bank against it.* (Isa. xxxvii. 33.) These were the very terms of His engagement. Well then, in order to fulfil them, nothing more was required of GOD than that He should drive back the affrighted Assyrians. He had only to distract the counsels of Sennacherib by stirring up some ill feeling among his chief officers, or spreading a mutiny among his soldiers. And yet, as not satisfied with this, what did He do? That very night He despatched an Angel, who invaded the camp with a drawn sword, and after a tremendous slaughter left in the field, as a prey to the vultures, no less than one hundred and eighty-five thousand dead corpses. Take another example. In the case of Solomon the promise of GOD would have been strictly performed by His simply bestowing on him that wisdom, which he had asked for with a view to the right government of his people. (1 Kings iii. 12.) And yet, GOD, in addition to this, gave him riches. Once more. The promise of GOD would have been perfectly kept with Jehoshaphat by simply giving that water, which he desired for the timely relief of his army. And yet, in addition to this, GOD gave him a victory. (2 Kings iii.) And thus, if you search the Scriptures, you will find that He not only performs what He promises to do, but that He does it with a surplus; as S. Chrysostom intimates, "He keeps His promise right liberally."

3. Oh, my hearers, this is a fidelity indeed, widely differing from that of your friends. And whence does the vast difference arise? Must I tell you? It arises from this: because these persons, these friends of yours, are friends to what they will get, rather than friends to what they will give, in their dealings with you. I will explain myself. To *what* do you consider certain people, generally, to be friends, people, who compass you about with so much deference, so great flattery, and so many smooth smiles? Do you consider them to be friends to your person? Oh, the good easy folks you are, if you think so! They are friends of that handsome sum of

money, you have invested, as a settlement on the marriage of your daughter. They are friends of that piece of preferment in your gift. They are friends of that patronage, they hope to obtain from you. They are friends of your rising prosperity. They are just such friends to you, as bees are to the flowers, to extract the sweetest honey; as vines are to the elm, to get a lift higher for themselves. GOD is the only friend, who is desirous of being so, that He may give us of His own. All He enjoys, all He has, He wishes to lay out for our advantage. It has indeed been His gracious will that a mutual interchange should subsist between us of what we both severally possess, according to the famous maxim, that "what friends have, they have in common." But who ever heard of an interchange like this? He has given us, on His part, nothing but riches and glory: He has taken from us, in return, nothing but pollution and poverty. To us He has given all, that Deity has of grandeur; for Himself He has taken all, that humanity has of lowliness. To us He has given His merits; for Himself He has taken our miseries. To us He has given His Immortality; for Himself He has taken our death. To us He has given the Happiness of His Kingdom; for Himself He has taken the sorrow of our banishment. What more shall I say? "He came," writes Peter Chrysologus, "to bear our infirmities, and to give us His strength; to seek for Himself the things of man, to provide us with the things of GOD; to accept infamy for Himself, to heap dignities on His people." And where will you find any other such a friend, ready to strike with you a similar bargain? a friend, who will ask of you nothing but your grief, and who will impart to you nothing but His joy?

4. Let us pass on to another reflection. Of whom in this world does GOD profess Himself to be the friend? Know you, what class of persons they are? The poor, the afflicted, the oppressed, the despised. *To that man will I look, that is poor, saith the Lord.* (Isa. lxvi. 2.) The Israelites had good proof of this: for if GOD ever showed them a special favour, it was at the time, when they were reduced in Egypt to the lowest state of destitution and decay. Look at Elisha. Did

God ever work more illustrious miracles in his behalf, than when He saw him made an object of ridicule, even to children. Then it was, that He roused the wild beasts from their forest dens on his account. Look at Lazarus, the renowned brother of Martha and Mary. On what occasion was the love of CHRIST towards him most conspicuously displayed? Was it not, when he was become a loathsome corpse, offensive even to his own sisters? *Behold how He loved him!* (S. John xi. 36) was the exclamation of the Jews, astonished at those signal proofs of affection, which CHRIST manifested at his sepulchre. But " Oh, ye evil-minded men," the Angelic Doctor T. Aquinas says in reply to them, " why did they say 'He *loved* him?' They should rather have said, '*loves* him now,' when the SAVIOUR was actually giving so clear a proof of the constancy of His affection to His friend, even when putrifying in his grave." " The misery of Lazarus was on the increase; CHRIST's friendship suffered no decrease." Surely our human friends do not act in this way. For what is the fact? They no sooner perceive you reduced in your circumstances, than they quickly sound a retreat; they fly away from you, and will even openly desert you to your shame and disgrace. The very persons, who well-nigh adored your rising sun, now your rainy day is come, will not even appear to know you. Should your house ever show any symptom of weakness, and threaten a fall, alas! how soon, at the first shake and crumbling of the walls, would you witness the immediate flight and dispersion of all those swallows, that nested themselves under your roof!

Poor Job! what had he failed to do, that he might deserve the aid of a trusty friend in his day of necessity? He had defended the widow; he had maintained the orphan; he had clothed the naked; he had fed the hungry. Yet, notwithstanding all this, on his sinking into that sad state of affliction, well known to you all, he was left so utterly destitute, that, when unable to borrow the use of a shed, or a piece of matting, or common sack, he was compelled to lie down, like some dead dog, upon a vile dunghill. *My brethren have dealt deceitfully with me as a brook, and as the stream of brooks they pass away.* (Job vi. 15.) But you will answer me by saying that Job, at this very time, had three friends, who one and all went to comfort him. At the first sight of him, you will say, they burst out in lamentations, like a set of desperate men, sighing, groaning, defiling the very hair of their heads in the dust. I grant it: but these three friends are my very witnesses, to confirm the truth of what I say. For, tell me, with all their intense sympathy and sorrow, did they not leave poor Job, as they found him—in the very same forlorn condition? Did they relieve him with a farthing? Did they supply him with a single rag? So far from this, hear what Job himself said: he told them that they were frightened at the sight of him—*Ye see my casting down and are afraid* (vi. 21.) Afraid! and of what! What fear could these dignified personages entertain in seeing their friend brought so low? Was it a fear lest they should be involved in the same calamity? a fear of catching his disorder? "Reflect," Liranus acutely observes on this passage; "they were afraid, lest Job, driven to it by extreme necessity, should apply to them for pecuniary relief." You smile, my hearers, at this comment, as if disposed to regard it as more fanciful than sound. But Job with his own mouth confirms it; *Ye see my casting down and are afraid:* and then immediately adds; *Did I say, Bring unto me? or, Give a reward for me of your substance?* From this it is quite evident that their fear chiefly arose from an apprehension of being called upon to part with their money. I therefore draw this inference. If we must not ordinarily expect anything beyond kind words, even from friends of a more tender and compassionate spirit, like these men, who so loudly proclaimed their grief, tell me, I beseech you, my hearers, what can we possibly hope for from persons of a sterner character? Will they not cruelly leave us to pine away in our misery, not even favouring us with a word of comfort, with a recognition, with a single look? Ah! these pitiless men will surely refuse us every help, and perhaps even combine to aggravate our sufferings by all the means in their power; resembling in this respect certain people, who, having during the heat of the summer enjoyed the cool refreshing shade of the spreading beech-tree, and indulged under its shelter in all kinds of diversion and festivity, nevertheless, at the approach of winter, when they see it dried up, are the first to take the axe, and recklessly to cut away at it right and left, root and branch.

5. However, we will suppose your friends to be more kindly and liberally disposed, and really desirous to help you in your necessities, yet, with all this, how rarely would they assist you to any extent, without making an ostentatious boast and display of their services, and often rating them very far beyond their value! Nay, the smallest attentions they show you, the most trivial obligations men confer now-a-days, are expected to call forth an overwhelming sense of gratitude. The debt incurred must be distinctly acknowledged: you must protest that you are bound to them for ever: for in vain shall we now seek for benefactors, content to show us kindness without its being known, whose quiet course is like that of the silent subterraneous stream. In Ecclesiasticus it is expressly written of the worldly friend, "He giveth little and upbraideth much" (xx. 15.) Whereas GOD—how does He act? We may reply in the elegant language of Eucherius, "He gives us many things, of which we are quite unconscious; nor is His secret beneficence towards us less than His openly declared." Those favours of His can scarcely be numbered, which He bestows upon us so secretly and without ceasing, that we are not ourselves aware of receiving them; and, if some of His other benefits are more publicly conferred, He then acts towards us with such retiring modesty, as if, in His view, it was only by some happy accident that He had it in His power to do us good.

In all my study of the New Testament I have found it difficult to light upon one single instance of any kindness, conferred by CHRIST, which He did not gracefully ascribe to some good quality in the recipient. To the Canaanite He grants the recovery of her daughter, *O! woman, great is thy faith; be it unto thee even as thou wilt.* (S. Matth. xv. 28.) He heals the woman with a bloody issue: He says to her, *Go, thy faith hath made thee whole* (ix. 22.) He removes the darkness from the eyes of the blind man: He says to him, *Go thy way, thy faith hath made thee whole.* (S. Mark x. 52.) He pardons the woman, who had been a sinner: He says to her, *Thy faith hath saved thee.* (S. Luke vii. 50.) This was the unassuming rescript, which He usually affixed to the petitions He received. But I have a still more striking instance at hand. Our LORD was one day entreated to condescend to go and restore life to the daughter of the Ruler of the synagogue. He complied with the request, and went. But Oh, what a studious dissembling of His power was here! We dwell not on the fact of His putting forth from the house the assembled people and the mourning minstrels, of His letting down the vestibule curtain, of His enjoining secresy, of His imposing strict silence in a matter of this great importance. We pass over these circumstances, to observe, particularly, how, on His approaching the dead body, He did all He could to lower in the minds of the parents any sense of their obligation to Him for His intended act of kindness. He prefaced the miracle by a kind of Divine equivoque, saying, *The maid is not dead, but sleepeth.* (S. Matth. ix. 24.) What! *sleepeth?* And what man, possessing the same power with CHRIST, would not have done the very reverse of this? It is pretty evident that any other person would first have established beyond all doubt the fact of her being dead. He would have addressed the bystanders to this effect; "Draw near: pay attention: mark well, if she retains any symptoms of life in her: feel her pulse, if it beats; feel her heart, if it moves: observe her eyes, if they have any animation: take notice, if you can perceive the least breath playing upon her lips: make yourselves quite sure that she is really cold, stiffened, discoloured, and, all over, of a deadly pale." Thus, in order to blazon forth to the utmost his intended act of kindness, he would, it seems, have been at the greatest pains to make them feel their absolute need of his help. But CHRIST did nothing of the kind. He would have it appear that He was simply banishing sleep from the eyes of the slumbering damsel; that hereby, as I think, He might put to shame those, who arrogate to themselves so much praise for their paltry services; whereas He lessened the vastness of His benefits by the unpretending way, in which He conferred them.

Again, among all the persons, whom He miraculously healed, do we ever find Him retaining a single one of their number to be His disciple, His attendant, His votary? No, not one. He cured in the Pharisee's house the man with a dropsy; but instantly commanded him to depart. He healed in the country of Nazareth the paralytic; but forthwith bade him *go to his own house.* (S. Matth. ix. 6.) He raised the young man near the gates of Nain; but at once *delivered him to his mother.* (S. Luke vii. 15.) Nor did He deal differently with that demoniac, whom He dispossessed near the borders of the Gergesenes. This man earnestly entreated to be allowed to follow Him by land or sea, or whithersoever He went; but nothing would induce our LORD to comply with the request. *Jesus suffered him not; but saith unto him, Go home to thy friends.* (S. Mark v. 19.) So true it is, that in these particulars of His conduct CHRIST resembled the sun; which, imparting, as it does, light to the stars, does not exact from them the least remuneration of any kind; but rather that, where it appears, they should immediately retire. And now, my hearers, what say you? Produce your worldly friend, who will treat you in this fashion? So far from it, no sooner has he done you any service, however trifling, than he directly lays his claim upon you for your daily attendance in serving him. He requires you to be henceforth always at his elbow, and to be giving him continually every possible proof of your gratitude, of your devoted, ay, of your slavish attachment to his person.

6. But come; let us advance a step further. We will allow that there are friends in the world, so nobly disposed as to divest their favours of all ostentation, and to exact from you in return no kind of acknowledgment, deference, and submission. For all this, I still maintain that you have not therefore yet found in the world any faithful friends. And why so? Observe my reason with attention. Without any fault whatever on your part these friends may withdraw their affection from you. Pharaoh confined for a long time in the depths of a dungeon his two most favoured servants, the chief of the butlers and the chief of the bakers. He imprisoned them, because, as we read in Scripture, they had *offended* him. (Gen. xl. 1.) Now can any of you inform me, what was the mighty offence they committed? Did they attempt to poison

him? Did they try to cheat him? Did they compass high treason against him? Did they aim a daring blow against his government? Not at all, if we may credit what the Hebrew tradition says in this matter. How then did this happen? Why, their fault was a mere accident. "*It came to pass*, that they had offended their lord." The chief butler was found guilty, because the king detected in his cup a little fly; and the chief baker, because he discovered in his bread a little stone. So very small a trifle suffices to deprive us of the smiles of mortal man: ay, such a mere nothing as this! What then do I say? May not some slight suspicion, however groundless, which he has conceived of your conduct, rob you of your friend? A scandal, told him about you, may be the cause of your losing him; as Joseph lost the favour of Potiphar, whose shameless wife had falsely accused him. Some envy, conceived in his bosom against you, may rob you of him; as David lost the favour of Saul, when the daughters of Israel so extravagantly sang his praise. A natural fickleness of mind, such as is common to man, may rob you of him. A quarrel, caused by a joke, may rob you of him. A word, spoken in fun, may rob you of him. Some root of bitterness, springing up in worldly matters between you—an opposing interest, a controversy, a lawsuit—any of these may rob you of your friend. Could any alliance promise more stability than the one cemented between Lot and Abraham? between Abimelech and Isaac? But a contention arose; in one case, between the shepherds about some right of pasture; and in the other, respecting some right to a well: and so Abraham must separate from Lot, and Isaac must depart from Abimelech. (Gen. xiii., xxvi.)

If we would know how very easily some private interest can deprive us of the friendship of any one, listen to a fact of this kind, which is very remarkable. It is related in the Sacred Book of Judges, that there was a person of great eminence, Micah by name. He had erected at his country residence a small and decent Chapel, suited in every respect to Divine worship. He had set over it, as officiating Priest, a Levite; whom he kindly treated, as one of his sons, assigning to him a comfortable apartment, two changes of raiment, a handsome annual stipend, and his daily food. Moreover, that he might never be in want of ready money, the Sacred text adds, that he had *liberally supplied him* in this respect. (Judg. xvii. 12, Vulg.) All this kindness, on the part of Micah, was fully reciprocated by his Priest. And so one day it came to pass, that, on his observing certain soldiers of the tribe of Dan entering the Chapel with a view to plunder, he boldly confronted them, reproved them for what they were about, kept them at bay, and, single as he was, ventured to stand up in defence of what had been consecrated to GOD. *What do ye? What do ye?* Now was not this a marvellous attachment to his master, and a most valiant deed? But listen to what follows. When the soldiers saw him offering this resistance, they cried out, "Gently, gently: don't you see that you are nothing more in this Chapel than a ridiculous little parson, a poor chaplain of the lowest grade? Do, as we wish you: be satisfied with keeping quiet. We will present you to a much better living, than this, to look after. *Hold thy peace; lay thy hand on thy mouth, and go with us, and be to us a father and a priest. Is it better for thee to be a priest unto the house of one man, or that thou be a priest unto a tribe and family in Israel?*" (xviii. 19.) Would you believe it? When this good honest man heard talk of preferment and of a better living, it was not enough for him to keep quiet, which was all the soldiers required him to do; but he was the very first to lay his hands upon the Altar and to plunder it, to strip the walls, to clear the credence-tables, to make off with the censers, to steal the images: and so he scampered off at full speed with the soldiers.—" O! my friend, O! my friend, is it thus, that you betray me? Is it thus, that you desert me? Is it thus, that you turn your back upon me?" Micah may lose his breath in crying aloud to his heart's content; for lo! his priest is now far away, and quite out of hearing. Now what think you, my hearers, of this transaction? Was it possible for Micah to have done more, than he had done, to secure the fidelity of this man? Had he not treated him with the highest respect? Had he not reposed in him the fullest confidence? Had he not acted towards him with the utmost liberality? Yes, Sirs; but this was, from time immemorial, the way of worldly friends; to side with the highest bidder; to imitate flies, who hasten to the best furnished table; to imitate doves, who go, where the nicest seeds are to be found. But this, you say, may be a custom, which in our day no longer exists. Oh, my hearers, excuse me from any reply to this, lest I should cast too deep a shame on our present times.

7. Let us then fall back upon our design; and let me ask, how can we ever firmly rely on those friends, who, without any fault or even any demerit whatsoever on our part, are capable of forsaking us? Fault or demerit of ours, did I say? Why, the very useful services we render them, the very kindness, the very love we feel towards them, may prove the cause of their forsaking us. "Men's bad temper," says Seneca, "has reached such a height, that it is a most dangerous thing to confer singular obligations on any person." For, so long as the party obliged is unable to requite his benefactor in any proportionate way, he begins by little and little to regard him under that sinister aspect, with which we look on our creditors: he begins to avoid him; he begins to dislike him; and sometimes turns out, at last, his most ungrateful enemy: and all from no other motive than a morbid feeling of shame at the idea of being his friend, and yet a friend unable to show the full gratitude he ought. And is this, my hearers, what we are to call a solid friendship? a true friendship? an enduring friendship?

8. We will now take the opposite view of our subject. We will speak of GOD, and trace the analogy between His ways and ours. In regard to the particulars I have mentioned, can you have any fear of GOD? Tell me, then; what? that His love will cool without any fault of yours? that, although you behave well, He will disdain you? that, although you show Him love, He will abandon you? So far from this, the great wonder here is, that we are at liberty to forsake GOD without any fault on His part, but He has no liberty to forsake us without any fault of ours. "He does not forsake us, unless He is Himself forsaken." We have no cause then to stand in fear, in regard to Him, as to any inconsistency, any rancour, any detraction, any disposition on

His part to quarrel with us, or to suspect us, or to be allured away from us. It is of our own selves that we must be apprehensive. S. Paul triumphantly declares that nothing should be able to *separate him from the love of Christ, not angels, nor principalities, nor powers, nor things present, nor things to come, nor height, nor depth, nor any other creature.* But have you noticed? S. Bernard here very shrewdly observes, that, among all these particulars, the Apostle has not mentioned *himself;* "he omits to add, *nor our own selves.*" And why? "because only with our own free will we can forsake GOD. Excepting our own free will, there is nothing; absolutely nothing, for us to fear." We ourselves only can do ourselves that harm, which a GOD Himself, with all His terrible Omnipotence, cannot do us. And, if this be so, seemeth it not, my hearers, that we possess a mighty advantage in having none but ourselves to complain of, should we ever come to lose so good a friend? Oh, what comfort! Oh, what peace! Oh, what security is here! If I fix my love on man, I must be continually on my guard against a thousand accidents, which may alienate me from him. If I fix my love on GOD, I need only protect myself from myself. Henceforth, let others offer Him the most magnificent presents, the most splendid fortune, a more than princely inheritance: on no such accounts is there the slightest danger of His preferring them to me, so long as the love I bear Him shall exceed theirs, however inferior my outward condition may be. He is not like Micah's priest, who sided with the highest bidder. He sides with those, who love Him most, in preference to those, who give Him most. And so it was seen, when He had to elevate one of His Apostles to the Primacy. He did not promote the disciple, who distinguished himself, when first called, by the greater sacrifice of riches abandoned for His sake (for in that case He would have fixed upon Matthew;) but He preferred the man, who cherished the most ardent affection of love towards Him. Just so, when He had to award the highest praise to the one, or the other, of the two sisters, who received Him under their roof, He gave it not to her, who had taken such trouble, in providing for Him the most expensive entertainment, (for, in that case, Martha would have had the prize ;) but He assigned it to her, whose tender heart loved Him most. And those millionaires, who cast such heaps of money into the treasury, could not, with all their offerings, bribe Him to prefer them to, or even to put them on the same level with, that poor widow, who with such great pains laid up in store her two farthings. (S. Mark xii. 42.) Blessed be GOD, who does not allow Himself to be decoyed by the gifts of men. He esteems His friends by what they are in themselves; not by what they give. *God loveth a cheerful giver.* (2 Cor. ix. 7.) Paul does not say a liberal, nor a splendid, nor a munificent; he says, a *cheerful giver*—a quality this not of the hand, but of the heart; not so much an outward act, as an inward principle.

9. Nor let it once be supposed that this arises from GOD'S scorning, as men do, to be indebted to any one for any considerable benefit. Quite the contrary, says S. Chrysostom. "GOD delights as much in having creditors, as we delight in having debtors." The pleasure we take in seeing those, from whom we hope to receive something, is exceeded by the joy He has in seeing those, to whom He means to give. Notice in this respect a striking contrast. The man, who, when in trouble, was privately relieved by persons beneath him in station, on his recovering his former prosperity, and finding himself again rich, again in favour, again courted and flourishing, feels quite ashamed to meet those, at whose doors he so frequently went a-begging : nothing will exasperate him more than to hear that one of these persons, actuated by some proud or contemptuous feeling, was going about saying, "Only look at him—how he now launches out in such fine style! Why, I remember to have seen that very man with my own eyes coming, and that more than once, coming to my door, and begging the smallest pittance of relief!" How very different from this is GOD'S way! With the blast of the trumpet at the Last Day He will assemble the whole universe before His presence : and for what? To publish aloud the very smallest gift He once received in private from us. In His highest exaltation to Glory He will not be ashamed to recognize, one by one, His old benefactors, nor to acknowledge, that, when He was upon earth reduced to the most abject poverty, He

had from this person, as a charitable offering, a rag to cover Him; and from that person, a piece of bread; and from another, a cup of water. *When the Son of Man shall come in His glory,* what will He do? He will say, *I was an hungered; and ye gave Me meat. I was thirsty; and ye gave Me drink!* (S. Matth. xxv. 35.)

10. Oh, friend, friend indeed, the only faithful friend in the world! Oh, rare uprightness! Oh, perfect truthfulness! Oh, incomparable fidelity! Had I not reason, think you, Christians, to cast into the distant background every other object of your contemplation, but Him, in whom our truly wise centurion so entirely confided? Tell me yourselves, if you will candidly speak the truth, were you not on the point more than once of breaking out with that saying of the wise man, *A faithful man, who can find?* (Prov. xx. 6.) In short, can you in this world find a friend, on whom to depend? Has not your experience taught you, that, generally speaking, they deceive and betray us, and that, like falcons, intent only on their own prey, they elude our grasp, just at the very critical time, when we deemed them most certainly in our power? Keep now well in mind what I have said, whilst I rest a moment: and during this short interval prepare your answer to a very important question, which, much to your edification, I shall propose to you.

The Second Part.

11. The important question, which I intended to propose to you, is simply this. If God alone can justly be called a true friend, if all others are liable, more or less, to prove unfaithful, how is it possible that any one, merely to please a friend, should ever offend God? Are you silent, my hearers? Tell me your thoughts, I beseech you. Perhaps I have not clearly stated what I mean. I will repeat then my question. I ask, how is it possible, that, for the sake of pleasing a friend, whether by complying with his requests, or following his counsels, or humouring his fancies, any should ever offend, dishonour, and provoke God; thus proving true to that friend, who is so faithless, and false to Him, who is so

faithful? Does not this look like a question well worthy of your consideration? What say you then to it? Solve the difficulty; satisfy me about it: or, at least, give me something of an answer.—Oh, the immense ingratitude of Christians! It is evident that not one has the courage to make the least attempt at an answer, because there is not one, who probably is not himself guilty of this monstrous wickedness.

'Tis our vain and frivolous mind, our inconsiderate mode of living, that carries us on to such an extreme : and, if this be the fact, should it not overwhelm us with shame and confusion of face? Pericles is generally commended for the reply he made to a person, who from self-interested motives asked him to swear to a falsehood. He allowed—the story is well known—that he was the man's friend, *usque ad Aras*, " even to the very Altars !" And yet, Plutarch is so far from commending him, that he blames him for this reply, declaring that he went too far. " Even to the Altars !" " Even to the Altars"—Ah, what imprudence! *Nimis propè accesserat.* He had already got too near it. For how many improper concessions must Pericles have made to this friend, before the latter became bold enough to ask him to commit Sacrilege! Hear now, how I shall apply this to your case. The friendships, you form, must not extend to the altar : no : this is going too far : they must reach, but to the threshold of the Temple, so as not to embolden your associates to tempt you beyond. What! are they not then already well persuaded that GOD stands far more high in your esteem, than they do? Can they have any remaining doubt upon this point? Can they feel any uncertainty about it? Oh, the immense wrong you are evidently doing GOD, that most noble of all friends!

12. And with what a countenance will you presume in the hour of your need to appear before GOD, when stung with the keenest sense of jealousy, He will say to you, " Depart hence, go now, and apply to those your most deserving friends; those friends, who were so dear to you, whom you prized so infinitely beyond Me? Have you not entirely centred your affections on men? Let men therefore deliver you from death ; let men therefore restore to you life ; let

men therefore give you Paradise: let men therefore save you from hell! *Where are your gods in whom ye trusted?* (Deut. xxxii. 37.) Take courage then; *Let them arise, if they can save thee in the time of thy trouble!"* (Jer. ii. 28.) And you, Christians, what will you reply to this? Can you hope forsooth that those same friends, who caused you to offend GOD, will now intercede with Him in your favour? that they will confess to Him that *they* are really the guilty persons? that *they* are to blame; and that, in consequence, *they* ought to consent to suffer the penalties prepared for you? So far from anything of the sort, they will be the first, if the matter presses, to raise their voices against you, and to overwhelm you with their accusations. The Divine Scripture relates that Absalom, on being defeated by Joab, as he was hastily effecting his escape through a thick forest, met with this sad misfortune. His hair, blown aside by the wind, got entangled in the branches of a tree; his mule took fright, and ran off; and thus he was left suspended in the air, having no means whatever to escape by flight. A soldier of the enemy, on seeing this, ran off with the intelligence to Joab, who said to him; "Why didn't you, with such an opportunity, kill him at once; for I would have rewarded you with at least ten shekels of silver?" "Oh, on no account," replied the soldier. "Had you been able to give me a thousand, no consideration would have induced me to kill him; for the King has expressly commanded that Absalom's life should be spared. If I had allowed my impetuosity to get the better of my loyalty and discretion, the King would have most severely resented it; and probably you yourself, either to give him some comfort and satisfaction, or to keep with him on good terms, or for some other motive, well understood by you, practised courtiers, would have been the first person to inform against me; *Thou thyself wouldst have set thyself against me.*" (2 Sam. xviii. 13.) Oh, how well and how wisely did this plain common soldier plead in his own justification! "Thou, who dost now advise me to commit so grievous an act of disobedience against my King, thou wouldst be the very person, not merely to decline afterwards taking any part in my defence, but to denounce me in the

Royal presence, as a rash, impudent, sacrilegious wretch and villain, and to exert thyself in packing me off with the least possible delay to the gallows—*Thou thyself wouldst have set thyself against me!*"

13. Now this is precisely the thing you ought to say within yourselves, my hearers, whensoever a companion entices or urges you to do what is wrong. Trust him not; believe him not; rest perfectly assured that, on your. appearance before the Divine Tribunal, he will be the most determined accuser and spiteful enemy you have. He now invites you, as your friend, to go with him to that profane comedy. Yes, Sirs; but afterwards he will *set himself against thee*: he will say that you encouraged him to do this by your excessive fondness for amusements. He now invites you, as your friend, to accompany him to that house of bad fame. Yes, Sirs; but afterwards he will *set himself against thee*: he will say, that you furnished him with the occasion by your open and unblushing wantonness. He now invites you, as your friend, to go shares with him in that unlawful contract. Yes, Sirs; but afterwards *he will set himself against thee*: he will say, that you suggested the speculation by your notorious insatiable love of money. Be prepared for all this: mind, as far as he possibly can, he will always be the first person to lay his own blame at your door. And, for the sake of such miserable traitors as these, will you suffer yourselves to be brought to offend GOD? Oh, what blindness! Oh, what stupidity! Oh, what infatuation! What claim, I ask, have such wretches upon you, what earthly ground and reason, that obliges you on their account to turn your backs thus upon Him, to whom you must finally apply for help in your last desertion.

14. Look, my hearers, upon the LORD JESUS. See Him suffering and bleeding for you. Wander, where you will, to this point we must all come back at last; even here, at the foot of His Cross. That hour will arrive, when, overcome with pain and given over by the physician, we shall find nought of this mortal life remaining to us, but our repentance for having employed it so badly. Who, among our friends, will then be the person to visit and to console us? Some

one, it may be, who is expecting a place in our will. As for the rest of them, Oh, what a complete desolation! . . . And can we conceive what, at such a crisis, our heart-rending anguish, our groans, our ravings will be! To see, for a certainty, we are already forsaken by every one else; that there is no other hope left us, but in GOD; no other consolation, but in GOD; no other happiness, but in GOD; and yet that to Him, this same GOD, we must be constrained to say, "Thee I despised; Thee I despised, for the sake of pleasing a set of ungrateful men!" How earnestly shall we then implore the prolongation of one year, a single, single year; for time enough to publish it abroad that we no longer care for any mortal friends! This indeed is a worthy design on our part, and a godly resolution. But the last breath is even now trembling on our lips, and we must needs die. And then conceive with what bitterness of soul we shall behold the face of our injured LORD, with what intense shame, with what inward torture! GOD only prevent us in His mercy from being goaded on by a sudden frenzy, the effect of which would be that we should yield to the horrible suggestions of the enemy, despair in our last moments, and so destroy ourselves! To escape such tremendous perils, what then must we do? I show you the way. This very morning, by a firm determination of purpose, let us choose GOD to be, what He really is, our Supreme Friend. Let our relations indeed be dear to us, but less than GOD; let our companions be dear to us, but after GOD; let our masters be dear to us, but under GOD; nor let us ever be ashamed openly to avow before every gainsayer, *My God, in Thee I trust. I will not be ashamed!* Who is he, that can ever feel offended, because we regard him less, than we do the Being, who has made us, who has redeemed us, and who will render us happy for ever? But should any be found, capable of taking such an offence, we have in this very circumstance good ground for less regarding him, inasmuch as so bad a friend cannot be worthy of our love.

SERMON III.

A DISSUASIVE AGAINST REVENGE.

S. MATTH. v. 44.

"BUT I SAY UNTO YOU, LOVE YOUR ENEMIES."

1. WE are indebted to the prelate S. Gregory for the striking observation, that CHRIST called the fishermen to the Apostleship, while they were standing on the shore; not in the act of drawing their nets, but of casting them into the sea. This was to show us that the preacher of the Gospel is not obliged to catch and to convert souls, but only to employ with diligence the means, conducive to that great end. His duty is to spread the net of the Divine Word over his hearers, and never to abandon his task from any sense of weariness, arising from long-continued toil and from the sweat of his brow. Then, should any sinners, like fishes of a more subtle nature, contrive to elude his snare, or, when captured, to effect their escape, *that* is their business: it by no means follows that the unhappy preacher should take his failure too grievously to heart; but rather recollect that the wages of reward will be proportioned to every man's labour, and not to his success. *Every man shall receive his own reward according to his own labour* (1 Cor. iii. 8,) and not according to the fruit of that labour. Certainly, were it otherwise, nothing, I believe, would have ever induced me to appear to-day in this pulpit. I too, like a second Jonah, should in that case have fled in despair *from the presence of the Lord* (i. 3;) with this differ-

ence, however, that whereas he fled from a fear of the people's repenting, I should fly from a fear of their remaining impenitent. And do you doubt this? In to-day's Gospel CHRIST bids me command you in His Name to forgive your enemies, to overlook every injury, to pardon every ill usage. *Love your enemies.* And would you fain have me entertain a sanguine hope that you will obey this command? I might indeed waste my breath and exhaust my strength in calling you to this duty: but what will it avail? We have here to deal with a passion so unruly, that it pays no regard to reason; it rejects all good advice; it yields to no expostulation; like an infuriated asp, it refuses to hear, lest it should no longer have to bite. Therefore, there is scarcely any probability of my being able to acquit myself with honour in this undertaking... Still, a view to your happiness urges me on. Oh, my brethren, it is this, that animates my soul; it is this, that inspires my tongue: because I clearly perceive that, in order to indulge a passion of this blind and headstrong nature, you will involve yourselves in numberless inconceivable sorrows. Show me then, I beseech you, as a favour, no other honour than this—to hear me patiently, whether I speak the truth: and then resolve for yourselves, as you like.

2. I am well aware, my hearers, how passion obscures the understanding to such a degree that, as in a very dark night, it quite prevents us from discerning between good and evil. *Mine eye is troubled through anger,* said David (Ps. xxxi. 10, Vulg.) *Mine eye is dim by reason of indignation,* said Job (xvii. 7, Vulg.;) and Paul still more emphatically adverts to the same effect, when he says, *Let not the sun go down upon your wrath.* (Eph. iv. 26.) He meant, if we may believe T. Aquinas, that the sun of our reason should never go down upon our anger. "Let not your sun set; that is, let not the dictates of reason be darkened." Did any beam of that most beauteous sun still illumine your minds, you would see at once that the mischief, you are doing yourselves by taking revenge, exceeds the good, which you are doing your opponent by granting him pardon. Though he may receive your pardon, yet be assured, his own sense of remorse—those inbred

furies, the goads of a guilty conscience—will not allow him to pardon himself. Do what he will, either in this present life or in the life to come, he will suffer far more heavy penalties than any he can suffer from you. Whereas, in your wish to avenge yourselves, what miseries do you not incur? Anger, beyond all doubt, is the most impetuous of all our passions. It is "a brief madness." He, who acts under its impulse, must always act rashly and never wisely. He supposes all difficulties made smooth, every danger averted, every contingency in his favour; and rarely considers how often the man, who was most confident of his success, turns out the loser. It was on this account that Aristotle compared anger to a dog. You have noticed a dog, when he hears a knocking at the door: he immediately barks and rages; he rushes out, ready to tear the first comers in pieces. He takes no precaution, whether they be many or few, strong or feeble, well armed or defenceless: and hence he is frequently compelled to turn back crest-fallen, and at times well beaten: but this would not have happened, had he first only waited a little, to see who was coming; and then, having discovered the person to be an equal match, had challenged him with barking, or actually flew at him with his teeth. The angry man will be found, on consideration, to act just in this way. He, like the unwise dog, makes a hasty rush to attack any opponent whatsoever; nor does he pause to ascertain first, as he ought to do, what is the risk he ventures upon, what is the strength of the opponent, and what his own: and hence it often happens that, seeking to inflict an injury, he is injured himself, and, instead of requiting some old wrongs, he receives other new ones. Now what is your security that this very thing may not also befall you? For, even should you be so successful, as to drive your enemy out of the world, do not others survive to take his part? Very seldom does an act of revenge completely prosper. You may have succeeded in utterly annihilating your adversary; but then you have offended his family, you have exasperated his party; so that, for the one, who falls dead, a hundred living may spring up from him. How many therefore have had to regret that ever they avenged themselves, yea, what a sore grief has it proved to many, that they have triumphed! I find it so stated by Tertullian. They reckoned by their success upon making themselves sure, and afterwards they discover that they have done no more than cut off the head of the hydra; so mightily do their dangers increase: and hence what a troubled prospect is now before them; and all in consequence of their unwillingness to live on terms of peace with a single individual. They must lose his friends, by their evident ill feeling towards all, who belong to him. They must lose their recreations, by absenting themselves from all the societies he frequented. They must lose their independence, since now they cannot go about in safety, as they might wish: for they must needs despatch some one in advance to ascertain what person, or persons, they are likely to meet out of doors: every new face they see excites some suspicion; every weapon near them causes some alarm. At their meals, they must suspect some poisonous mixture in their food; in their walks, they must apprehend some traps set in their way; at night, they must have a misgiving, lest they be treacherously surprised in their beds. They must consume the best part of their income in keeping servants to protect them; in bribing spies to give them information; in maintaining ruffians to use the stiletto for them; and in keeping open house for a set of people, whose mouths are said to be like the devouring flame, which is never satisfied, who never say, "It is enough."[1] And don't we see every day of our lives how, in consequence of this, families are brought to ruin by their quarrels, splendid patrimonies are wasted, large establishments are broken up, and the noblest alliances are brought to desolation? How then is it possible for you to be at ease in a condition so wretched, as this must needs be, in which the evil you have to suffer is so certain, and the good, which will come of it, so uncertain? Speak, and tell me: for you must, I am sure, be already quite convinced that I have no design to preach in favour of your opponents, but rather to plead the cause of your own near relatives, of those dearest to you; in a word, of your own selves.

3. You have only two ways before you of replying to this.

[1] What a picture of Italian society in the seventeenth century!

You may say, first, that, for the sake of revenge, you are content to sacrifice everything you possess. But behold the sun of reason is now set in your mind! Excuse me, if I tell you so: it is evening with you—your sun is gone down! Oh, what folly! Oh, what childishness! This is nothing else than to fall into the notorious absurdity of that Tribune of the people, named Drusus, as the story is related by Pliny; who, not knowing any other method of blasting the character of his enemy Quintius Cepio, and doing him an injury, adopted this wonderful expedient. He swallowed the blood of a filthy goat, a thing as deadly, as it was disgusting; and committed suicide with the hope that his death would then be laid at the door of his well-known enemy. "And is not this," says Chrysostom, "to act like a madman, like a fool, like an idiot? What, I ask, is more absurd than to punish your own self under the notion that you are taking your revenge on your neighbour?" If however you do not say you are content to sacrifice everything you possess, there is another way still left you to evade the force of my argument. You may say that you have not anything to lose; that you are quite your own master, that you are absolutely independent, that you live alone, that you have no interest to care for, no family to provide for, and that, when your enemy is once dead or rendered powerless, you will then have not a soul in the world to fear. But, if you speak in this manner, I must at once stop your mouth: for then it is not evening with you, as I supposed; it is already dark dreadful night! *Will ye not fear Me? saith the Lord.* (Jer. v. 22.) If there be nobody in the whole world left to cause you fear, GOD surely is still left. Will you not fear Him? Oh, did you understand what an atrocious injury you are doing Him, in thus taking your private revenge of an offender, however in the wrong—Oh did you understand this, believe me, you would not so readily allow your anger to transport you thus far.

4. Represent to your mind a Prince, as benevolent as powerful; and that, being anxious to prove his attachment to some favoured subject, should address him to this effect; "My friend, I wish to conclude a treaty with you. Therefore listen. I wish to have it publicly decreed throughout

my dominions, that whosoever dares do you a wrong should be held guilty of high treason, just as if he had committed the outrage against my own person. Henceforth I shall consider all the injuries, all the affronts, all the base treatment, done to you, as done to me. But then I expect from you, in return, one condition, which is this: that you must leave it entirely to me to execute all worthy vengeance for such offences. I declare myself to be the receiver of them, as being mine; as mine, I wish to avenge them." Now, tell me, supposing the case of such a Prince, thus addressing one of his inferior subjects, would not the latter deem himself very highly honoured? And were he to decline the condition, as though it were a hard one, would he not be set down for a fool, and even condemned as a low-minded churl? And think you, that such a Prince, however benevolent his disposition, could ever afterwards regard this audacious subject with any favour? Would he any longer interest himself in his welfare? Would he be at any further pains to provide for his safety? So far from it, I believe that he would banish him from his presence, and, instead of defending him from the assaults of other men, would be himself the very first to proceed against him.

Now, consider all this as exactly describing our position. GOD has most plainly protested that He will take all wrongs done to us, as if done to Himself in this same way. This is an undeniable fact. Salvianus so states it. "Our most kind and merciful GOD has in common with His servants both the honour and the dishonour, they receive in the world; lest any one, who injures a servant of GOD, should suppose, that it was only a man, whom he had injured." Accordingly, none can harm, none can grieve us, who does not at the same time harm and grieve Him also; while every sin, committed against a neighbour, is in like manner committed against GOD. *He, who despises you, despises Me.* (S. Luke x. 16.) Could He have given us any greater proof of the intense love He bears us? But then what follows? As He has protested, that He will consider the personal injuries we receive to be His, so, as the second part of the contract, He has declared, that He has reserved to Himself the office of avenging them. *Vengeance is Mine: I will repay, saith the Lord.* (Rom.

xii. 19.) Now, were we to be dissatisfied with this condition, has He not every just cause to be highly displeased? Or, by imposing this condition, has He laid on us a heavy burden? Has He done us a wrong? Has He oppressed us? What evil has He thereby brought upon us? We are compelled to acknowledge that we must entertain one or other of these two opinions concerning Him; either, that His arm is not sufficiently strong to maintain our cause; or, that He has no heart to commiserate our ill-treatment. But who among you can fall into such absurd and crazy notions? Ask S. Chrysostom; he will tell you, that GOD is so implacable in resenting the injuries, done to us, that He would far sooner fail to retaliate what affects Himself, than what affects His servants. "It is often the way of GOD to pardon the sins we commit against Him, when He most severely punishes the sins we commit against our neighbour."

The wretched Cain was guilty of two flagrant acts of wickedness; one of them was directly against GOD, whom he affronted by his sacrifice; the other of them was directly against his neighbour, whom he murdered through envy. Who would not have considered that every obligation was laid upon GOD to punish with the utmost severity the former of these offences, as being personal to Himself? Cain's was the first act ever committed in the world directly against Religion: and hence it seemed to call for some very signal castigation, so as to secure for the future the respect of mankind for the Divine Worship. Nevertheless, remarks S. Chrysostom, observe how very slight a sense of injury GOD manifested on this occasion. He was content with simply declaring to the offender, "Thou hast sinned." He did not punish him in the character of a Judge, but merely admonished him in the quality of a friend. But, when the same wretch went out breathing savage slaughter against Abel, Oh, then it was that an offended GOD was unable to contain Himself. With His own mouth He execrated the villain; He drove him from His Presence; He banished him to the wild woods; He haunted him with terrors. During the remainder of his life He would allow no peace to that mind, which ever afterwards was torn and distracted by as many furies, as Cain had thoughts by day, or dreams by night. How then can you possibly entertain the notion that GOD will never resent the wrongs you do Him, with this certain fact before your eyes, that He punished so far more severely the first crime, committed against a man's neighbour, than He ever did the first act of Sacrilege, perpetrated against the very Deity Himself? But, on the other hand, if GOD so warmly interests Himself in your behalf, why do you not trust Him entirely with all your concerns? And then, seeing you are nothing better than His most subordinate menial servants, how can you dare claim the authority of your Sovereign LORD? Is not this to dispute with Him His judicial power? Is not this to repudiate His protecting care? "What homage of due respect shall men present to GOD, when they presumptuously undertake to defend themselves?" I ask you this in the words of Tertullian. When you have sustained an injury, if you constitute yourselves to be judges, if you draw out the case for yourselves, if you pronounce the sentence for yourselves, if you execute justice for yourselves, what remains for GOD to do, but to sit still? You make Him, who is really the sole and the absolute Judge of your contentions, to be nothing more than an idle spectator.

Why, if this be so, it will henceforth be quite needless that we should tire ourselves with repeating the words of the Psalmist; *O Lord God, to whom vengeance belongeth, show Thyself.* (Ps. xciv. 1.) No; for as long as you will not allow Him to act in this character, you disown Him, as your avenger. *The God to whom vengeance belongeth, hath acted freely* (Vulg.:) and He has no pleasure in your wresting the spear from His grasp to flourish it about, as you please. In accordance with this character, Oh, how keenly must He resent such an odious outrage against Him. To usurp the jurisdiction of your LORD! Why, know you not this to be the very point, on which every Prince is most jealous? Therefore see at once what you gain by desiring to avenge yourselves. It amounts to this; that, whereas had you no such desire, GOD would then stand on your side, and avenge you of your enemy; now He will stand on the opposite side, and avenge your enemy of you! Choose then, which you will have. Do you prefer having GOD on your side against your enemy? or, do you prefer having GOD on your enemy's side against you? Think a little. You cannot come to any other terms. You must needs fix your choice between the one or the other. Will you then be so unwise, as to fear having a man for your enemy, and therefore labour to effect his overthrow; and yet not to fear having a GOD for your enemy, and therefore not to beware of offending Him? Hear how GOD Himself speaks by Isaiah, *Who art thou, that thou shouldest be afraid of a man, that shall die, and forgettest the Lord thy Maker?* (li. 12, 13.)

5. I hear the excuse, which you are ready to plead. You say; were you to decline executing justice with your own hand, your reputation must suffer for it; that you have been the person offended, and therefore you must take your turn to be the offender: otherwise, did you consent to leave your vindication in the hands of One, so vastly your superior in power, you will be looked down upon, as in the same proportion inferior to your adversary. Is it really so? A mighty, a most mighty disproportion! I grant. But, my hearers, let me here heartily congratulate myself, as well as all you, that this should be the first action in all your life, reflecting any discredit on your reputation; just as if it was no discredit whatever to persons of your rank to frequent, even though married men, houses of known bad character; to maintain the most improper connections, even in public; to go on year after year keeping back his wages from the poor labourer; to be so insincere in your words and general behaviour; to flatter your inferiors, with a view to your own interests; to calumniate the innocent for the gratification of your envy; to hinder to such an extent the happiness of others out of mere spite and bad feeling. And is it possible then that you—you, I say—who without the least scruple can commit the most disreputable actions to the injury of your souls, can yet fear doing any one such for their decided benefit? But whence is it that you infer all this loss to your reputation, as if Solomon deserved no credit, when he said, *It is an honour to a man to cease from strife* (Prov. xx. 3)? Is it because the laws of worldly honour have so ruled it? But what, if we should find that persons, more noble than our-

selves, have obeyed this duty of forgiving an enemy, without having the fair lustre of their characters in the least sullied by it; and have done it too before this same world? Shall we then be above following their example? For how stands the case? Will you call the Basils disreputable men, the Nazianzens disreputable men, the Chrysostoms disreputable men, because they left behind them such signal instances of forbearance? Will you impute it to men, like these, as something degrading, that they refused to act upon the wicked laws of worldly honour, and would rather follow the holy instructions of CHRIST? I wish you to decide this matter for yourselves. Who will think it scorn to be infamous in the sight of the world, while he is in such noble company? Be then glorious, if you prefer it, with the Adonibezeks, with the Abimelechs, and with the Rehoboams, men accounted so many prodigies of impiety. This is nothing to me. I am content to be infamous, yes, infamous with those, whom I have cited, as such patterns of meekness. After all, I know how it happens. *That, which is highly esteemed among men is abomination in the sight of God.* (S. Luke xvi. 15.) And whose saying is this, that I have ventured to utter? Is it the saying of some modern or some ancient philosopher? It is the Word of CHRIST. If any doubt it, I refer him to the sixteenth chapter of S. Luke: there let him read it for himself.

And are we still so blind, as to require further arguments? Oh, just consider what it is, for the sake of which so many rush to their destruction, while their glory is to triumph over their enemies, to crush them, to trample them in the dust under their feet. That, which in the unmeaning language of the world, men call glory, what is it in the sight of GOD? It is *abomination.* Yes! CHRIST declares it. *That, which is highly esteemed among men, is abomination in the sight of God!* And you, of your own free choice, take this glory for your portion. Keep it then. I give it you. As for me, I rather choose to be infamous. I choose to be infamous. *I will yet be more vile* (2 Sam. vi. 22:) only let me be infamous in company with the followers of my LORD. *It is better* (Oh, how Divinely expressed by Solomon in the Proverbs,) *It is better to be of an humble spirit with the lowly, than to divide the spoil with the proud.* (xvi. 19.)

6. Not that I can at all concede this glory to you, that you hope for. For, tell me, do you think that, if you would lose so much credit with many of your acquaintances by granting pardon, you would not just as much lose your credit also with other persons by taking revenge? You grievously err, if you think so. Because, in a case like this, the shrewdest observers will invariably say, that, though you might perhaps be a most formidable worldly-wise man, yet that you behaved at the same time in a brutal blood-thirsty manner. They will say that you showed more effeminacy in your anger than real manliness; since, in spite of all the reasons urged to the contrary, and all the kind intervention of friends, you could not bring your mind to adopt that noble resolution, on which David once acted towards Saul, and Octavius towards Cinna, and Philip towards Nicanor, and Murena towards Cato, and Cæsar towards Marcellus. They will remark that you have simply done no more than what every viper and wasp is capable of doing; namely, of biting or of stinging the person, who provokes them; and that, if this is to be your assumed plea for glorying, then the most cowardly animals are most to be commended, since, of all others, they are most sensible of an injury. Now then, if both parties will speak ill of you—the good and the wise, if you take revenge; the wicked and the foolish, if you grant pardon—is it not better you should be spoken ill of by the silly populace, than by the wise men? I said, by the silly populace; for, to speak to the point, who are the persons, whose reproofs you have been taught to consider so formidable? Are they the Constantines, the Justinians, the Theodosiuses, men, who have approved themselves among Christians, as the Lycurguses of the people? But these men never breathed a single word in disparagement of pardoning. Eminent, as they were, for wisdom, they well knew that whatever is right cannot be otherwise than to the same extent honourable. They, whom you hold in so great fear, are none other but a certain lewd set of licentious men, half infidels, half heathens, half atheists, the proud calumniators of that Gospel, which

they ought to acknowledge. Hear how they are described by the Apostle; *If any man teach otherwise, and consent not to wholesome words, even the words of our Lord Jesus Christ, and to the doctrine, which is according to godliness, he is proud, knowing nothing.* (1 Tim. vi. 3, 4.) What a censure have we here! He declares that every such person should be looked upon as *proud*, as *knowing nothing;* as an aspiring ignoramus, an ambitious fool. And are you prepared to make the opinion of such men your rule of life, to confine your praise to their approbation, and from them to receive your reward?

7. But if, after all, you find these reasons unsatisfactory, and still stoutly maintain that you will forfeit more honour by granting pardon than by taking revenge; be it even so. What then do you infer from this? that you are quite at liberty to disobey the positive injunction of CHRIST? No; you must bow submissively to His authority, and willingly sacrifice to Him this mad and vain aspiration you have after worldly distinction. Your character, you say, is gone. Well, let your character go. This then is the path appointed unto you, that is to bring you to Paradise. It is rough; it is difficult: it is painful: I allow all this: yet what can you do? None were ever known to have reached Paradise by stepping over flowers and leaves, but by wounding themselves with thorns and briars. "My delicate ones have gone through rough ways." (Baruch iv. 26.) Gaze on those holy men, who were most sensitive, those holy women, who were most delicate. Ah! through what paths did they make themselves a way to Heaven! They shuddered at the mere sight of what was before them. . . . And does it seem a mighty thing that Heaven should cost you, to get it, some little loss of worldly reputation? Men, you pretend, will ascribe your declining to take revenge, not to your religious principle, but to your cowardice, to your want of spirit. Be patient; let them so account for it. Is not everlasting happiness bought cheap at the cost of any temporal suffering whatsoever? *In your patience possess ye your souls.* (S. Luke xxi. 19.)

8. But, to conclude, just reply, if you can, to this remaining concise argument, which I would fain leave, as a dagger, infixed in your heart. You are placed in such a dilemma,

that of necessity you must choose one or other of these alternatives: it is a question, whether you should give up your reputation, or GOD should give up His. If you fail to avenge yourselves, then worldlings will despise you; but, if you avenge yourselves, then you will despise GOD. Which of these two things therefore seems most befitting? Shall your honour be sacrificed? or, shall the Divine honour be sacrificed? Yes, yes, I quite understand you. You mean to say, "Let the honour of GOD go, provided our honour be preserved." Is it indeed so? Then I have no more to say. I have done. O my poor SAVIOUR, why take so great pains with this people, and weary Thyself in Thy counsels and entreaties, that for Thy love's sake they should *forgive their enemies?* Why repeat so often in their ears, *But I say unto you—But I say unto you?* Ah! let us hear no more such words from Thee. Pardon me, if I express my deep regret that they should ever have escaped Thy lips! Dost *Thou* say unto us? But on this account will men consent? On this account will they act? On this account will they obey? *Thou* sayest unto us. But, because of this, will men's angry passions be appeased? *Thou* sayest unto us. But, because of this, will their instruments of murder be cast away? Simply because *Thou* sayest it, will they for the time to come cease from rushing, as they did before, to revenge and defamation, to blood and the sword, to slaughter and carnage? O my Treasure, who art so despised of men! No more of those words, *I say unto you,* from Thy mouth; no more, I pray: for these Christians of Thine attach more weight to the least particle of their own reputation than to all Thy wishes, all Thy counsels, all Thy commandments. And dost Thou see and observe this? *Behold, the Word of the Lord is unto them a reproach, they have no delight in it.* (Jer. vi. 10.) They will leave Thee to be taunted with reproaches, and will not scruple even to band themselves together against Thee, under the pretence of Thy requiring of them things, not only difficult, but impossible; yea, degrading to them and disreputable. And what wilt Thou say, in reply to their arguments? With Thy single word, *I say unto you,* dost Thou expect to stop their mouths? This, I allow, was once the boast of the ancient philosophers.

With an *Ipse dixit* every opposition, raised against a Pythagoras, was at once triumphantly silenced. But Thou art not held in the same high esteem. Our great folks lay claim to knowing far more, than *Thou* knowest about these points of worldly honour—*Thou,* who wast born in a manger; *Thou,* who wast bred in a workshop; *Thou,* who art dead (must I even tell Thee this?) *Thou,* who art ignominiously dead upon the cross from Thy love to this very people—what canst *Thou* possibly know about points of honour?—Christians, my very heart is breaking; whether from zeal to GOD or from abhorrence at the impiety of men, I know not. I feel unable to say more. Do you also wish to be found among those, who in this manner put CHRIST to an open shame? Do you also wish that He should remain so degraded, so vilified, so overwhelmed with confusion, in order that you may not lose an atom of your honour?· *Let not the sun go down upon your wrath:* I say it again, *Let not the sun go down upon your wrath.* Oh, let not passion cast you down into such utter darkness! Accordingly, while you now consider how with becoming wisdom you ought to act, I will take rest.

THE SECOND PART.

9. There are some, who will readily deny the application of this sermon to themselves, because they do not profess any open hostility. They speak the truth. They do not profess it, because they keep it concealed. Oh, how many are there, who brood in their hearts over the enmities they bear, and keep them shut, like mines, closed now, that at the proper time they may be exploded. They wait for the opportunity; they bide the critical moment: beyond this you cannot trust them: for, as was shrewdly observed by Ecclesiastes, *anger resteth in the bosom of fools* (vii. 9.) You may sometimes observe a person of this class, which by the world is called wise, but by GOD foolish. He has learnt so thoroughly to dissemble, while in your presence, every old grievance that you would feel positive that every emotion of anger in him was quite extinct. No; it is not extinct: it only slumbers. Rouse it a little, and you will soon see it shake off its sleep.

For what, if here and there some abstain from downright injuries to their neighbours? this arises from their lacking the power: in other respects, they still harbour their malicious thoughts. They live upon their inward malignity and feed upon their angry resentments. Let them but hear the name of the person, who has given them offence, mentioned in society, all of a sudden they feel their blood boil within them. They will show him no kindness, nor even common civility in word or in deed. And, should they ever depart from this rule, it would only be to blind his eyes and throw him off his guard; so as more effectually to indulge their spite against him by some underhand contrivance. And do not these persons then exceedingly displease GOD? Oh, what a delusion it would be, were any to suppose that the most hateful acts of revenge alone, such as massacres, assassinations, and such like enormities, were so offensive to GOD. Hear what He declared by the prophet Hosea, *Ephraim provoked Me to anger with his bitterness* (xii. 14, Vulg.) Have you marked the expression? He does not say, with his furious wrath; He does not say, with his outrageous misdoings; no, with his *bitterness:* because those feelings of bitterness, which you cannot consent to eradicate entirely from your minds, these, these are what so highly displease GOD. And, while you are in this state, will you have no fear to join in the Sacred Ordinances of the Church and to receive the Supper of the LORD?.. But come, whatever the animosities be you still retain in your bosom, whether great or small, secret or open, I invite you this morning to offer them all alike, as a gift to CHRIST, who now by my mouth demands them all of you.

10. In His Name I have delivered my message, *Love your enemies.* And now what answer am I to convey to Him from you? Will you obey Him? Will you submit yourselves? Will you forgive? Tell me, what do you mean to do? Are you still in any doubt? Oh, heavens! Surely, after all, we are somewhat indebted to CHRIST. It is to you He speaks. It is of you He makes the demand. *I say unto you.* Did He entreat a set of strangers, for whose welfare He had done nothing; well and good: but He demands it of you, to whom He has given souls and bodies, riches and health, children

and friends, education and influence, and all the good you
enjoy here below—of you, I say, for whose Salvation He has
endured so many affronts—of you, for whose ransom He has
poured forth such torrents of Blood! And are you then the
persons to deny Him this favour? Abigail in her distress
was able to pacify the wrath of David, and to prevail upon
him graciously to overlook the uncalled for insult he had received from the churlish Nabal. Ambrose was able to prevail
upon the Emperor Gratian, that he would pardon a man, who
had publicly ridiculed his august person. A Genovefa was
able to prevail upon King Childeric, that he would pardon
many, who had daringly rebelled against his Royal Majesty.
And Pelagius, the deacon, casting himself at the feet of Totila
near the entrance of the Vatican—of Totila, when still a barbarian and a heathen—was able to prevail upon him by the
Holy Gospels, the Book he held in his hands, that he would
of his clemency save from destruction the city of Rome, which,
before hostile, was now lying prostrate at his feet. And is
CHRIST unable to prevail upon you, that, for His sake, you
would forgive your enemy and overlook a wrong, an affront,
a slight, a mere trifling word? What more would you have
CHRIST do? Would you fain have Him prostrate Himself
in supplication before you with this petition? I may almost
venture to say that He would consent to it. For, if He hesitated not to stoop before such a traitor, as Judas, to wash his
feet, to dry them, to kiss them, I believe He would consider
it no indignity to be seen on bended knees before you. But
do you require all this, before you will grant His request?
. . . Do you need all this entreaty from a GOD, who for you
was crucified? Oh, what a disgrace! Oh, what a shame:
Oh, what a reproach!

More here may still be urged. For it is not only in regard
to the past that you lie under such vast obligations to CHRIST;
you are also materially dependent upon Him for the future.
Tell me, have you reached such a state of perfection, as never
once in any wise to have offended Him either in thought,
word, or deed? You have not. On what ground then can
you hope to obtain His gracious forgiveness? Hear His own
announcement, and, while you hear it, tremble for yourselves:

If ye forgive men their trespasses, your Heavenly Father will also forgive you. (S. Matth. vi. 14.)—You are quite sure then, as a matter of faith, that, if we pardon our enemy, GOD will pardon us—*But if ye forgive not men their trespasses, neither will your Father forgive your trespasses.* Hence too we know by faith and for certain that GOD will not pardon us, if we do not pardon our enemy. What say you therefore to this? Does it in no wise concern you, whether GOD will show you mercy for your sins committed against Him? Are you in love with death? Are you in love with destruction? Are you resolutely bent on damning your own souls? If so, why then there is an end to our discussion. Let the earth open its jaws; let hell discover its depths: make your desperate headlong plunge into those flames, that you may burn in them for ever! But, should your desire be to receive mercy of the LORD, then I ask (venting my soul in the words of S. Augustine) "With what face, or with what confidence, can that man look for the forgiveness of his offences before the Tribunal of CHRIST, who, when GOD commanded him to forgive his enemies, refused and would not?" With what boldness can you presume to implore the least pity of Him? with what assurance? with what countenance? And yet—Oh, their folly!—no persons show such a reluctance in granting pardon to others, as they, who are themselves under the greatest need of asking pardon from GOD. How strange is this! Holy men, having comparatively no sins to be pardoned, when they are injured, give thanks; when they are cursed, return blessings; when they are persecuted, repay in acts of kindness: and all for fear, lest hereafter GOD should treat them by the measure of that severity, which others have found at their hands: while we, miserable sinners, who, every moment of our lives, should sink down into hell, did not GOD with a strong arm bear us up, we cannot with all our impieties and wickednesses on our heads, hear a word said to us about being reconciled to our enemies! No amount of amends made can satisfy us; no weight of authority can prevail upon us. Let GOD command,—let Him entreat,—let Him threaten, —we still clamour for blood, for nothing less than blood. We would have our enemies despatched, or, at least, suffer all the mischief we can do them. The revenge, that we are unable to take by means of the ball of the pistol, we would have by means of the ball of the voting-box: the revenge, that we are unable to take by means of the poniard, we would have by means of the pen: what we cannot compass by acts of violence, we would have by words of malice. But is it possible that, merely for the sake of gratifying this brutish propensity of ours, we should throw to the winds all our happiness, make GOD our enemy, banish ourselves from heaven, and thrust our souls into hell? At the foot of the Cross let us form a more generous determination. Yes; approach the Cross of JESUS, and embrace His very feet, streaming as they are with blood. Why hesitate? "If you deposit your wrong in His hands, He is your avenger; if your loss, He is your Remunerator; if your grief, He is your Comforter; if your very life, He is your Resurrection." In these words does Tertullian encourage you. Cannot you trust GOD? Cannot you feel assured of His power to reward you abundantly for this well-pleasing and dutiful service, done for His sake?

11. Yes! yes! draw nigh; for I wish this morning to take the pen, and, as in the immediate presence of GOD, to steep it in His Holy wounds; that I may write down the formulary of pardon with their very Blood! "LORD, by virtue of the office, which I unworthily hold in this place, I declare unto Thee, in the name of this people, that all the injuries we have received in times past, or shall hereafter receive, we lay them all down at Thy most Sacred feet! Here we offer up our resentments in sacrifice to Thee; here we mortify and kill our angry bad passions, as so many victims, to Thy honour. And, though it may grieve us sore to lose the sweet satisfaction of revenging ourselves, yet, notwithstanding this, because it is *Thou*, who commandest, we will obey. We will ourselves propose terms of reconciliation, should they not first be made to us; and, when they are first made by others, we will accept them. Only do Thou forgive us, according to the same pity, which we extend to our offenders: and when before Thy most terrible Tribunal our own sins shall accuse us, be Thou our SAVIOUR, be Thou our Defender!" Christians, is there one among you, who refuses to come forward and sign this

formulary of pardon? Is there one such person? If there be, let him declare himself: for then, in the burning indignation of a holy zeal for GOD, with this very same Blood will I write down the dreadful sentence of that man, *because he remembered not to show mercy* (Ps. cix. 16.) *He shall have judgment without mercy, who showed no mercy.* (S. James ii. 13.) . . . . But let every one of us prostrate ourselves humbly at the feet of our LORD; there let us implore pardon for our enemies, pardon for ourselves—pardon, pardon for all, who have sinned!

SERMON IV.

HUNGER AFTER THE FOOD OF GOD'S WORD.

S. MATTH. IV. 4.

"MAN SHALL NOT LIVE BY BREAD ALONE, BUT BY EVERY WORD THAT PROCEEDETH OUT OF THE MOUTH OF GOD."

1. THAT, which to the body is its proper food, the Divine Word is to the soul. This is a certain truth, unless we are disposed to refuse credit to a S. Chrysostom, who expressly affirms it: Gregory and Ambrose declare the same, and so does the concurrent testimony of holy men. Nor is there anything strange in this. This Word preserves in the soul its vital heat, so that it does not die; it nourishes the soul, when faint; it strengthens it, when feeble; it restores it, when sickly; yea, it has a peculiar excellent virtue beyond all other kinds of food. They, however pleasant, or wholesome, or substantial they may be, can have no effect upon bodies, that are not alive: the Divine Word is able to impart life to souls, that are dead. Who therefore among you will feel any great surprise at hearing CHRIST this morning affirm, that *Man shall not live by Bread alone, but by every word that proceedeth out of the mouth of God?* With good reason may indeed He affirm, not only in a figurative, but also in a literal sense, that man himself is nourished by the Word of GOD; inasmuch as the soul, which is the noblest part of man, is nourished by it. The Divine Word, nevertheless, must give

place (if I may say it without offence) to the food of the body in this respect; it is not so universally hungered after, nor so vehemently desired, among men. But why is this? Is it not a food equally good? We have already shown it to be superior. Is it not dainty? yes, in the highest degree. Is it not delicious? yes, exceedingly so. Whence then does it arise that so few feel hungry after it? The cause, if I mistake not, is this. No person, who desires first to fill himself with every word, that proceedeth out of the mouth of the devil, can have a relish for *every Word that proceedeth out of the mouth of God*. And can you fail to observe the multitudes, who are every day feeding their souls with the vilest garbage, with impure discourses, with immodest representations, with instructions, larded with ribaldry, detraction, satire, and every species of vanity? What wonder, then, if their taste for any more wholesome nourishment should be utterly spoiled? It is absolutely impossible, that those, who *turn unto fables*, should not *turn away from the truth* (2 Tim. iv. 4.) Whatever be the cause—and I do not pretend to know it—the effect is beyond measure deplorable: for God can inflict no more terrible scourge on any people at variance with Him, than that of depriving them of this spiritual appetite.

2. Hunger is a most stimulating thing: its property is to impel every animal to procure the food it desires. It will not allow the timid stags to rest in their caves, nor the goats, who are unable to defend themselves, to abide in their retreats: it will prompt even the little birds to leave their beloved nests at the imminent risk of their lives, to light upon the ground, and there, for the mere sake of a few seeds, to expose themselves to the danger of falling into the snares of the numerous fowlers, who, like silent thieves, stand watching for them in the thicket. What then have you to say? Do you pretend to have really any stimulating sense of hunger after God's Word, while it has not the power, except seldom, to draw you from your houses to a place so noble, so secure, as a Church; where, while you gather in your supplies of food, you need be under no fear of meeting with any violence, or any snare, or any insult, or even of incurring the very smallest expense? When in a time of famine the Patriarch Jacob heard

that corn was selling in Egypt, though at an exorbitant price, he immediately bestirred himself, and turning to his children said; *Why do ye look one upon another ?* (Gen. xlii. 1.) What neglect and indifference is this, that I see in you! What apathy! What indolence! *I have heard that there is corn in Egypt; and here you are, standing idle to be starved to death! Get you down thither and buy for us from thence, that we may live and not die.* Away! away! This is no time for allowing one's self rest, when the famine presses so sore. What then would Jacob have said, had he heard that corn in Egypt, instead of being sold at an exorbitant price, was actually given away? Would he not have been far more indignant? Would he not have been much more disturbed in his mind? Dear Christians, the Word of GOD is not sold in this place to any hearer: it is given away for nothing. *I have preached to you the Gospel of God freely* (2 Cor. xi. 7.) So I can say with S. Paul. You have nothing to pay, nothing to contribute; and yet you are negligent: you come not here every day under any anxiety to provide yourselves with seasonable instructions, as you would seek for food. Ah why, why is it so? It can only arise from your want of a real appetite. "They, who will not seek what is placed within their reach, pine away with a fastidious apathy," saith S. Augustine.

3. I am quite aware that staying at home is an excellent thing; but it is not so during the time of preaching. Nor, in saying this, do I allude only to the male sex among you, who, to my knowledge, are going about then in the eager pursuit of their worldly interests. I allude likewise to the female. The celebrated Shunammite was a lady of rank, a lady too of most retired habits. But in what terms did Elisha speak to her, when he foresaw, a few months before it came to pass, the severe famine, destined so grievously to afflict the whole land of Israel? Did he forsooth say, "Remain quietly where you are; don't leave your home; don't stir from this place; attend to the female department of your family." No; he said quite the contrary. *Arise and go thou and thy household, and sojourn wheresoever thou canst sojourn* (2 Kings viii. 1.) But alas! holy prophet, what are you doing? Are

you not well aware how highly becoming it is in women to be shut up at home? Know you not that they are all like crystal, which is safe only, so long as it is well guarded; and like precious ointment, which is fragrant only, so long as it is well covered? How then can you now advise her to set out on a vagrant kind of life, and wander about in any land, or among any set of people? *Go and sojourn wheresoever thou canst sojourn!* Oh, surely, such a life would be to her dishonour! There is no denying this; it would; but not in a time of famine. Whosoever is starving for want of food let him *arise*, let him help himself, let him use all the means in his power, provided they be honest; for necessity has no law. Such was precisely the conduct of the Shunammite. *She arose and did after the saying of the man of God: and she went with her household, and sojourned in the land of the Philistines seven years.* Hereby she confirmed the truth of that saying of Hegesippus, that "famine gets the better of every affection of our minds, and chiefly of our sense of shame." But why speak I only of this Shunammite? Did not Ruth in a time of famine leave her paternal home, and did she not more than once, poor young widow as she was, betake herself to the fields to glean the ears of corn, that had escaped the sickle and hands of the reapers? (Ruth ii.) Was not Sarah on account of the famine seen accompanying her husband Abram even so far south, as Egypt? Was not Rebekah on account of the famine seen travelling with her husband Isaac to Gerar? And ought then the women of our day to tarry at home, intent only upon their household affairs, when there is preaching in the Church? And should they leave it to their husbands to go there without them, while they willingly renounce their own share of the spiritual food, comfort, and support? Never let this be charged against them! For such conduct will be found, on consideration, not to arise from any love of seclusion on their part; no: in some it springs from the want of all devotional feeling, in some from indecision of character, in some from indolence. And therefore I tell you that it is their duty, not only on Festival days to assemble together here, like other folks; but that, despising all superfluous finery in dress, the cause why they waste so much of their precious time, the value of which is only discovered on a deathbed, they also ought to be here, coming early and in good time: for let them remember that impatience to get one's food is another sign of genuine hunger.

4. Is it not so, my hearers? Suppose a sumptuous banquet to be prepared for a numerous company of guests, such as the one, which Samson once made for his friends, or Solomon for his servants—who are the first to make their appearance? Who are the punctual people? Why, the hungry. The late-comers are either indifferent to the feast, or wish, as a fine thing, to be thought so. What then must we say of ourselves? Must we say that any hunger after the Word of GOD prevails among those, who are so late in their attendance on the sermon; not late occasionally by some accident, but invariably and intentionally late, just as at a dinner when half over. No; we cannot possibly say this. The hungry are they, who have not even the patience to wait for the time appointed. They are the first to appear in Church, to occupy the benches and to secure the chairs, regarding every other business quite subordinate to the hearing of the Word of GOD, when preached to them. *Teach a just man*, declares the HOLY SPIRIT, what will he do? *He will make haste to receive.* (Prov. ix. 9, Vulg.) He will make haste to devour your instruction with more awakened eagerness, than doves rush to their seed, or fishes to their food. Reprove him; *he will make haste to receive:* solve his doubts, *he will make haste to receive:* advise him; *he will make haste to receive:* propose to him some new and approved spiritual exercise; *he will make haste to receive.* In a word, *Teach the just man, and he will make haste to receive:* he will do so on common days, he will do so on Festival days; at any time, in any place, on any occasion, like a hungry man, *he will make haste to receive.* We know that a man will become restless under a craving desire for food. He scolds the servants; he disturbs the whole house with his complaints, because the dinner is not on the table. . . . Hence let none among you consider himself, as at all hungering after GOD's Word, who when he hears the Church bell calling him to the sermon, as to a feast of Royal dainties, can still remain idling in the streets.

So far from *making haste to receive*, such a one continues his chat. He sees others leave on their way to Church; but he *makes no haste:* he hears them ask him to join them; but he makes no *haste:* he hears even the last chime, but it does not move him: he makes no *haste to receive:* he cannot bring himself to quit the bench, where he is lounging: he cannot tear himself away from his club, where he sits abusing his neighbour.

5. There must, moreover, be but a very slight feeling of hunger for the Word of God, when people are become so refined, when they expect that sermons should be daintily served up. "Hunger is not fastidious," said Seneca. The hungry man cares nothing for display, in what is set before him; he is not caught by condiments; he is no admirer of high seasoning. He has so little discrimination, as to what he eats, that he exemplifies that true saying of the wise man, *To the hungry soul every bitter thing is sweet.* (Prov. xxvii. 7.) He will gather the wretched wild grapes of Galgala, even as though they were the celebrated clusters of Engaddi. On this account, there is no describing the pleasure, afforded to a hungry appetite by the commonest articles of food. Artaxerxes, King of the Assyrians, when compelled, after his defeat in battle, to support himself under a cottage roof with barley bread, made it a matter of complaint against his gods that, up to that hour, he had never eaten with so great relish. Ptolemy, King of Egypt, when, having left his baggage on the road, he was constrained to appease his hunger in a squalid hut with bread made of bran, protested to his courtiers that he had never before tasted such a delightful morsel. . . . So true it is that hunger is not fastidious, and that the things, as holy Job testifies from his own experience, that disgust our palates, when pampered, become quite delicious, when we are well-nigh starved: *The things, that my soul refused to touch, are as my sorrowful meat* (vi. 7.) How think ye then? Never to hear a sermon, that pleases and contents you, but to grow every day more squeamish and particular,—suppose ye this to be a spiritual hunger? One person laments, that the sermon is so dry and overlearned; another, that the style is so coarse: here, the language is considered so common; here, it

has so few points, or striking passages. And we are expected to call this spiritual hunger? No, Christians; no: it is nothing of the sort; and let us hear no more of it. Instead of longing after such nice delicacies, get a hearty good appetite; and you will all at once be well satisfied. Seneca writes, that, if one has to serve up a dinner for hungry folks, it is soon accomplished: every cook is good; every kind of cookery suffices. "It is easy to feed with a little those, who simply desire to be filled." Habaccuc soon provided in a bowl a dinner for his poor reapers. Elisha soon got ready upon a plough a dinner for his common labourers. But Oh, what vast trouble is required in catering for a people difficult to please! It is necessary with the Kings of Persia to advertize promises of reward to any one, who should discover in the world some new method of gratifying the palate, since the old established methods are now despised. *The full soul loatheth an honeycomb.* (Prov. xxvii. 7.) With men, like Apicius, we must lay in a store of nightingales' tongues: with men, like Heliogabalus, we must provide a stock of parrots' tongues: we must even with men, like Vitellius, furnish our tables sometimes with the livers of lampreys, imported on the swiftest galleys from the Carpathian sea. And therefore, my hearers, I tell you the truth. If you have any hunger after the Word of God, I have no doubt, during this Lent, of my being able to satisfy you: but, if you have no such hunger, I give it up as hopeless. I know well in this case you will seldom come to hear me; and that, even should you come, you would sit here, like people without an appetite; you would derive no pleasure, no benefit, no nourishment from what is set before you; if perhaps you did not go so far, as to surrender to your neighbours that very food, which you ought to be eager in securing for your own portion. Now what do I mean by this?

6. A hungry person during meals has no idea whatever of helping the people sitting near him from his own plate: his only care is to replenish himself; and, just as if the entire provision on the table was intended for him, he is, to use the words of Ecclesiasticus, "unsatiable," and "greedy after meats" (xxxvii. 29.) A spiritual hunger then will in like

manner constrain you to appropriate every portion of the Word of GOD to your own use; and you will never be like those hearers of a sermon, who are for ever treating other people by applying all they hear to their neighbours. Oh, how this remark exactly fits that courtier, who is so artful! Oh, how this describes that nobleman, who is so proud! This was certainly meant for such a lady, who is known to patronize every place of frivolous amusement. Oh, if she had but heard it! Attend, I say, attend to what is on your own plate: for most assuredly the food, that is left by you for other persons, can never nourish yourself. "A man of sense will praise every wise word he shall hear and apply it to himself." (Ecclus. xxi. 15, Vulg.) And do you know how he does this? He acts like the cinnamon tree, planted in a marshy land, that draws away for its own nutrition the neighbouring water to such an extent, as quite to dry up the morass around. He acts like the cypress-tree, planted in a grassy land, that draws away for its own growth the adjoining moisture to such an extent, as quite to impoverish the soil close by. Do you wish to be edified by our preaching? Come, and listen to it with a hungry appetite: for in so doing you will be like those, of whom CHRIST said, *They hear the Word of God and keep it.* (S. Luke viii. 15.) You will exclusively apply to your own instruction everything you hear. You will mind yourselves. You will think of your own profit; and, after the pattern of Gideon's fleece, you will absorb, to the full, all the dew, that comes down upon you from above, without leaving one single drop of it to fall beside you.

7. But, after all, the great mischief is that we experience so little hunger. Hence it arises that so few among us at sermon-time are wholly intent upon themselves, but rather allow the evil spirits so easily to rob their souls of every good instruction; so little jealous are they of the same. You must have observed, on grand festive occasions, how some of the servants about the table are waiting, like so many harpies, instantly to snatch away your plate from before you. This is what these evil spirits do here. They are on the look-out to snatch the wholesome food of GOD's Word from your hand; nor from your hand only, but from your very heart. *Then*

cometh the devil, and taketh away the Word out of their hearts, lest they should believe and be saved. (S. Luke viii. 12.) Who shall count the numberless devices, which they have employed, in order to nullify among any class of people the Divine ordinance of preaching? . . . . When you sit listening at Church, do you ever feel a sudden sensation of weariness creeping over you, which disposes you for some reason or another to quarrel with the sermon? Sometimes you are oppressed with drowsiness; sometimes your imagination is too busy; sometimes you are unable, do what you will against it, to keep your eyes from wandering about to notice who is entering, or who is leaving, the Church; that I may not say to observe, whether it be some fine lady, coming to the service, much in the same spirit, that Ahasuerus wished Vashti his wife to appear at the feast; not to partake of it, but to be herself admired.

What is the meaning of all these sad distractions, within so short a space of time? What do they mean? The evil spirits are cunningly at work to divert your attention, and then to snatch the food out of your grasp: they would make you lose that particular word or sentence, which would have been most profitable to your souls. They are the harpies of hell, flying about the Church, in order, as S. Ambrose observed, that "they may take away the Word from the listless or hypocritical hearer." They are those ravenous birds, which so greedily pounced upon the basket, that contained Pharaoh's bake-meats. (Gen. xl. 17.) They are those eagles, which so audaciously came down upon the carcases, that Abraham had spread in sacrifice to GOD. (Gen. xv. 11.) Give heed then unto preaching, my hearers; give heed, I again say: for, if you suffer all these monstrous birds of prey, such as are now plotting their invisible siege against you in this place, to have their desire, you will, beyond all doubt, have to go home empty, at the close of the sermon; or rather, as I should say, you will scarcely bear to sit it out. You will behave like another Judas, who got up from his seat, when the supper was half over, and departed: he *immediately went out.* (S. John xiii. 30.) For how will you ever feel disposed to pay attention, when you have no hunger? This, this, after all, on a review of the whole subject, is the prime cause of every loss you sustain, of every irregularity you commit. You have no appetite for the Divine doctrine : and, if your souls be strangers to this appetite, (must I declare it?) O GOD, how great is the misfortune, the wretchedness of your state! Ye are dead men!

8. This certainly is a strong expression, my hearers: and yet I did not let it escape from my mouth without good reason. Hear what Cassiodorus says: "To be strangers to all appetite for the Law of GOD is a grievous disease; it is a calamity much to be deprecated." Hunger after the bodily food is one of the most certain signs, whereby to know the healthy condition of the body; and hunger after the spiritual food is one of the most indubitable proofs of the healthy condition of the spirit. All holy men agree in teaching us this. S. Chrysostom, S. Bernard, S. Ambrose, S. Augustine, and S. Gregory expressly affirm it. Yea, CHRIST Himself distinctly taught the same, when He furnished us with that notable mark for discriminating the elect from the reprobate, assuring us that the elect hear willingly the things of GOD discoursed to them, and that the reprobate hear them unwillingly. *He, that is of God, heareth God's words; ye therefore hear them not, because ye are not of God.* (S. John viii. 47.) These words He addressed to the wretched Jews of His day. Nor ought they, my hearers, greatly to surprise us. For the ordinary method, instituted by GOD for the salvation of His elect, is, that they should hear the truth preached to them. *Hear,* He says by Isaiah, *and your soul shall live.* (Isa. lv. 3.) Other ways, beyond all doubt, He had to save them; such, for instance, as by means of heavenly visions, or of immediate inspirations, or of the sudden illumination of their minds, or by the use of religious instructions: yet GOD has chosen none of these to be His ordinary methods; it may be, as S. Bernard remarked, in order that "Life may reach us at the very same door, at which Death had before entered." Death entered at the ear, that was opened to listen to the preacher of lies (for this was the serpent's character in the earthly Paradise;) and so Life also must enter now at the ear, that is opened to listen to the preachers of Truth. "The

ear was the first gate of Death; let it first be opened to admit Life."

Nebuchadnezzar, king of Babylon, was an eye-witness of the fall of that stately tree, which was the emblem of his empire: he saw all its fruit decay; he saw all its flowers wither; he saw every leaf it had dry up; he beheld how suddenly it was deserted by the wild beasts and birds, that in such vast crowds had either nested under its shelter, or sported among its branches. Well: did this spectacle serve, of itself, to impress his mind? By no means. In addition to this, it was necessary for him to hear the living voice of such a man, as Daniel. (Dan. ii.) David, however of a yielding disposition in other matters, was never moved to repent of having killed that incomparable soldier Uriah, until he had heard the living and reproving voice of a Nathan. (2 Sam. xii.) Jehoshaphat, however scrupulous a man in other matters, was never moved to an abhorrence of the league, he had formed with that infidel king Ahab, until he had heard the living and upbraiding voice of Jehu. (2 Chron. xix.) And to the same purport, independent of the testimony of Sacred Scripture, I could show you, that, out of a hundred remarkable conversions, such as now occur among us, ninety-nine are the effect of the power, attending the preaching of the Word of GOD. The case of a S. Augustine may be accepted in full credit for them all. All his wonderful natural talent was not sufficient to recover him to GOD: all his vast erudition, all his unwearied application, all that invincible ardour, he ever displayed in the pursuit of truth, none of these sufficed for this purpose. It was necessary that, like a child, he should imbibe his earliest lessons from the lips of S. Ambrose; nor was he brought to resolve on a true repentance, until such time, as he had heard those exhortations in public, and those encouraging words in private, that succeeded in winning his soul. O foolish foolish man, whosoever then thou art, that, with such examples before thee, hast dreamed of being able to find some easy return to GOD by any other than the beaten highway! There must be preaching! There must be preaching! What you shall hear on a particular day, in a particular place, from a particular Minister, *that*, I emphatically say, *that that* is it, which shall, after all, strike upon your heart. For *it* your conversion is kept in reserve by GOD, if you are living in sin; and for *it* your confirmation, if you are in a state of grace. Believe me, Christians, believe me. It is not without reason that the HOLY SPIRIT so much and in so many varied forms of speech inculcates upon us this duty, that we should hear. *Hearken, O! daughter, and consider, and incline thine ear.* (Ps. xlv. 10.) *Bow down thine ear, and hear the words of the wise.* (Prov. xxii. 17.) GOD well knows the path, by which He has it in His mind to enter into our hearts. But 1 pass from this to another consideration. The Elect, you know, are in the Scriptures represented as wise, and the reprobate as foolish: they appear in the famous parable of the Virgins, five of whom were entertained by the Bridegroom, and five rejected by Him. Arguing from this fact, can you point out to me that particular feature, which the HOLY SPIRIT has assigned as indicating the peculiar property of the wise, or the peculiar temper of the foolish? Here it is. When any person speaks to each for their profit, the wise are most ready, and the foolish are most reluctant, to hear. *He that hearkeneth unto counsel, is wise.* (Prov. xii. 15.) This text proves what I say, in regard to the wise. *The ear of the wise seeketh knowledge.* (Prov. xviii. 15.) So does this. *The heart of the wise seeketh knowledge.* (Prov. xv. 14.) So does this. . . . . On the other hand, when the discourse addresses itself to the foolish, what do we read? Listen, listen, I beg you, for it is something quite fearful. *A fool hath no delight in understanding* (Prov. xviii. 2;) and again, *A fool despiseth his father's instruction* (xv. 5;) and again, *Fools despise knowledge* (i. 7;) and again, *A scorner heareth not rebuke* (xiii. 1;) and again, *A scorner loveth not one, that reproveth him; neither will he go unto the wise* (xv. 12.) Hence it was, on the strength of these weighty authorities, found in Solomon, that Isaiah, anxious to point out to the Israelites the worst of the ills, that had befallen them, called them "a rebellious people; lying children; *children, that will not hear the law of the Lord*" (xxx. 9.) This was as good as telling them, that they were dead men.

To come, then, in conclusion, to the main business of this

discourse, what say you, my hearers? Does the total want of that hunger I have been describing seem to you only a trifling disease? It is rather a desperate condition of the soul; and such is the unanimous verdict, pronounced upon it by those spiritual physicians, whose summary decisions on the matter of eternal death we have in our possession; decisions, not of men, fallible; but of GOD, infallible. "The beginning of our departure from GOD," writes Palladius, "is when we conceive a disgust at His teaching, and when we no longer relish that, which every soul, that loves GOD, hungers after." What therefore must you do, as ever you wish to get rid of so gloomy a prognostic of your damnation? Excite within you to the utmost of your power this hunger after Heavenly doctrine. Excite it by all proper means. Excite it by ceasing to frequent those theatres, which I have sometimes seen open, even on Sacred days and seasons. Excite it by withdrawing yourselves from all impure talk and conversation. Excite it by giving up unprofitable society. Excite it by a fixed resolution to taste no more of the poisoned cup, furnished you in those frivolous popular works, which you so greatly relish. Above all, excite it by your more frequent attendance on this course of Lent sermons. For this is a distinction, much to be observed, between the nourishment of the body and that of the soul: to have a relish for the former, we must practise abstinence, or only seldom take food; but to have a relish for the latter, nothing is more effectual, than the habit of eating both often and plenteously.

THE SECOND PART.

9. Do you suppose that I am not perfectly well aware of what you will say among yourselves this morning, as you return home? You will be ready to say, that it was not entirely from a pure godly zeal that I preached to you in this way, but from an apparent regard to my own interest. You will suspect me of a wish to obtain a more crowded congregation; and that with this view I magnify so much the importance of that hunger, which will every day fill my Church. How do you wish me to answer this reflection? By saying

that I derive no pleasure from seeing the Church crowded? Did I pretend to this, I should be foolishly giving myself out, as a more holy man, than an Augustine, who in his homilies on the Psalms frequently commended his people for their readiness in crowding to hear him; as a more holy man, than a Bernard, who, in his Septuagesima sermons, spake of his monks in high terms of praise, because of the attention, with which they listened to him; as a more holy man, than a John Chrysostom, who very seldom preached without expressing his grief at the diminution, or his joy at the increase, of his congregation; in this respect comparing himself to a mother, whose tender heart is sore-affected, should she perceive one of her dear children to be absent at meals, so that she anxiously and distressfully inquires of all present, what is become of him. GOD forbid that, poor sinner as I am, I should ever assume an air of indifference, and say, that it matters nothing to me, whether I see before me few, or many hearers. Willingly would I see you all here every day, were it possible. But, when I acknowledge this, you wrong me in supposing that I have my own glory in view—and yet, it may be so: knowing, as I do, how deeply pride is lodged in my heart, I cannot absolutely forbid the idea. "There is an exquisite subtlety and the same is unjust." (Ecclus. xix. 25.) Howbeit, I still hope I am not in this sense to blame. Did I say that you should exclusively come to hear *me?* There will not be wanting, this Lent, preachers of greater piety and learning than myself, who will prepare for your spiritual refreshment more sumptuous entertainment, than I can. Therefore have a simple eye to your own edification; and, wheresoever you find the pastures most wholesome and nourishing, there go. My only entreaty is, on no account starve your souls. Ah! my dear Christians, is it not a serious thing to do so much, to suffer so much, to spend so much for the support of a vile body, and then to have no care whatever for the soul? Who will give me tears, adequately to mourn over such exceeding folly; yea, words, groans, and howlings to express my abhorrence of it? Every one complains, if the body passes one single day without its food: the soul goes empty, not one single day, but even weeks and months together, and no one regrets it. Oh, if you knew all the good one sermon diligently attended to could do you, believe me, you would, for the sake of hearing it, manage to overcome every obstacle and inconvenience.

10. And, could you but discern how many came out of Church, after the sermon, so different from what they were, when they went in to hear it, what prodigies of grace might you hope to find effected in yourselves! What changes! What transitions! S. John Chrysostom ingeniously remarks, in reference to this point, that the animals, which went out of Noah's ark, went out the same, as they came in. The crow went out, a crow; the wolf, a wolf; the fox, a fox; and the porcupine, all armed with its living arrows, was a porcupine still. Just as the ark received the animals, so it retained them. "But," the holy man proceeds to observe, "the Church transforms the animals she receives into her bosom: not by any change in her substance, but by the extirpation of their sin." Like unto a crow, that sinner entered the Church, who, having hardened his heart by delaying repentance, ever croaked to the same tune—"To-morrow, to-morrow:" now, behold, little as we expected it, he goes out mourning, like a holy dove. Like unto a greedy wolf, that usurer entered the Church, who grew fat on the blood of the poor: and, behold, he goes out, more gentle than an ewe, and willing to spare the very wool from his back, that the naked may be clothed. Like unto a spiteful fox, that swindler entered the Church, who built his house on the ruin of his competitors: and, behold, he goes out more harmless than a lamb, willing to sacrifice his own interests, if thereby he can get any deserving persons promoted. And that excitable quarrelsome man, who made every one smart, who touched him, came here, like unto a bristly porcupine; and, behold, he goes away, like a loving spaniel, tractable and gentle to all. And what new creatures have we here! They are, as every one knows, moral transformations, wrought by means of that Divine Word, which, when tasted, can work in the souls of the faithful such strange enchantments. The magic viands of a Circe formerly metamorphosed men into brutes; but such is not the effect of our gracious food. It

rather changes brutes into true men; yea, more than this, it changes them into Angels. . . . Who then will not hunger after a food so distinguished, a food so sustaining, a food so miraculous? Yes, yes; with all my heart and soul I repeat what I said before. Get this hunger, if a stranger to it; seek and secure it. Ask it of GOD with earnest importunity; quicken and excite it in your souls. The prophet records of those poor starving wretches in Jerusalem, that they would have given all the most precious things they could find, for the sake of getting something to eat; neither retaining their gold, nor keeping back their silver, nor valuing their jewels: *They have given all their precious things for food to relieve the soul.* (Lam. i. 11, Vulg.) And so ought you. For the sake of getting this nourishment of the Word of GOD, you ought to despise everything in comparison; your *precious things*, my hearers, your *precious things*, whatsoever they be. When there is preaching to be heard, then it is no time for looking after other interests; for minding the farm, for minding the lawsuit, for visiting your neighbours, for inquiring about worldly things. Did Esau, when he was hungry, care at such a time about his primogeniture? So far from it, as all of you know, he bartered it, to his infinite disgrace, for a mess of pottage. Others, pressed by hunger, have pawned their furniture; others, pressed by hunger, have pawned their clothes; and the famished Egyptians willingly surrendered all their land to Joseph, who provided them with corn. Come on, therefore, come on. Provide also for the soul its dear beloved food; and care not, if you risk everything else.

SERMON V.

THE SINNER PUT TO SHAME AT THE LAST DAY.

S. MATTH. XXV. 31, 32.

"WHEN THE SON OF MAN SHALL COME IN HIS GLORY. . . . . BEFORE HIM SHALL BE GATHERED ALL NATIONS."

1. AND to what extremes will men have the audacity to go, in their abuse of the all-loving kindness, which GOD has condescended thus far to show us? Has He hitherto kept silence, as if He were quite insensible of every outrage? But what then? Do we not hereby learn, that patience, after long provocation, turneth into fury? Arise then, O ye Angels, ye destined heralds of the last tremendous Day; blow aloud your trumpets, and prove to sinners whether what I say be true! Ye Heavens, shroud yourselves in darkness, and refuse them in their consternation every light, but the flash of the thunderbolt! Rain down, ye flames, upon them, and greedily turn their possessions into ashes! Open thy jaws, thou earth, and like a famished one swallow up their dwellings! Scour the land, ye beasts of the field, and, meeting these wretches at the cavern's mouth, whither they fly for refuge, let none be able to boast that he has escaped your indignation!—But what am I now doing? All these are judgments, which over and over again have been sounded in the ears of sinners without producing the least effect. I myself too am conscious of having, in my early days, described them with all the terrifying eloquence I could; and yet never,

to my knowledge, did they make one face turn pale, one heart feel cold. But now, for once, it has occurred to me (since I have to speak on the Universal Judgment,) that, setting aside every other kind of punishment, I should confine myself to the exhibition of one alone, which is far less regarded; but which, because it peculiarly affects the nature of man, ought by an easy consequence to tell upon the fears of those, who have in them any remains of humanity. I said, it peculiarly belonged to man. For what is that correction, which, among so many, we can inflict upon man alone? Is it hunger? or stripes? or the flame? or wounds? or death? No; says the pious Archbishop of Valentia: of all these kinds of correction the brute beasts are capable. The punishment proper to man is Shame. "The beasts can be beaten, or slain, or burnt; they cannot be put to shame." And then he shrewdly proceeds to remark, "When man for his offences is put to public shame, then it is, that, as man, he is chiefly punished." Do not, therefore, expect, my hearers, that I shall this morning display before your eyes, as others do, fiery vapours appearing in the sky with a lurid glare, the rattling of thunder, the clouds of smoke, the deluge of fire, the hail-storm of arrows; nor yet the sun, clothed in mourning apparel, nor the moon, distilling human blood, nor every star, transformed into a comet with streaming hair, in signs of woe. No, Sirs. You will simply have to gaze on one single appalling spectacle: it will be this—The sinner put to shame in the sight of the universe! But don't you think this will be the most terrible of them all, the most affecting, the most painful? You cannot but admit as much, if ye be men; men, especially, of that ingenuous disposition, so civilized and so refined, as you are reported to be. Therefore attend; and let the person, whose soul is not affected by what he hears, tremble for himself; lest, through the deceitfulness of sin, he be not from a human being imperceptibly changed into a brute beast.

2. If ever there was a most notorious indignity in the world, it certainly was the one, which Hanun, king of the Ammonites, practised upon the ambassadors of David, in utter contempt of all common decency. He ordered the

heads of every one of them to be shaven close, as if they had been so many slaves. He had their beards clipped in the most ludicrous fashion, as if they were so many buffoons; and their nether garments cut away in the middle, so as to render the exposure of their persons most degrading. In this state he compelled them to appear before his Nobles at court. In this state they had to parade the streets before his subjects. And, lastly, having thus turned them into the utmost ridicule, he sent them off, just as they were, and overwhelmed from head to foot with shame, to their own country. I leave you to consider how deep a sense of indignity must have oppressed the minds of these unhappy men. I content myself with the simple record of Scripture: *the men were greatly ashamed.* (2 Sam. x. 5.) I can imagine the poor wretches not daring to lift up their eyes, nor to utter a word; and that, sooner than submit to such a degradation, they would have preferred leaving their heads on the hard and fatal block. But, if this be true, how, Oh, how will it fare with those reprobate sinners, who will have to endure a far more scandalous and cruel usage; not in one single city, not in one single court, but in the presence of the entire race of mankind? They will see the Eternal Judge sitting upon the clouds of heaven on the most Majestic throne of His power; then the countless orders of His assessors, Apostles, Patriarchs, Prophets, Martyrs, arranged according to their respective ranks on their elevated seats; companies of Confessors, of holy men and of holy women; and together with them not so much companies, as vast regiments of Angels clad in complete armour, who, while they cover the plains of the firmament on every side, will swell the number, and much more heighten the splendour, the gorgeousness, and the magnificence of this immense assemblage. And before such an assemblage, a very congress of Kings, more brilliant each of them than the sun, the miserable condemned (still retaining, as they must, the feelings of our common nature) will be forced to appear in all their filth, in all their deformity, in all their brutishness, without the vilest rag to cover them, blazing, for so they will, with their shame. What confusion will they experience, think you, on finding themselves exposed to the gaze of so vast a world—especially, when they see themselves furiously thrust, like convicts, into its presence by a savage set of devils, who, as if proud to parade before heaven the prey they had captured from it, shall lash and torment them, as they advance, with every kind and degree of insult and cruelty? Piso, a noble Roman, when summoned to appear before the Senate in the degrading dress, usually provided for criminals, no sooner beheld all the formalities ready in the court for his condemnation—the Judges ascending the tribunal; his accusers, taking their proper places; the people crowding to get a sight of him—than, quite unable to bear up under the shame of being the common gazing-stock, indignantly, after a brief pause, drew forth a dagger from beneath his cloak and killed himself. Conceive then what these wretches would do, could they only command the use of any weapon, capable of terminating their existence. Who then would be able to stay their hands? who to curb their impetuosity? who to restrain their desperation? But, in spite of themselves, they must submit to all the infamy of having their case fully investigated. *They must bear,* as Ezekiel writes, *their own shame,* and (which is more grievous still) must be *confounded in all that they have done* (xvi. 54.)

3. I said more grievous still: for, if their mere appearance only before this Tribunal shall cause them such intolerable shame, how will they feel, when *the Lord shall bring to light the hidden things of darkness* (1 Cor. iv. 5)? when, in other words, the Court will proceed to read aloud the indictments against them, to publish their most hidden acts of meanness, and to expose their most secret infamies? I can devise no readier method of helping you to conceive what their shame will then be, than by the following illustration. Suppose me to be miraculously gifted with a perfect insight into the characters of every individual among you; and that I was now to stand up and begin to say, "Do you observe that female yonder, who is so modest in her appearance? She is living in adultery; and that young man, who seems to be all absorbed in his devotions, is her paramour. Do you see such a one? It was he, who committed that felony. Do you see such a one? It was he, who committed that theft. And that

man further down—do you know who he is? He is a devil in disguise, who, in order secretly to assassinate a certain enemy of his, is even now plotting some mischief against him." Supposing, I say, that I had the power to communicate to you in this manner whatsoever I pleased, and beyond the possibility of any man's contradicting me; who can describe the glowing blush of shame, which would lighten up every countenance in the Church? You would all of you instantaneously rise up in a tumult against me. One would try, even from a distance, to stop my mouth with his menacing gesticulations; another to frighten me down with his looks; another to stifle my voice with his loud cries: nor would others fail, as their wisest course, to effect their escape, getting at once out of my reach, lest I should put them to shame. And yet where are we now? We are in a town: we are in a Church. Is it then so serious a matter for us to lose a little credit in the sight of a few individuals? I leave you hence to infer for yourselves, what it must be in the sight of an assembled Universe! Dissemble then for the present, as much as you like, in the particular confession of your sins; keep in the back-ground your worst offences; gild and gloss them over: think you, forsooth, that you will be able to do this at the Last Day? Alas! how will you then be compelled to make a full, undisguised, unreserved confession, and with your own mouth to disclose what you would fain conceal from the observation of the world. Some will disclose acts of theft; some will disclose acts of felony; some will disclose acts of adultery. Do you doubt my words? Then hear the words of the prophet Hosea: "*The iniquity of Ephraim is bound up*" (xiii. 12.) The sinner at present *binds up* his sin with as much care, as a mother hides her new-born babe in her bosom. He hides it from his superior; he hides it from his parents; he hides it from the person, who is in CHRIST's stead, in regard to his soul. *His sin is hid:* but what comes next? *The sorrows of a travailing woman shall come upon him.* Have you observed a female very near her confinement? She can no longer conceal her condition; she is forced by her own cries and groans to publish it. So will it be, according to Hosea, with every sinner. *The sorrows of a travailing woman shall come upon him:* in other words, he must, however reluctantly, discover himself. But what overpowering shame will it cost him to do so ! . . . In spite of himself, he must appear in public before all the world a totally different character from what he wished to be thought; an object of disgust, hatred, and general execration: nor will all his clamour and howlings be able to procure him the smallest pity. What say you to this, my hearers? Is it not indeed true that in that Day sinners will be most dreadfully ashamed of themselves? *They shall be clothed with shame* is the expression in Job (viii. 22;) and, to use the phrase of the Psalmist, *They shall cover themselves with their own confusion, as with a cloak* (cix. 29.) Alas! poor wretches that we are ! To what purpose are all the careful contrivances we resort to, in order to keep our wickednesses under cover? our managing to indulge our envy under the mask of zeal? to forward our own interests under the show of justice? What avails it that the night now lends us its thick shadowy mantle entirely to mask our basest actions? What avails it that under a counterfeit smile we now hatch the most relentless hatred ? What avails it that under an honest-looking face we disguise the most depraved heart? All the greater, in proportion, will be our confusion hereafter.

4. And don't pretend to tell me, that, exaggerate, as I will, the greatness of this confusion, you cannot see it in the same light with me for this reason; because there will be such numbers of people, after all, to share it with you. I positively deny your conclusion. It involves a fundamental error. Are you aware whence it arises, that sinners are now so little ashamed of their misdeeds, on knowing that they have such numbers to keep them in countenance? It arises from this. They estimate the evil of sin, not by its intrinsic malignity, but by the common opinion of the world about it, which often regards it, as being a credit to a man, or a mere trifle, or something not worth noticing. But in that Day they will not so regard it. In that Day they will judge of sin, as sin really is in the sight of GOD. "Then," as T. Aquinas remarks in his Summa, " then our shame will have respect to that estimate of GOD, which is according to Truth."

By means of a light, so true and so terrible, what shame will a man feel in detecting himself to be the parent of such a monster! Imagine the confusion of that illustrious lady, who, if I remember right, in the time of Pope Martin IV. brought forth at Rome a child, covered all over with hair, like a bear, with a rough shaggy fleece upon it, with sharp crooked talons, and with the ferocious look of a wild beast. Those mothers among you, who sigh for beautiful children, or who, having them, feel so proud of them, will readily enter into the wretchedness of this unhappy woman, when she gave birth to such a frightful object. What then will a reprobate sinner have to suffer, when he is made conscious of being the parent of sin, an offspring so far more disgusting? Sin is that monster, horrid beyond all imagination, to which no equal was ever generated in the pools of Lerna, or the lakes of Asfaltidis, or the muddy sloughs of Cocytus. This is that monster, which the Gorgons, the Scyllas, the Cerberuses, the Sphinxes, the Hydras, the Geryons, the Minotaurs, the Pythons, all own to be their superior: yea, rather; this is that monster, from which all these miscreated beings derived their birth into our world; that monster, on account of which the spirits once so glorious are now so debased; that monster, on account of which mortal man is become so miserable; that monster, solely on account of which, CHRIST, when wearing its likeness, was so abhorred in the sight of the FATHER, looked so hideously deformed, appeared so covered with leprosy, and, as the Apostle wrote, was unable to avoid the ignominy of one accursed. *He was made for us* (yes, I will speak it out,) *He was made a curse!* (Gal. iii. 13.) On what grounds then do you flatter yourselves that the reprobate shall never feel the enormous shame to themselves of having given birth to such a monster; one, that they cannot conceal by burying it under ground, as some incestuous offspring; one, that they cannot make others believe to be no child of theirs?

5. This, however, in my view of the matter, will sink into insignificance, as compared with the far deeper shame they must experience, when they shall hear CHRIST with an awful look of Majesty reprove their ingratitude, shown towards His

own Person, His own precious Blood. My brethren, in our present state we cannot understand the full import of the words —*Christ Died for us!* But, when arraigned before His Divine Presence, we shall understand it: and then, finding ourselves to have been, in return, so unmannerly, not to say so stubborn and so brutish, in our dealings with Him, as to have declined rendering Him any service, or doing any good work on earth for His sake, yea rather to have made it always our chief boast that we have dishonoured Him, what shame, think you, will overspread our faces on these accounts?

Alvaro Bassano, a great Admiral, a man most renowned for his many enterprising voyages and his splendid victories at sea, received an order from Philip the Second, King of Spain, to collect together that vast naval force against England, which afterwards was so miserably destroyed. Having many ships of war to get ready for so grand an undertaking, with the supply of stores and of ammunition, and with the manning of his fleet, he was prevented from pushing on his preparations so expeditiously, as the King imagined he would have done; who therefore, feeling irritated in his mind against him, summoned him to Court, and with a troubled countenance, and a stern tone of voice, said to him, "It is quite clear that, in executing my commission, you have not acted, as I had reason to hope you would, and as it was your duty to do." He said nothing more than this. But was not this enough? enough, think you, to break the man's heart? Alvaro left the Royal apartments with his face all in flames: he returned home: he took to his bed: and after a very few days he died. Christian friends, I am quite sure that there is not one among you so silly, as not to attribute to the voice and countenance of CHRIST, acting as Judge, a far mightier power than to the same in any earthly king. Conceive then what will become of you in that hour, when, placing you before His august Presence, He will pour forth His indignation—*He shall speak unto them in His wrath!* (Ps. ii. 5.) And He will not have to reprove you for any excusable negligence or slowness in His service, but for so many tremendous intolerable outrages. He will say, "After I had gone so far, as to give My last breath for thee on the bitter Cross, I surely believed that I might fairly expect some slight respect from thee in return. But tell me, ungrateful man, what hast thou ever done to correspond with My excess of love towards thee? What rather hast thou not done to injure Me? Thou hast despised My Name; thou hast calumniated My servants; thou hast profaned My Temple; thou hast ridiculed My Word; thou hast even dared basely to blaspheme My very Blood. Was it peradventure that I made too high demands on thy gratitude? I asked of thee only so much courteousness and so much deference, as would preserve My Name from the degrading reflection that thou didst scorn to be reckoned among My followers. Shivering with cold, I asked of thee a rag for warmth. Starving with hunger, I asked of thee a morsel of bread to save My life. But thou —what hast thou done? Hast thou not been far more willing to waste thy substance in lewd theatres, in profligate company, in riotous debauches, in vile houses of ill-fame, than bestow it upon Me? Behold then the very utmost, that I am able to obtain from thee, after I had Died on the cross to Redeem thee: I occupy the very lowest place in thy affections; there is no one so much affronted by thee, as I am." Thus will He address you: and on hearing such words, who will then be so stout-hearted, who so impudent, as to raise his eyes from the ground for a single moment? *Who can stand before His indignation?* (Nah. i. 6.) Ah, Christian people, I know that thou hast at present *a whore's forehead: thou refusest to be ashamed.* (Jer. iii. 3.) Thou hast now a forehead so hardened, that no such reproaches, as these, seem to require of thee the least change of countenance. But, believe me, you will not find it so hereafter. Hereafter the flame, that shall be on thy cheek, will appear to thee, as outburning Hell itself. And mark well what I now say, or rather what a Jerome tells you in my stead; that, in your inability to endure so profound a disgrace, every hour will seem to thee a thousand years, in thy longing for CHRIST to come and finally pronounce the dread sentence of thy damnation, permitting thee at once to go down quick into Hell. "For it would be better for the finally lost to endure the pains of Hell, than the continued Presence of the LORD."

But soft: we have not yet done. With a view to thy more abject exposure, He will bring in company with Himself, to put thee to shame, those Gentiles, who, though entire strangers to the faith and destitute of all the graces of the Sacraments, yet never committed any sins, equal in atrocity to thine.

6. ... Wilt thou not be very sore confounded, Christian, when born, as thou art, in the bosom of the Church, in the midst of so many oracles of Scriptures, so many doctrines of Fathers, so many examples of Saints, thou shalt yet see many heathens outstripping thee in goodness? so that, excepting only thy faith, which, being without works, instead of adding to thy glory, shall only serve to heighten thy disgrace, thou shalt find thyself, on the stage of these momentous proceedings, placed in other respects below an Aristides, in justice; below a Zeleucus, in rectitude; below a Palemon, in chastity; below a Socrates, in patience; below a Pericles, in truthfulness; below an Antigonus, in meekness; below an Epaminondas, in disinterestedness—men, all of them born in the deep darkness of heathenism, who therefore to their misfortune were never favoured, as thou hast been, with any knowledge of Eternal Life, with any Gospel, with any traditions, with any Creed, with any Prophecies, with any Miracles, with any Sacraments; who had never seen a GOD Dying for their sakes in His exceeding love towards them, and in such dreadful agonies, as thou hast seen. Wretched man! What sayest thou to this? What is thy reply? Hast thou any defence to make? Dost thou believe that this circumstance will materially tend to deepen that confusion, which on other grounds so oppresseth thee already?. Were it not to have this effect, never would CHRIST have put us in fear with that denunciation, *The men of Nineveh shall rise in judgment with this generation, and shall condemn it. . . . The Queen of the South shall rise up in judgment with this generation, and shall condemn it.* (S. Matth. xii. 41, 42.) On this passage what was the exclamation of S. Chrysostom? Simply this. "Never forget how great will be their raillery." What! a Christian, reprimanded by a Tartar! A Christian, accused by a Turk! A Christian, condemned in the judgment by an infidel! Oh, what a sad opprobrium! "How great the raillery; how

great the raillery!" Who will ever be able to express it? Boleslaus, the first King of Poland, observing that one of his Counts Palatine showed great cowardice in a battle, was content with sending him a beautiful golden distaff, a present for him to spin with. The nobleman with a kind of look, such as you may easily imagine, received the present, as coming from the King; and thereupon, quite unable to bear up against the shame of being thus by this significant act compared to a woman, in a fit of despair tied a halter round his neck, and strangled himself. How then will it fare with the Christian on his seeing himself confronted with a heathen? ay, not only confronted, but even placed beneath one, which is tantamount to preferring the weak to the strong, the defenceless to the armed, the low-born slave to the illustrious Royal heir? Will not this be a keen cutting disgrace, quite a match for every other? Ah, I can well understand how every such Christian hiding his face with his hands, as quite ashamed that any should recognise him, will then reiterate his lamentations and pour forth his complaints anew. And "Oh, wretch that I am," he must needs cry out in the words of the Psalm, "Oh, my misery! Oh, my affliction!" *The shame of my face hath covered me, for the voice of the slanderer and the blasphemer, the enemy and the avenger* (xliv. 16, 17.)

7. One thing alone must here be noticed, in order to prevent mistake. It is this. As far as we can gather from these Scriptures, the heathens, I have alluded to, will not come to perform any judicial act against the reprobate. Wherefore CHRIST, if we carefully weigh His words, did not say of them that they should sit down and condemn, which is the proper office of a Judge, but that they should *rise and condemn*, which seems rather the office of an accuser. His Saints alone, together with CHRIST, will exercise any judicial authority over the reprobate. Who is there ignorant of this? *The Saints shall judge the world.* (1 Cor. vi. 2.) But pay attention to this fact, as it greatly strengthens our argument, and when duly considered, supplies us with fresh evidence of the intensity of that shame, concerning which we speak. On what class of reprobates will each of the Saints exercise a like authority? Upon them all? You are right: upon them all.

Yet there can be no doubt that they will exercise a more particular authority against those, from whom in this life they received a particular ill usage. Such persons will be specially handed over to their jurisdiction, according to that notice, given in the Book of Wisdom, "Then shall the righteous man stand in great boldness before the face of such as have afflicted him and made no account of his labours." (Wisd. v. 1.) The righteous will have to make a special inquiry into the case of these persons; they will have to produce a special statute in regard to them; they will even have to pronounce a special tremendous sentence against them. Pause then awhile and consider with me, how grievous, under this supposition, will be the shame, evinced by a Herod in his having publicly for his Judge that same Baptist, whom he beheaded; how grievous the shame of a Nero in his having that same Peter, in his having that same Paul, whom he kept so long in such ignoble bonds; of a Diocletian, in his having that same Sebastian, whom he made the arrow's mark at the stake; of a Valerian, in his having that same Lawrence, whom he caused to be roasted on a gridiron. The proud Queen Cleopatra, sooner than be led in triumph by Augustus, against whom she had waged war, did not scruple, as we all know, to take the infuriated asp to her naked bosom, and so to die: and yet we cannot doubt but that Augustus would have treated her otherwise, than with the highest distinction, or have refused her, when alive, the respect he paid her, when she was dead. Conceive then what the reprobate would be willing to do in that Day; what would they not gladly suffer, if, at any sacrifice, they might be allowed to escape that far more oppressive load of ignominy; I mean, their having to lie prostrate at the feet of those same beggarly wretches, those same despised outcasts of this earth, whose labours they once "accounted as madness." Oh, what a terrible disgrace! Oh, what a bitter and atrocious shame!

Behold here the prediction of Isaiah verified, that the slanderers of the just man shall one day fall down at his feet. *The sons also of them that afflicted thee shall come bending unto thee* (lx. 14.) Behold the Senators, behold the Consuls, behold the Governors, all of them imploring mercy in vain at the hands of those same poor brethren of theirs, whose importunities they would not listen to, whose pleadings for the Faith they could not answer. See the gluttons asking favour of those Lazaruses, to whom they refused the crumbs, which they yet willingly gave to the dogs under their table. See the Ahabs humbly beseeching those Naboths, whose property in their insolence they scrupled not to plunder. See the Holoferneses groaning at the knees of those Achiors, whose words they feared not in their pride to ridicule. What shame, in your judgment of the matter, can possibly exceed this? Is it not enough that the ungodly should see their enemies raised above them to such heights of Glory? This is not enough. No. Besides this, on their bended knees they must have to appear before their judicial presence; by them they must have to hear themselves examined; by them judged; by them convicted; and by them, which is the completion of every other dreadful circumstance, by them condemned to everlasting death! And, when that hour is at length come, when, every charge against them being proved and every malefactor among them brought in guilty, the sentence is about to be passed by the Judge, who can describe with what loud and unanimous acclamations the Saints will bear their part in pronouncing that sentence? With one voice they will exclaim, in unison with CHRIST, "Away, away! *Depart, ye cursed, into everlasting fire.*" (S. Matth. xxv. 41.) . . . Then will the wicked experience that very shame, spoken of in the Psalm, where it is written, *Let the ungodly be put to confusion and put to silence in the grave* (xxxi. 19.) For, if the confusion of Adam and of Eve were so great, on seeing themselves banished from the earthly Paradise that they might till the ground; and if the confusion of Hagar and of Ishmael were so great, on seeing themselves expelled from the house of Abraham, that they might wander in the desert; and if Miriam, the sister of Aaron, blushed all over, when, as infected with leprosy, she saw herself expelled from the camp (though indeed after seven days she was to return, as cleansed and purified,) what will it be with those miserable sinners, who, excluded from the society of the Angels, from the communion of the Blessed, from the Empyrean palace of all perfect bliss, shall find themselves thrust down to the lowest depths of the abyss below, that they may there dwell with the evil spirits; and that, not only for a few days, or for a few years, but for ever and ever! *I will bring an everlasting reproach upon you and a perpetual shame; which shall not be forgotten.* (Jer. xxiii. 40.) These are the words of Jeremiah —and Oh, what words they are!

8. Onwards, then, my hearers, towards our conclusion. Is there a single person here, who does not shudder at the thought of his being liable one day to incur such infinite degradation? Alas! in your notions of worldly honour you are so exquisitely sensitive, that a mere trifle hurts you, a chance word goes to your quick, and, on any affront received, however trifling, off you fly, in eager haste for satisfaction, to the sword, to blood, to destruction, and to death. And shall it be possible that you, highminded gentlemen as you are, can so undervalue that infinite disgrace, which awaits you at the last Day? a never-ending disgrace? a disgrace of the very worst kind? a disgrace, which will serve to exasperate you through all the ages of Eternity, which *shall not be forgotten?* Why, after all, an affront, shown you in this life, does not last long; but that disgrace lasts for ever. Do you mind what I say? It lasts for ever. For it is a certain fact that the damned will for ever have in their constant view that identical horrible shame, which was inflicted upon them at the last Day in the sight of the Universe. And that shame, if we at all credit S. Basil, that shame will be enough, of itself, to enrage them for ever, to madden them for ever, to goad them on for ever to the most inhuman and frantic acts of desperation. "The shame, which they will retain through Eternity, shall torment them more, than the penal fire." If then a less affront offends you to such a degree, Oh! what folly, Oh! what blindness, Oh! what mad infatuation must it be in you daringly to expose yourselves to an affront so incomparably greater!

The Second Part.

9. Just now tell me, in real truth, my brethren, does not what I have narrated this morning seem to you a mighty pretty fable?—O Father! and what a strange unlooked-for question is this, you put to us? How is it a fable? Are

you speaking seriously, or in play? How is it a fable? We regard it, as being Evangelical history and Truth eternal: and, if you have given it any high colouring from your own imagination—which we are not sure of—*that* must be your affair. For, of a certainty, we do not regard the future Universal Judgment of the world to be a fable. We hold it to be an Article of our Faith.—Ah, is it so? What good news to me, if only they were true! For, to speak plainly, my opinion was, that if not all, yet that many among you, regarded it as fabulous, just as the majority of people everywhere else do.—Ay, but not of Christians.—Yes, I say, of Christians.—Well then, not of Catholics.—Yes, Sirs, of Catholics.—Of what use in the world then are our houses of Inquisition?—Think for yourselves. If all those, who look upon the Judgment Day as nothing but a fable, were to be cast into the Inquisition, alas, my dear Pisa,[1] all thy prisons would prove far too narrow for the purpose of receiving them! .... However this may be, as I should be sorry to speak too boldly before such a distinguished congregation, will you permit me to transfer the remainder of my sermon to a great Prelate, illustrious for his birth, his experience, his doctrine, and his sanctity? Will you be at all offended, if I bring Salvian to this pulpit on the wing from Marseilles, and let him here pour forth his flood of Divine eloquence? Come; let him now decide the point between us. He is the Master; and I, as his pupil, will merely put the questions to him. "O most wise Bishop, what sentence dost thou pronounce? These hearers of mine, to whom I have preached

[1] No particular town being mentioned in the original, these sermons having been preached in divers cities of Italy, the translator has taken the liberty of giving the preference to Pisa, and of inserting it here. For Cardinal Noris in a letter, written by him to Magliabecchi from Pisa in the year 1677, states that Segneri was then preaching there, and adds the interesting fact that the Grand Duke of Tuscany always went to hear him, and even prolonged his stay at Pisa, solely for this purpose. This then was some earnest of the still higher honour and success, which afterwards crowned his labours, as a preacher, at Rome. It may here be mentioned that Segneri dedicated his *Quaresimale* to the Grand Duke, reminding him of the affection he had shown towards it, even before its birth, as published; for in two of his principal cities he had been one of the most constant and attentive hearers. It was first published at Florence in one vol., folio, by Jacopo Sabatini, A.D. 1679.—See Tiraboschi, Tomo viii. P. ii. B. 3, S. 11.

this morning—tell me, do they all regard the Universal Judgment, as something true, or as something fabulous? a fable, or a reality? Let me ask you plainly, Do they believe it, or do they not believe it?" The venerable man most cautiously removes the case beyond this congregation, and, stating a general proposition, so as to avoid giving offence to any one in particular, he settles the point in this way. No person believes that he will have to be judged by God, that most righteous of all judges, so long as he does not strive to the very utmost to escape an adverse sentence, and also do all he can to secure a sentence in his favour. "No one, who regards it as a thing certain, that he must take his trial before God, ever fails to employ the means, whereby he may receive for his good works Eternal good things, and may not have to suffer for his evil works Eternal evil things." Is this then the decision? It is quite enough for my purpose. I need go no further. I have now no fear of again offending a single individual among you. Answer me, therefore, my dear Sirs. If you believe in the last Judgment, what are you doing, to the intent that you may obtain in that Day a favourable sentence with all its blessed consequences? At least, what are you doing, so as to escape an adverse sentence with all that bitter shame and deplorable loss, which I have so fully set before you? I perceive that, when called upon to take your trial in any important cause at some earthly tribunal, you secure your attorney, you fee counsel, you wait upon officials, you stoop to men in authority. I observe that you allow yourself no rest by night or day. To-day you are seen in one antechamber; to-morrow in another: to-day you have a conference with one lawyer; to-morrow with another: you read, you study, you write; you get covered with dust in routing out old long-forgotten family papers. I observe, that you are ready to incur great expense: to this person you send a present; and to that you offer a bribe. You procure at any cost the countenance of persons of high station. You fail not to employ all the means, that occur to your mind, so as to secure beforehand, if not a triumphant decision in your favour, at least the fair hope of it. Now tell me. Do you take any such mighty pains to procure a verdict in your favour at the Heavenly Tribunal, where the cause to be solemnly decided is an affair of Eternity? Answer me at once. It is no use your wincing. It is no use for you to attempt to evade this my question. Do you take any such mighty pains? O GOD, why only to hint at such a thing is itself the deepest shame! Do we exhort you to receive the Holy Communion once a month? You say that it is too often. Do we prescribe to you some wholesome act of repentance? You say it is too difficult. Do we propose to you some regular plan of devotion? You say it is too wearisome. Well then, we try again. At least, we ask you, to give up a certain society—I cannot. Frequent no more that place of amusement—I will not. But surely you might spare a short quarter of an hour every night to examine and settle your conscience?—It affects my head. Surely you might attend the daily morning Prayer at Church?—I have no time. Give then, at least, some trifle in alms to those wretched objects, that crawl about our streets, so that they may put in a word for you at the Day of Judgment. *Make to yourselves friends of the mammon of unrighteousness.* (S. Luke xvi. 9.)—Only think; how can I? I am burdened with debts; I have my own family to provide for; I am eaten up by lawyers.[1] And do you then really believe that you will have to be judged by GOD, while you thus refuse to make even half the exertion, which you readily submit to, when you believe that you have to be judged by a man? "You do not believe! you do not believe!"—I will take the very words of Salvian out of his eloquent lips, and use them as my own— "You do not believe; you do not believe; and, though you may pretend to do it by what you say, you deny it by what you do." Is it then, that the Judgment-seat of GOD may be less formidable, than that of man? Is it then, that the cause may be less momentous? Is it then, that the opponents may be less powerful? Is it then, that the case may be less intricate? Is it then, that the Judge may be less scrutinizing? Is it then, that justice may be less pure? Is it then, that the power of appeal may be less impossible? Why then nothing else can be said, than that you have no belief that you must appear before such a Tribunal. "You do not be-

---

[1] A propensity to litigation has at all times been a common fault among Italians, and is frequently adverted to in this *Quaresimale.*

lieve, you do not believe! And, though you may pretend it by what you say, you deny it by what you do!"

I should be quite willing to allow that you did believe, could you give me this one simple proof; namely, that you refrained from openly ill-treating that Judge, who will be the person to try you. . . . But how, ye profligate men and women, for to you I am speaking, "how can you talk about your believing in a Judge to come, when no one in your estimation occupies a less or a lower place, than this very Judge Himself?" You believe that you will have to be judged by CHRIST. Well: and whence is it then that you can speak evil of CHRIST in all your sports and pastimes? blaspheme CHRIST in all your transports of anger? swear falsely by CHRIST in all your contracts? offend CHRIST in all your amusements? How is it then that you prefer displeasing CHRIST to displeasing your friend? How is it then that you prefer giving up CHRIST to giving up that improper female connection? How is it that you prefer squandering your money in every kind of foolish, immoral, scandalous, and utterly worthless expenditure, rather than giving it to CHRIST? Am I to suppose that you treat with such rudeness any mortal man, who is to be your judge? Do you speak against him with so much freedom in every society? Do you hold him up to contempt with so much wantonness on every occasion? Are you bold enough to insult him to his very face with the same utter unscrupulousness, which you show towards CHRIST (can worse be said of you?) in His own Churches, where He is mystically present in the most Holy Sacrament, and where, nevertheless, you do not hesitate to chatter, and gossip, and laugh, and sometimes even to pay your idolatrous adoration to some living Venus, who may be sitting near you? You may say what you like, never will you convince me that you have any belief in CHRIST, that He will come to be your Judge. "You do not believe, you do not believe: and, though you may pretend it by what you say, you deny it by what you do."

10. But why not believe it, my dear Christians? Why not believe it? Do we not know, for a certainty, that none among us shall be exempted from this judgment? *We must all appear before the Judgment-seat of Christ* (2 Cor. v. 10,) exclaims the Apostle—*all, all.* What then are you doing? Do you hope

that by some special favour you may absent yourselves? Do you hope by some clever trick to get out of the Court? Do you hope to escape altogether by flight? Ah, if you have ever been foolish enough to cherish such a notion, your hope is delusive. Itansura, King of Scythia, once sent to King Darius, his principal enemy, an extraordinary present. It consisted of three animals, a mole, a fish, and a bird; animals each of a genus most opposite to the other. Together with them he also sent a poisoned arrow. This was to intimate to Darius, as S. Clement of Alexandria relates, that, if he had not lurked low under the ground, like a mole, or had he not dived deep into the sea, like a fish, or had he not vanished high into the air, like a bird, the arrow, shot from the King's arm, would unquestionably have sooner or later reached him. This was clearly the empty boast of a barbarian, you will say to me: but, tell me, would these means have been sufficient to save him from GOD? No; replies David. They would not have been sufficient. *If I climb up into heaven, Thou art there.* Mark GOD's arrow! When, as a bird, I fly aloft, it reaches me in the air. *If I go down into hell, Thou art there also.* Mark GOD's arrow! When as a mole, I hide myself, it finds me underground. *If I dwell in the uttermost parts of the earth, there also Thy hand shall find me.* Mark GOD's arrow! When, as a fish, I plunge into the deep ocean, it hastens even there in its fleet career to strike me under the water. Far too fondly then are we flattering ourselves, when we trust by any means to escape GOD. Wherever we go, we are always in some territory subject to His dominion. Everywhere does He assert His authority; everywhere does He retain His ministers; everywhere does He support His armies; so that in every place we must of necessity fall under His power. "It is not possible to escape Thy hand." (Wisd. xvi. 15.) And yet fear ye Him not, tremble ye not at Him, as not believing so much as this, that *it is a fearful thing to fall into the hands of the living God?* (Heb. x. 31.)

My GOD! Do Thou enlighten the minds of this people! Do Thou soften their hearts: for I quite despair of all power to do so, even were I to spend my last breath in suppliant entreaties at their feet. I despair of it; I despair of it. But why? Is it because they are hardened? Is it because they

are perverse? Is it because they are stubborn? Ah no, my
God: it is rather, because I myself am a sinner. And how
canst Thou expect *me* to convert any of my hearers, when it
may be that I myself am worse, than any of their number?
Do Thou, therefore, do Thou mercifully supply my lack of
service: and grant me this favour, I now ask of Thee. Give
me, at the least, one soul in this congregation! One single
soul, I beg of Thee, O LORD, out of this vast assembly; and
choose that soul for Thyself, as it seems good in Thy sight.
I demand it of Thee by that most Holy Blood, which Thou
hast poured out on the Cross, by those stripes, by those
purple wounds, by those cruel and intense agonies, which
Thou didst endure for us! Oh, how happy should I be in
being accounted worthy of so bright a conquest this morning!
How should I thank Thee! How should I praise Thee!
How should I bless Thy goodness from the bottom of my
heart! Yes, yes; one soul at least, I will hope for at Thy
hands. But then?—whose soul shall it be? Take courage,
O woman, for that one soul may be thine; thou, who hast
grown old in a life of sin, so as to render thy deliverance a
seeming impossibility. Or, that one soul may be thine, O
thou man, who art become a devil in thy furious passion; or
thine, thou gambler; or thine, thou adulterer; or thine, thou
assassin; or thine, whosoever thou art, who, in spite of the
sharp goadings of thy conscience, hast so long refused rightly
to confess thy sins. A soul is the thing I desire: and I desire, moreover, that it be the soul of a most abandoned trans-
gressor. LORD, what dost Thou answer? Art Thou unwilling to give it me? Ah, yes; I see why it is. I have done
Thee a wrong by limiting my request to *one* soul. Many
many souls I would now earnestly hope from Thee: yea, I
would even hope to gain them all. Have we not every one of
us hereafter to assemble together in the valley of Jehoshaphat?
O LORD, suffer not me and this people to be separated from
each other in that Day; but so order it by Thy grace, that
we may all of us be found at Thy right hand, all of us in
peace, all of us in safety, all of us invited with great triumph
to Thy Glory, none of us excluded from it *with shame and
everlasting contempt!*

SERMON VI.

THE FEAR OF GOD FROM THE SENSE OF HIS POWER.

S. MATTH. XXI. 10, 12.

"AND WHEN HE WAS COME INTO JERUSALEM, ALL THE CITY WAS MOVED, SAYING, WHO IS THIS? . . . AND JESUS WENT INTO THE TEMPLE OF GOD AND CAST OUT ALL THEM THAT SOLD AND BOUGHT IN THE TEMPLE."

1. I KNOW not from whence it came, that all the world, under its sad old state of delirium, should have preferred the worship of gods, who were vile and mean-spirited, to that of those, who were noble and generous. Only review in your minds, my hearers, the various nations of forlorn heathenism. You will see that each emulated the other in the adoration, paid by it, to a multitudinous set of senseless deities—of stones, that could not move, of stumps, that could not speak, of metals, that could not hear. This went so far, that in Egypt you could scarcely find a common peasant, who had not his own gods growing up in his garden. He had only to take his mattock, and he could raise them: for every leek, springing up there, was a new deity; every onion was a fresh object of worship. That truly was a fortunate time for brute beasts, and, particularly, for those of the baser sort, when lizards and grubs received more distinguished honour than eagles and lions. What animal indeed is there more grovelling than a beetle? Yet a beetle was regarded by the

people of Syene, as their favourite god. What more clumsy than a tortoise? Yet a tortoise was worshipped by the Troglodites. What more stupid than an ox? Yet an ox was worshipped by the inhabitants of Heliopolis. What more offensive than a goat? And yet a goat was worshipped by the inhabitants of Mendes? Whence, my hearers, did all this absurdity arise?

Do we not all know the vast influence, in other respects, of pride, among men? How then was it, that they were not ashamed to prostrate themselves before a rabble of such vile, misshapen, and disgusting little brutes, as these? Actually on their bended knees they would burn incense on the altars of those very animals, whom in their walks afterwards they crushed under their feet. The solution of this question, if I mistake not, is not so very difficult. All these idolaters were men of most abandoned lives; and since the common instincts of nature obliged them to recognise some Divine being in the world, they naturally preferred being subject to a god, who, however contemptible, was yet weak, rather than to one, who, however noble, was yet strong. The Divine power is a sore object of hatred to wicked men. They will adopt any god, provided he be one of slow perception and incapable of taking vengeance. This was exactly the dream of the foolish Marcion. I am supported in my opinion by the authority of Theodoret, who maintained that it was on this account the Philistines adored the fly, as being an animal, unclean and loathsome, it is true, but to the same extent harmless and volatile. They reckoned upon their being able to commit every sin with impunity, while they had a god, who was so entirely in their own power, that, were he to cause them the least annoyance, they could banish him with the wave of a fan, or a shake of their finger, or a puff of their breath. Hence what, when alive, they could blow away in a moment, when transformed into an image they called a god. If, peradventure, in this our day, we have ever countenanced any such crazy delusions, as these, let us unlearn them. The God, whom we worship, is not, ye sinners, a god of that senseless character, that ye would attribute to Him. He is well able, in spite of you, to do far above what you would have

Him; and therefore it is your part and duty to respect and fear Him. For have you not observed His behaviour this morning in our Gospel? The people are curious to ascertain, *"Who is this?"* What then does He do? Without any delay He lays hand upon His weapons; He rebukes them; He scourges them; He fills every soul with alarm; and thus He convinces them of His power to command their respect, after they had dared to carry their outrages beyond His own Person to the walls of His Sanctuary. What therefore will ye do, in order to escape His mighty arm? Where, ye unhappy men, will ye find your place of concealment? where your refuge, so that He may not overtake you? Far better for you to follow the advice I now am ready to give you; which is this: on no account depart from this Sacred building without having first acknowledged with fear and trembling the power of your GOD. Reflect with me this morning on the brutish stupidity of every sinner, while he has no fear,—(who would believe it?)—to stand up in arms against the Almighty. For, as Job declares, *He stretcheth out his hand against God and strengtheneth himself against the Almighty. He runneth upon Him with a lofty neck.* (Job xv. 25, 26, Vulg.)

2. In truth, are we not all struck with horror at beholding CHRIST in this Gospel, how, with nothing more than a simple rod of small cords in His hand, He routed the multitudes, overturned the benches, scattered the animals, and filled all the Temple with confusion, all the city with alarm? We justly look upon that power, as being greater than any other, which by the help of weaker means can effect its object. Were I to tell you, by way of example, that the brave Samson was able with a mere lifting up of his spear to keep at bay a whole army of Philistines, you would surely think him a man of mighty power; but, if I were to tell you that he was able to do this with the help only of a sword, would you not think him possessed of a power still more mighty? and of mightier and mightier still, were I to tell you of his doing the same with a wooden club? But if, advancing still further, I should tell you that he accomplished all this with the mere jawbone of a dead ass, then your estimate of him would

rise proportionately high, and you would be disposed to smile at those pretences to what men call power, which are so much lauded in the princes of this world. To consider indeed such persons powerful, only because we see them go abroad preceded by many thousands of horses and soldiers, of spearmen and fusileers, is quite a mistake. All this is rather a sign of their weakness. We would admit them to be powerful, in the true sense of the word, if, like Samson, with a jawbone in their hands they could march against the combined forces of the enemy, slaughter them, disperse them, and throw them all into confusion and disorder. For, just in proportion as any power can produce the greater effects by means of the weaker instruments, must be the degree of the intrinsic value, which it possesses. Now this is that very power, which shone so miraculously in our GOD: and therefore, according to the judgment of S. Chrysostom, GOD gave us to understand His true nature after a most magnificent fashion, when, having to subdue the haughtiness of the Egyptians, He subdued it, not by having recourse to wild beasts, which are the terror of the forests, but by those paltry reptiles, which are the scum of the fens. "A truly grand spectacle did GOD exhibit to the whole universe, when He beat down the pride of the Egyptians, not with lions and bears, but with frogs and flies." Granting this to be so, come near, ye, who are Christians; and just tell me, whence arises that pride of spirit, which prompts you at times to provoke GOD? From whence proceed all your exceeding boldness and your fearless presumption, so that, instead of ceasing from the affronts you offer Him, you are induced to heap upon Him fresh indignities?

3. It is not, however, of so much importance to me, that I have your own confession in this matter. Of mine own self I discover plainly enough, what it is, which adds to your boldness in sinning. It is commonly your abundance in worldly goods, and, particularly, your great riches. Nor is this surprising. Money is that, which ultimately everything else subserves. *Money answereth all things.* (Eccles. x. 19.) Solomon has long ago settled this point for us; and hence it is, ye moneyed men, ye, who have found out this truth by long

continued experience, that ye come to say among yourselves —" What can I possibly want? I have it in my power to order matters, just as I like. Do I wish to gain such a lawsuit? That attorney will do my pleasure. Do I wish to gratify my passion for that young female? She will do my pleasure. Do I wish to take revenge of my enemy? That hired assassin will do my pleasure." And thus you rise up audaciously against GOD, fearing no evil, because you abound in money, to which all earthly good is obedient. *The rich man's wealth is his strong city and as a high wall in his own conceit.* (Prov. x. 15; xviii. 11.) But perceive ye not that, while your money commands everything else, it does not command Him, who is the Lord of your money? Suppose GOD to have a design to level with the dust a certain tower, as lofty as you please to make it. Does He, in your opinion, require some pieces of ordnance for this purpose? You have your property, most of you, in farms or in enclosed land; and therefore exposed to the open day. Tell me; must GOD, in order to deprive you of such possessions, renew the wonders of the preceding century, when He rained down stones in Bologna, or of this present century, when He has rained down lead in Buda? So far from this being necessary, He can carry His will into effect by the most insignificant means; for instance, by what He did to Ahab, that is, by withholding the rain in its season; or by despatching the particles of hail, or the thin mist, or the tiny insect, to attack your crops. Any dense troop of caterpillars or locusts, that He may commission to march against you, will suffice to reduce you to beggary. And what famous conspiracies has He not utterly defeated by such poor, weak, little troopers as these? Not only did He by their instrumentality drive the Canaanites out of their land, that He might plant in it His own people; but by the same means He subdued a Persian army, led by Sapor their king, under the walls of Nisibis; and routed another army of the Franks, encamped with Charles their king, near Girona. And is He not able to devastate your few inches of arable land by the same means? Question the historian Diodorus, as to the dearth, which was occasioned in Media by a set of poor little sparrows? Ask Sabellius, what a desolation was brought into Thracia by the most diminutive frogs; Cromerus, what havoc was caused in Masovia by the lightest grasshoppers; Pliny, what waste was introduced into France by the pettiest flies; Sigonius, what famine was produced in Italy by the meanest caterpillars. And from these instances you will be able to inform me, whether GOD has it not in His power with a mere trifle to render you miserable.

But perhaps your property may not be invested in land; and therefore you laugh at all fear of drought, inundation, vermin, and wild beasts. In what then is it invested? In bills of exchange? but how deceptive they are. In mortgages? but how liable to fail they are. In trade and in commerce? but how full of hazard they are. For is the vessel, in which you ventured to embark your merchandise, so independent of GOD, as not to require of Him any favourable winds? Forsooth, it must cost Him wondrous toil, either to grant it a prosperous voyage, or to dash it in pieces on a rock, or to strand it on a sand-bank, or to let it fall into the hands of the corsairs! Ye then, who traffic on the waters, how can you dare provoke GOD at that very critical time, when the bulk of your property goes floating on the wide sea? Did you know it to be already reaching the port, not even then should you dismiss your apprehension. For, as Tertullian observed, GOD is wont to reserve nigh unto the shore His hidden under-currents and His calms, whereby to cause shipwreck. How much more fearfully exposed must your vessel be, far out at sea, where GOD retains in His service such mighty storms, and billows, and whirlpools, and rocks, and sea monsters, and hurricanes, where *He breaks the ships of the sea through the east wind* (Ps. xlviii. 6)? Proceed we further. If He gives an order to the least spark of fire, are not all those houses, on which you raise your rents, immediately consumed? If He commission the pestilential vapour, are not those flocks and herds, from which you derive your income, immediately infected? If He speak the word to the subtle penetrating damp, does not your standing corn immediately rot in the ear, and the grain perish, on which you built your hopes of a more abundant harvest in a season of prevailing scarcity?

Even if your dollars are closely lodged in the chest, placed under the guardianship of iron bars, and of steel hinges, you must not consider them beyond the reach of Him, who, as on this day, with a scourge of small cords *overthrew the tables of the money-changers.* Oh, simpletons, that ye are! Oh, how great your delusion! A lawsuit, in which He may engage you against any one, an enemy, a calumny, a quarrel—how rapidly may these consume your wealth? Ah! He had the best of reasons to tell us by the mouth of His Prophet, that all the gold and all the silver belonged unto Him. *Mine is the silver and Mine the gold* (Hag. ii. 8.) And yet, knowing this so well as you do, you can still be ready to provoke Him. Only tell me. Did any potentate keep under his own lock and key all your riches, just as Joseph had the controul over the riches of the Egyptians, so that it should be entirely at his disposal whether you should have them or lose them, could you ever be guilty of so great a folly, as to brave his displeasure, or openly to pick a quarrel with him? And yet, you will quarrel with GOD? Oh, what blindness, infatuation, and insanity! It is from the fact of your being possessors of great wealth that you take occasion to offend Him. I tell you, that on this very account, because you are possessors of great wealth, you ought to respect Him the more. If you were poor, you would be liable to one punishment the less; but, being rich, you are thereby capable of receiving one punishment the more; which is, you may be reduced to poverty.

4. But come, I will grant that GOD permits you to continue in the entire possession of your income; yet how easily can He deprive you of the advantages, which arise from it! Riches surely are not to be coveted merely for themselves, but, as the philosopher teaches us, for the fruits we reap from them, such as honour, friendship, advancement, connections, entertainments, divers pleasures: and does not GOD equally bear all these fruits in that hand of His, in which S. John saw *the seven stars;* in other words, those seven planets, that dispense them to mankind?[1] Were I to speak particularly of

---

[1] Segneri, in thus referring to the supposed Providential influence of the planets on human affairs, shows that, notwithstanding his professed character

each of these advantages, the detail would be too long. I will mention, however, one, that comprehends all the rest. Are you not all quite convinced that health is the life and soul of every other blessing?. "There is no riches above a sound body," says Ecclesiasticus (xxx. 16.) To what avail do you possess your fine villas, your beautiful gardens, your magnificent palaces, if, chained down to a sick bed, like King Asa, you are never in a state to enjoy them; but are cut off from every source of consolation and relief, save that of having your doctors holding their consultations about you? All the benefit of our earthly goods consists, not in the possession, but in the use of them. And accordingly the same Ecclesiasticus decided that " Better is the poor, being sound and strong of constitution, than a rich man that is afflicted in his body" (xxx. 14.) For a poor but healthy man has at least a relish for the pittance he earns; whereas a rich but sickly man finds no enjoyment whatever in the abundance he possesses. Were then GOD to allow your orchards to teem with the most delicious fruits, your vines to burst forth with the most luscious grapes, and your preserves to be well stocked with all kinds of most exquisite game, it would profit you but little, did He, on the other hand, so derange your organs of taste, that these delicacies would prove to you rather unsavoury than otherwise. Let GOD only strike some acute pain into your head, and what pleasure can all your book-learning afford you? Was not Angelo Poliziano a most learned man? Yet there was a time with him, when his books afforded him so little gratification, that he wandered about his house, knocking his

of a reformer, he had still some remains about him of the old popular superstition. There is a passage in one of the sermons of Savonarola, which informs us of the strong and ridiculous hold that superstition, in respect to astronomy, had in his time, particularly among the Clergy. *Vuoi tu vedere che la Chiesa si governa per mano d'astrologi? E non è Prelato ne gran Maestro, che non abbia qualche familiarità con qualche astrologo, che gli predice l'ora e il punto che egli ha da cavalcare o fare altra cosa o faccenda. E non uscirebbono questi gran Maestri un passo fuora della volontà degli astrologi. I nostri predicatori ancora hanno lasciata la Scrittura Santa, e sonsi dati all' astrologia e alla filosofia, e quella predicano su' pergami, e fannola regina: e la Scrittura Sacra adoperano come ancilla, perchè e predicano la filosofia per parere dotti, e non perchè la deserva loro a esporre la Scrittura Santa.* (Predica xxiii. sopra il soggetto, *Quàm bonus Israel Deus.* A.D. 1493.)—See Dante, Purg. C. xvi.

head against the walls; so excruciating were those spasms he felt shooting through his temples. Let God only make way for the formation of a frightful cancer in your lungs, and what pleasure can all your power afford you? Was not Herod a most powerful king? Yet for years he derived thence so little satisfaction, that he was on the point of laying bare his bosom with a knife, so sharp-toothed were those worms, which, like as in a state of fermentation, came forth from his bowels. You would, forsooth, have a rare enjoyment of those soft well-shaken feather-beds, those splendid couches, those gaudy tapestries, should your lot resemble that of the ill-fated Mæcenas, who for three successive years could not prevail upon sleep, even for a single night, to close his eyelids. What more shall I say? A slight attack of fever alone suffices to render the happiest Prince in the earth miserable. Hence S. Augustine emphatically observed, "Human pleasures are only counterfeits; and, such as they are, the least indisposition of the body can rob us of them."

But you will say to me; Is it not *your* body, rather than ours, which is liable to all these ailments? Well; I must grant it: you are young, you are hearty, you are strong. What then? However vigorous your health be, must God endure hard toil and labour to deprive you of it? Is not a cough enough to do this? Is not a slight humour enough? Is not a stone enough? How then can you pay Him so little regard, just as if you never knew that *healing is in His wings* (Mal. iv. 2,) and consequently that with a gentle flap of those wings He takes health from one and gives it to another, and so retakes and restores it again? Oh, ye heavens! I see that a judge among men can manage to strike terror into the minds of the wicked; and how does he do it? He lets them see his many various instruments of torture, his dreadful apparatus of punishment, and all the power he has to chastise them. And cannot God then terrify us with the vast appliances and means He possesses: those diseases, which He lets us see so constantly arrayed against us in the pains, and infirmities, and many various degrees of malignity, under which the enfeebled bodies of our friends or relations from time to time are sinking around us? And yet, no human judge has for any convict torments at all comparable to these. At the utmost, the sufferings such judges can inflict are limited to a certain period, which is fixed by law: but those, coming from the hands of GOD, sometimes extend beyond the reach of years, and, by reason of their continual daily pressure, are frequently found so intolerable, that many sufferers have in their despair preferred a violent death to such a life of prolonged misery . . . . Tell me then; if the bodily evils be so many, so diversified, and so severe, by which GOD can avenge Himself for the insults we offer Him, is it not the height of folly to treat Him with so little respect, or rather with so much petulant animosity?

Certain people really seem, as if they imagined themselves composed of such solid materials, that nothing, short of the most deadly weapons, could penetrate into them . . . . Now I only wish that GOD would give them some near insight into their bodily frames by rendering them for a short time transparent, like glass. This would enable them to discover at a glance the many hundreds of bones, muscles, nerves, veins, fibres, arteries, cartilages, which form the component parts of the body. Is there one among you, who would not be shocked to see with what facility a system, so complicated as this, might become deranged. You will be disposed perhaps to smile, when I mention the case of a certain oddity, who was under a full conviction of his having been transformed into glass, and who, in consequence, reclined for years on a couch of the softest down, never daring to move, but crying aloud to people, even at a distance, for mercy's sake not to touch him, unless they wished to break him in pieces. For my part, I am more inclined to weep, when I reflect that we, who are more brittle than glass, should yet fancy ourselves strong as bronze. It was often wisely observed by S. Augustine in his discourses, that "glass, though in its own nature most fragile, yet only needed careful keeping to last long:" whereas man, however vigilant and whatever care he may take of himself, must needs perish . . . . Many indeed have met their deaths in various ways from the most trivial causes and seeming accidents . . . . And dost thou not fear for thyself? And dost thou not tremble? And dost thou not, besotted man, entertain some respect for One, who is so powerful? And *that God* (as Daniel most emphatically speaks on this subject,) *that God, in whose hand thy breath is, hast thou not glorified ?* (Dan. v. 23.)

I remember to have read, how a certain wild Indian, named Munatama, was falsely accused before Vasco Nunez, one of the conquerors of that country, of the flagrant crime of high treason. The poor wretch pleaded, as well as he could, in his own defence; but in vain: wherefore, in conclusion, by way of summing up all he had said, he threw himself at the feet of that celebrated warrior, and with much dignity of action placing on the hilt of his sword his trembling hand, briefly in these words exculpated himself from every charge. " And is it possible, that you could ever suspect me of having entertained any idea of doing you harm, so long as you carry at your side that mighty weapon, which with a single blow cuts a man in two ?" Thus wonderfully did the savage, taught in the mere school of nature, plead his cause; for it appeared to him to be quite an impossibility, that one, like himself, who, agreeably to the customs of those parts, went about naked, with nothing more about him than a wooden scimitar, could ever invite a quarrel with a man, who was always armed, and who knew perfectly well how to manage a sword of steel. Ah! my dear Christians, come nigh, and answer me. Can you then entertain any idea of inviting a quarrel with GOD, as if you knew not the vast difference, that subsists between you, the vilest worms, that creep on the earth, and Him, who is the absolute Monarch of the universe? Something beyond a sword of steel has He at His side! As many lightnings, as are in the clouds; as many savage beasts, as are in the woods; as many poisons, as are in the weeds; as many whirlpools, as are in the waters; as many flames, as are in the fires; as many quicksands, as are in the earth,—these all are His weapons, wherewith He is able to beat down our proud presumptuous spirit; and still do you not fear Him? If, on His simply giving the word of command to a cough, to a fever, to a cancer, to a humour, you are dead men, what would be the effect of His commissioning thunderings and lightnings, hurricanes and earthquakes? To cast down poor puny man with engines so stupendous, as these—is it beyond the power of that great GOD, who, if He touch the mountains, behold them turned to ashes; if He rebuke the sea, behold it dried up; if He upbraid the sun, behold it extinguished; if He forsake the earth, behold it utterly undone? Oh, how well is this expressed in Job: *I have seen that they that plough iniquity reap the same. By the blast of God they perish.* (iv. 8, 9.) Have you noticed the words? He does not say by thundering, or by casting forth lightning among them: no; *by the blast of God.* For, if it so please Him, GOD can with a single breath at once put an end to us all. *With the breath of His lips He shall slay the wicked.* (Isa. xi. 4.)

5. We may go further: because GOD not only has it in His power to take our lives with the most gentle breathing of His lips, that is, with the utmost possible facility; but He can just as well do this at the very times, which are the most inopportune, and the circumstances, which are the most untoward imaginable. Tertullian affirms that GOD can make Himself feared, whensoever He pleases, by determining our death; but chiefly so, by determining it at those times, when we desire most the prolongation of life. " Death," he says, " comes upon us much more violently, in proportion as it finds us in the greater enjoyment of worldly applause, honour, satisfaction, and pleasure." How now in this case, ye profligate young men, can you dare so highly to offend Him by assaulting that virgin innocency? Or ye, greedy traffickers, by accumulating those heaps of money? Or ye, ambitious statesmen, by getting yourselves into that office? Or ye unwise parents, by forming that family alliance?—when only by snapping asunder one single thread GOD can defeat your long-woven projects at the very time, when they most promise you success? Who can recount the immense hardships, endured by Bibulus the Roman senator, in order to procure the vain distinction of a Roman triumph? Oh, how many deaths did he carry with him from Rome to people of other lands; some on the wings of poisoned arrows, some on the points of the sharpest swords! But Lo! at the very height of his boasting, GOD knew how to devise a way of turning it into the

shadow of death. And did it tax His strength to do this? It was quite enough for Him to appoint death to meet Bibulus on his entrance into the Capitol; death, too, not necessarily armed with all the destructive engines of war, but with a mere common house-tile in its hand. Would you believe it? A common house-tile, while he was ascending the Capitol, fell on his head, struck him dead on his triumphal chariot, and thus converted his laurels into cypress, his joys into sorrow, and all that most festive holiday scene into a funeral. What meaneth it then, ye sinners, that GOD, as possessing so great power, can instil into your minds so little fear, that not only you scruple not the least to offend Him, but sometimes can even plume yourselves on this very account, like those, of whom Job speaks, who *daringly provoke God?* (xii. 6, Vulg.)

I confess that, with all my revolving the matter over and over again in my mind, I find myself quite unable to discover your ground of self-security. "O, father," I shall be answered by some of this ungodly class of persons, "don't trouble yourself to take any more pains about it; for we will at once tell it you. We too at first stood in mighty awe of that power, which you have so strongly impressed on our mind this morning; and therefore we took great care not to commit any daring sin. But afterwards our experience helped us to dismiss all such fear; because in the course of time, by way of test, we did commit a sin, and yet in consequence of it we didn't suffer any calamity. Then it was that taking courage we added new sins to our old offences; we advanced from fornication to incest, from spite to revenge, from foolish talk to blasphemy. And yet, we live; we have our farms; and they yield us fruit: we have our children; and they multiply around us: we have our friends; and we stand well in their opinion: and even, if we have any enemies, they know how to respect us. On what ground then can you expect us to stand in awe of that power, which, if it be so formidable to others, is in no wise formidable to us?" Not formidable to you? Dost Thou hear, O my despised GOD? Dost Thou hear all this arrogant talk, and yet dost Thou endure it? See here the fruits of Thy forbearance and long-suffering. *Thou hast been favourable to the nation, O Lord. Thou hast been favourable.* And what hast Thou got by it? *Art Thou glorified?* Quite the contrary. I must apply to you Isaiah's words (xxvi. 15, Vulg.) *Thou hast removed all the ends of the earth far off.* Where then are those thunderbolts, which you waste to so little purpose, now against the senseless tower, now against the consecrated temple? Is it not right that you should spare and reserve them for the ungodly? Otherwise, wherefore dost Thou command us Thy preachers that we should declare the terrors of Thy mighty arm, if Thou failest to carry them into effect? By this you cause us all to be put to shame, to be found liars. I can now quite enter into the feelings of Thine ancient prophets, those Jonahs and those Jeremiahs, who manifested so great a repugnance to engage in their ministry, for fear of becoming a laughing-stock to the heathen. I too hoped to have produced in the hearts of these sinners some deep impression of fear towards Thee; but, as far as I can discover, they are likely to return home more emboldened than ever; and my lot, who am every day crying out among them *Violence and spoil*, will be to get laughed at for my pains. (Jer. xx. 8.) Yet, fool that I am, why do I utter such vain words against GOD, who is so wise and so orderly in all His dealings? Well then, ye sinners, let's arrange our differences. I am quite willing to grant all you say. Up to the present time GOD has not punished you. He has rather granted you prosperity. Is it not so? Very well; come, what do you now infer from this? Have you less cause to tremble for the future? I deny it; I deny it. I conclude quite the reverse; it is on this very account you ought to tremble and fear Him the more. Listen; for I wish to prove this, not from any probable arguments, but from what is clear and certain, that I may thereby save you from error.

The fact of GOD's not having punished you up to the present time, according to your deservings, can only arise from one or other of these two causes—either from His having remitted your punishment; or, from His having postponed it. It cannot be ascribed to any other, than these two circumstances, at least by any Christian man. Let us suppose then that He may have remitted your punishment. You ought therefore the more to fear Him; because the more He has forgiven you, in regard to the past, the less probable it is that He will forgive you, in regard to the future. And do you not well know that patience, when it is long abused, becomes fury? GOD truly is merciful; but He is also just. *Gracious and righteous is the Lord.* (Ps. xxv. 7.) Since then His mercy has thus far discharged its office, it will now be the time for His justice to take effect. "For what sort of a GOD" (as Tertullian inquires) "would He be, were He to command duties, without the design of rewarding our obedience; or to prohibit sins, without the design of punishing our disobedience?" And what kind of a Ruler would he be, who should be always pardoning, and never punishing? Correction is the chief guardian of all human laws; that, which makes them respected; that, which promotes morality; that, which is the main prop of government. And, as frequently to abate somewhat of their strictness shows a compassionate and kindly disposition, so on every occasion to do this would indicate an unmanly weakness. Therefore, in proportion as GOD pardoned you the more in times past, so much the less will He pardon you for the time to come.

But if, as is far more probably the fact, GOD has not remitted your punishment, but has rather postponed it . . . . then the fact of His not having up to the present time avenged Himself of you should be so far from increasing your boldness, as to increase your fear; for this looks as if He will take His vengeance of you in a lump, once for all. And what then will be the full outpouring of His fury, if such be the first early drops? The scanty streamlets, while apart from each other, could do but little; but, when united, what havoc they spread around! The small sparks, while detached from each other, were almost harmless: but, when conjoined, what a conflagration they stir up! The soft breezes, when disunited, were inoffensive; but, when gathering their forces together, what a tempest they occasion! How appalling then will needs be that final outburst of the wrath of GOD, like *an overflowing scourge* (Isa. xxviii. 15,) since even in its first manifestations it has already proved so fearful! . . . By continuing in your sins, you are only adding fresh supplies to that vast reservoir, of which Ecclesiasticus spake, "As a flood hath watered the earth, so shall His wrath inherit the nations that have not sought Him" (xxxix. 23, Vulg.) But *when* will the time be? When will this vast reservoir empty itself upon sinners with such dreadful impetuosity? . . . .

The Second Part.

6. No one can know for a certainty, when that time will be, which God has appointed for the exercise of a vengeance, terrible in proportion as it is delayed. This must depend upon the secret disposal of those judgments, which *the Father hath placed in His own power.* (Acts i. 7.) For even the very heathen could say, "The gods have feet of wool." Hence they step so softly over thy head, that, with thy utmost attention, thou art not aware of their approach. Notwithstanding, if with any probability we may infer the future from the past according to the famous saying of S. Jerome, "Things future are known by things past," I think we may designate the very hour, with some probability at least, if not with certainty. Attend, that you may know when that hour will be. All among you must well remember the wonderful manner, in which the city of Jericho was assaulted by the soldiers of Joshua. He had given orders that, during the space of seven mornings, they should carry the Ark in circuit round the walls, that the armed troops should go before, that the unarmed people should follow after, and that the Priests, every time of their going the round, should cause the trumpets to sound. This was accordingly done; and precisely on the seventh day, at the sound of those trumpets, the walls fell down and the city was taken. Permit me now, in my own way, to offer a few weighty observations upon this victory, generally so well known. The first morning, when the besieged people of Jericho beheld from the top of their walls that imposing array and heard those trumpets, what a terrible panic must the poor souls have suffered! They must have fancied that the soldiers were even already deploying for the attack, even already leaping on the ramparts, even already

scaling the very battlements. But, when they soon afterwards perceived that all this noise was followed by no practical effect, they must have begun to breathe a little more freely. The second morning, when they witnessed a like repetition of the same performances, their fears must have assumed the form of surprise; not one among them being able to comprehend what was the meaning of this clamorous demonstration, that all ended in nothing. The third morning, their surprise must have degenerated into a disposition to smile; as was natural to people, who now knew by repeated proof that the whole assault vented itself in empty sound. But then, the fourth morning, and the fifth, and the sixth, when the besieged had more thoroughly recovered their spirits, only conceive what must have been the laughter, the ridicule, the hisses, and the shoutings, with which they saluted the enemy from their heights. I can quite realise the scene to my mind. "Yes," they in all likelihood exclaimed, "these fine trumpets of theirs sound beautifully. Take notice of their new invention for taking cities, not by the force of battering trains, but by the effect of sound! Blow on merrily by all means; for, while you are blowing, we can be dancing. Why, what, in all seriousness, do you mean by this? To frighten us out of our wits by your noise, when you are unable to subdue us by your valour? We are none of those big stupid birds, who are brought down from their nests by mere dint of clattering noises. If you have the hearts of men, take the trumpet out of your mouth; come on, sword in hand; and then we'll believe you." Thus with every possible insult they may have cried aloud from their walls during those days. But, if at any time their fear must have been at the lowest point and their raillery at the highest, it was, if I mistake not, on the morning of the seventh day, preceded, as that day had been, by so many circumstances, calculated to embolden their minds under a feeling of their security. And behold, it was on that very morning that the entire overthrow of their city took place. *At the seventh time, when the priests blew with the trumpets, the wall fell down flat.* (Josh. vi. 16—20.) Now you will conceive, whether this overthrow was not all the more terrible from its being the less expected. The wretched inhabitants find themselves with a smile on their lips, when behold their bastion walls on a sudden tumbling down, their towers falling headlong, and themselves too involved in the dreadful crash. And then—what with the groans of some, who were wounded, of others, who were mangled to pieces, of others, who were smashed under the ruins—one simultaneous universal outcry of distress must have deafened the air and affrighted the very stars. The Israelites, in the mean time, each soldier at his proper post, pushed forward intrepidly over the gaping breach, and making their way over the bodies of the enemy, buried before they were dead, advanced with their pikes lowered and their swords drawn. Taking different directions, they penetrated into the private dwellings, and scattering on every side blood, on every side havoc, on every side death, they quickly reduced the city to complete desolation.

7. We will now return to our subject. What was it you wished to learn from me, my dear Sirs?—The time, when destruction shall overtake the wicked? Do you know, when it will be? Why, when it overtook the people of Jericho; which is tantamount to saying with the prophet Isaiah, at the time, when they were least thinking about it; *whose breaking cometh suddenly at an instant.* (Isaiah xxx. 13.) For it is a reasonable thing that the wicked should be apprehended at that very crisis, when, more regardless of GOD than ever, they either disbelieve His threatening, or ridicule His power, and therefore are most at ease in their sins. Behold then the zealous Priests of the LORD, who, with the trumpet of His Divine Word, prepare to lay siege to the obstinate stronghold of the human heart. They sound, they threaten, they announce far and wide the fast approaching overthrow, conformably to the order every preacher has received from GOD; *Cry aloud, spare not, lift up thy voice, like a trumpet, and show My people their transgressions and the house of Jacob their sins.* (Isa. lviii. 1.) The ungodly, on their hearing the preacher for the first time, begin to feel greatly alarmed: they immediately arm themselves against the assault by praying: they put themselves in an attitude of defence by receiving the Sacrament, as if they saw the destruction even now already at their doors. The destruction, however, does not come:

and so, on their hearing the preacher for the second time, as he sounds out the same alarm, they convert their fear into surprise, and begin to say within themselves: "What do these men mean by their keeping up every day this useless disturbance?" The third time, they convert their surprise into derision; and from derision they pass on to contempt, and from contempt to disdain, and from disdain to mockery: and then openly at their clubs and their casinos they discuss the latter among themselves. *They hear the words of the Lord* (as Ezekiel has it,) *and they turn them into a song of their mouth* (xxxiii. 31, Vulg.) For, as by way of counterpart to the words of the zealous preacher, they say, "Did you hear how skilfully he blew his trumpet? What, pray, do these men aim at? to frighten us out of our wits by scolding us and clamouring against us? Well, you, if you like, may believe them: as for me, I have been long accustomed to hear them dealing out the same threats, and for ever harping on the same string; and yet I find it all ends in nothing, but a most intolerable brawling. Where are all the heavy judgments he announces to us? *Where is the Word of the Lord? Let it come now.* (Jer. xvii. 15.) Where are all the diseases? where is all the beggary? To my seeming, we are more comfortable and more jovial, than other people are, who believe in these preachers."—Oh, yes! these other people you allude to—they are miserable? Are they? Well, well; only wait; for now is the very time for you to prove what you say. At this very time, when your incredulity has attained its height, even then you shall see what was the meaning of that preacher's voice, what the message of his sounding trumpet. In the midst of your merriment the wrath of heaven shall fall on you; and, when you perceive how all of a sudden such irrecoverable ruin has overtaken you, "Alas! alas!" you will exclaim, "we are lost and undone! See the blood, see the slaughter, see the havoc, see the desolation, see the flames, see the plagues, see the death!" And amidst such outcries, as these, stunned and stupefied, you will terminate your lives, condemned, so to speak, even before you die. Do you refuse to believe this upon my word? Turn quickly to the sacred Scriptures and consider. When did Belshazzar. the King of the Chaldeans. trace that fatal handwriting on the wall, which foretold his death? (Dan. v.) At the time, when, least fearing it, he was sitting at a most gorgeous feast with his concubines, and was drinking with studied insult out of the rubied cups, those spoils of conquest stolen from the Temple. When did Nebuchadnezzar hear that voice sounding from heaven, which condemned him to the wild woods? (Dan. iv.) At the time, when, least fearing it, he was walking amidst his flattering courtiers, proudly expatiating on the success he enjoyed with so much magnificence in his sins. When was Antiochus, King of Syria, struck from heaven with that intolerable disease, which goaded him on to madness? (2 Macc. ix. 9.) At the time, when, least fearing it, he was ascending his chariot and threatening, in his insufferable pride, the same desolation to Jerusalem, which he had so fully heaped upon other cities. When did Sennacherib, King of the Assyrians, receive from an Angel that final defeat, which caused the loss of his whole army? (2 Kings xix. 35.) At the time, when, least fearing it, he was daringly and insolently blaspheming the power of GOD, as unable to deliver Israel out of his hands, hitherto accustomed to so many victories. Jezebel, Queen of Israel—when did she see fulfilled the tremendous denunciation that she should be devoured by dogs? (2 Kings ix. 33.) At the time, when, having got the better of her fears, or, at least, suppressed them, she stood shamelessly in her splendid attire at the window, in the hope of strengthening herself by means of a new marriage in her unlawful possession of the throne. After the same manner we may run through the catalogue of those sinners, on whose heads the fulness of GOD'S wrath was poured out at one decisive blow. You will find this befell them just at the time, when they gave no heed whatever to it in their recklessness, or, when they were even turning it into ridicule in the height of their audacity. And, if we partake of the same sin, why should we not equally share in the same miserable end? Yes, yes; the Apostle resumes the subject. *When they shall say, peace and safety*—(*peace* now, *safety* hereafter)—*then sudden destruction cometh upon them . . and they shall not escape.* (1 Thess. v. 3.)

8. Let it then be a settled point, that our GOD is not a

brutish God, such as the heathens of old loved to have; and, seeing that with a small scourge of cords only, that is, with the most insignificant weapons, He is able to take such fearful vengeance on sinners, and in so many ways, let us learn hence to stand greatly in awe of His power. But, if He has hitherto abstained from punishing, this should not diminish our fear, but rather increase it: for either He has remitted the punishment; and then we know that after long forbearance His severity will become more inexorable: or, He has postponed it; and then it is clear that after long delay His vengeance will become more terrible. And surely, if ever we ought chiefly to fear Him, it is precisely at that time, when continued prosperity either causes us to forget, or inclines us to despise the Day of solemn account and reckoning.

SERMON VII.

THE UNDERVALUATION AND NEGLECT OF THE SOUL.

S. MATTH. XII. 43.

"WHEN THE UNCLEAN SPIRIT IS GONE OUT OF A MAN, HE WALKETH THROUGH DRY PLACES SEEKING REST AND FINDETH NONE."

1. THERE was once a time, when people thought they had performed a wondrous feat, if they could only secure themselves from the attacks of the numerous wild beasts inhabiting the gloomy forests or the verdant plains around them. Their care was simply confined to this; to avert all danger of being strangled by bears, torn by wild boars, bit by serpents, or stung by scorpions. We are disposed at the present day to smile at the very moderate degree of courage, possessed by our ancestors; so far have we outstripped them in our spirit of daring enterprize and bold adventure. We have not been content with getting rid of every possibility of danger from these animals; we have managed to enlist them in our service. We have nobly discovered the way of clothing ourselves with their skins, of nourishing ourselves with their flesh, of making their very bones useful, and of turning their poisonous venom itself into antidotes against disease: so that it will be found, on inquiry, that many more men's lives are now preserved, than used once to be destroyed, by means of these wild beasts. It is precisely in this way that we should treat the Devil, who is unquestionably the very worst beast

in the world, *an evil beast* (Gen. xxxvii. 33.) But what good, you will ask me, can be got out of him? The very greatest, be we only willing. It is simply this; from him we shall learn to value our souls. So jealous is he over our souls, that, according to the declaration of CHRIST, when he finds them snatched out of his hands, he allows himself no rest; he strives with the utmost toil and anxiety to recover them. *When the unclean spirit is gone out of a man, he walketh through dry places seeking rest and findeth none.* And what, if he should succeed and recover them? Does this not at all pain us? Only consider how studiously he labours to get the possession of our souls. He winds round about us with his devices, as he did round Eve; he assaults us with calamities, as he did Job; he bewitches us with his tricks, as he did Judas; he tempts us with his glozing caresses, as he did CHRIST; he pursues us, he adapts himself to us, he flatters us, he offers us the most munificent gifts. We, on the contrary, will be at no trouble whatever for our preservation. Ah, dearly beloved, and is it then possible we can so deceive ourselves? Not to value our souls! Not to value our souls! . . . .

2. If any worldly business weighs much on our minds, one very obvious sign of it will be our talking about it, our reasoning over it, our asking and inquiring how we may get guided and assisted in it. Jacob, setting out to seek Laban in a strange country, is really anxious to find him: he makes particular inquiries of those shepherds, who he thinks can inform him. (Gen. xxix. 5, 6.) Joseph, setting out to seek his brethren in a desert place, is really anxious to find them; he eagerly questions the wayfaring man, from whom he hopes to receive tidings. (Gen. xxxvii. 16.) And Saul, leaving his home on no higher errand than that of recovering a few stray asses, belonging to his father, simply because he was sincerely anxious about them,—what means does he not adopt, what hardships does he not encounter, what attempts does he not make, in order to find them! Would you believe it? He does not think it enough for this object to scale mountains, to cross plains, to pursue his unwearied course through various towns; he does not hesitate even to apply to an oracle for some favourable intelligence, to consult a prophet, a pro-

phet, too, of no ordinary rank, yea, one eminent, yea, the very chief, Samuel himself. *Come and let us go to the seer.* (1 Sam. ix. 9.) What say you, then, my hearers? Can you bring yourselves to believe that the business of your Salvation really weighs upon your minds, so long as you never take advice on this important matter, never hold any consultation about it with intelligent and learned men?

S. Luke relates that the hearers of the Baptist, being alarmed by his preaching, felt an anxiety for their salvation, unknown to them before, springing up in their minds; and hence they went in pursuit of him among the caverns and asked him, *What shall we do?* (S. Luke iii. 14.) The common people went to him and asked, *What shall we do?* The publicans went to him and asked, *What shall we do?* The men of war, even they in a like state of anxiety, went to him and all asked, *What shall we do?* Now speak the truth; Have you ever asked of any one in good earnest *What good thing shall I do that I may have Eternal Life?* (S. Matth. xix. 16.) Sometimes, it is true, and none will deny it, you make your appearance in a sacred secluded cloister; but then with what object? 'Tis to enjoy the pleasure of the garden, and to talk with one of the holy men about the triumph of the Tartars, the defeat of the Transylvanians, or any news, which may come from Ireland.[1] But, as to any serious inquiries about the best way to save your souls, I am not aware of any instance of your having ever compelled a single monk to turn out of his cell for such a purpose. Yet what wonder you should consider this matter so little and discuss it so seldom,

[1] It was somewhere about 1660—70, that the *Tartars*, led on by the daring Tekeli, invaded the neighbourhood of the Danube; and, not long before, *Transylvania* had been up in arms: in fact, the whole country between the Black Sea and Vienna was in a state of great disorder and agitation, prior to the memorable Turkish invasion and siege in 1682. These events were then occupying men's minds in Italy. (See Serm. XV. s. 3.) *Ireland*, moreover, about the middle of the 17th century, was in a very troubled political state, such as might well suggest matter for general conversation; unless the sister isle is here to be understood, as representing any distant outlandish part of the globe, a fit subject for curious inquiries.

"Questi da l' alte selve irsuti manda
La divisa dal mondo ultima Irlanda."
Tasso (Ger. Lib. canto i. 44.)

when even among yourselves you are not in the habit of fixing your thoughts upon it? He, who is harassed and anxious about any worldly business, cannot prevent his thoughts, however much he may wish it, from continually recurring to that subject. He seems like the stricken deer, that, wherever it goes, carries along with it the arrow, that gives it pain. The man thinks of it by day, and thinks of it again by night; he has it even present to his mind, when he lies buried in profound sleep. Accordingly, Cicero tells us of Themistocles, the great Captain of the Greeks, that even when asleep he bitterly envied his rival Miltiades the trophies he had won: and so, Plutarch relates of Marcellus, the great Captain of the Romans, that even when asleep he sternly defied his enemy Hannibal to single combat: and so others, actuated by some vehement emotion of the mind, were wont even in their sleep to give it some spontaneous expression; precisely as we read of Solomon in Sacred history, that, when demanded of GOD in a dream what gift he would choose, *Ask what I shall give thee?* (1 Kings iii. 5,) he made his petition exclusively for wisdom, because this was the constant and only subject of his waking thoughts. "Wherefore I prayed, and understanding was given me," (Wisd. vii. 7.) How then can you pretend to any earnest anxiety to secure your everlasting Salvation, while you suffer whole days, not to speak of nights, to pass over your heads without giving it the slightest consideration? And since, when you are asleep, your minds will revert to the various amusements and pleasures of the world and of its jovial society—(so Micah intimated, *They work evil in their beds*, ii. 1,)—how much less, when you are awake, can you ever once feel your thoughts powerfully drawn up to high and heavenly things?

3. But, although you conclude that the total absence of all thought about your souls clearly evinces your little anxiety for them, yet there is a sign even more evident than this. It is to think of them, and yet not to care for them. And do I not plainly see that the service of the soul is made subordinate to every other interest, and that, as if it were the less important or the less pleasing thing to be attended to, it is invariably thrown into the back-ground, and deferred to the

last? Yes, yes, too clearly do I perceive this; and Oh, that I had eyes to lament it, as I have eyes to see it! Such a person among you is deeply convinced that his soul is laden with sin; he knows it, he feels it, and, while he ponders the imminent danger, that surrounds him, he is forcibly smitten, as it were, in his conscience by a call from Heaven, seeming to say, "Go, wretched sinner, go and inquire for such a Minister of GOD and 'open your grief'[1] to him." *Go, show thyself to the Priest.* (S. Luke v. 14.) What reply does he make to this call? " Up, let me be doing : I decidedly resolve to go and unburden my soul to him. But when shall it be ? This very day ?—Why, to-day I am invited to that agreeable party. I'll go to-morrow."—" This morning it's right I should attend Church : I will attend; that is, if there's time to spare for Church, after I have conferred with my solicitor about the lawsuit."—" This morning I should get good to my soul by hearing the Lent sermon. I will go; that is, if there's leisure for it, after I have settled my accounts at that mercantile house."—And so you go on talking in like matters, always wishing to pay attention to the interests of the soul, if there be only spare time left for it—wise for to-morrow. And is this your notion of an anxious concern?

Eliezer, the renowned servant of Abraham, after a tedious journey reached Nahor, a city of Mesopotamia, from whence he had to bring back one of the family of Bethuel, as a fit spouse for the youthful Isaac. No sooner was he recognized and hospitably received, according to custom, than the people crowd about him, each anxious to show him some token of respect: one would help him to unload; another would conduct him to a room; another, seeing him faint from the fatigues of the journey, would run to bring him some immediate refreshment, before supper was ready : *And there was*

---

[1] By the expressions, "open your grief" and "unburden my soul," the translator has here taken leave to avoid the reference, made in the original text to the Romish practice of *auricular* confession. It would, however, be very far from him, in his wish not to give offence, to hide or keep in the back-ground the inestimable benefits of Pastoral aid, guidance, and prayer, when sought by the penitent or the sad in heart, according to GOD's Holy will and ordinance, as set forth in Scripture. The true doctrine of Confession and Absolution cannot be better learnt than from our Book of Common Prayer.

set meat before him. (Gen. xxiv. 33.) How, think you, did he treat their hospitable preparations? "Not so quick, not so quick, my friends; take no trouble I beg, on my account: for I solemnly assure you that I will not taste a single morsel, until I have first delivered my message. *I will not eat until I have told mine errand.*" Accordingly, not waiting even to lay aside his travelling dress, he gets up to make a long statement and detailed report of the circumstances, relating to his journey—the desire of Abraham, the good qualities of Sarah, the primogeniture of Isaac, the ample riches of the family, the conversation, which had recently taken place at the well between himself and the courteous damsel Rebekah, the water, which she had drawn for him, and the gifts, which he had presented to her. What more? He was determined at that first meeting to hasten on to a favourable conclusion the business, so prosperously begun; in a word, to settle the marriage: nor did he cease, till it was said to him, *Behold! Rebekah is before thee, take her and go, and let her be thy master's son's wife.* (Gen. xxiv. 51.) "But why all this apprehension, thou noble servant? Dost thou fear, lest time should fly, and the opportunity escape thee? or, lest there should be some negotiation already in hand to bestow Rebekah elsewhere? I am certain thou canst entertain no such apprehension. Wait a little then, take some slight refreshment, accept our civilities, and do justice to the hospitality we show thee: afterwards, when thou hast rested and recovered thy strength, attend, as thou wilt then be better able to do, to the matter, which so much presses thee." What is it, they ask? that he should wait? Ah! the anxiety he feels to execute his master's commission will never allow it. The thing most urgent must in the first place be attended to; and therefore it is quite impossible for him to rest or take food. *I will not eat, until I have told my errand.* In saying this he proves, as Liranus well observes, that he really has at heart the trust confided to him. If this be a true remark, judge for yourselves, whether the regard you bear to your souls can be called an anxiety on their account, while you not only make them give place to the necessary refreshment of your body, but to your idle pastime, your frivolous, your unprofitable amusements? Is there one among you, who ever says to himself, "This morning I have committed a sin : well then, until I have discharged my soul of its deadly infection by confession and prayer, *I will not eat.*"—" I have defrauded that poor man of his due: until I have first got him out of his difficulties by paying him, *I will not eat.*"—" I have defamed the character of that competitor of mine : until I have first repaired the injury by retracting my words, *I will not eat.*"—" I have violated the discipline of the Church and treated my spiritual Superior with pride, disrespect, and contumely : until I have first humbled myself before him, acknowledged my fault, and professed my purpose of amendment, *I will not eat.*" Oh, my brethren, where is the man among you, who conducts himself in this way, and who does not rather mind his worldly business and his carnal gratifications in the first place, before he ever once thinks of settling his conscience in matters of religious obligation?

4. But I forget myself. What am I saying? Is it not a fact that many defer all serious reflection to their old age, and postpone it to such time, as when languishing in death they can scarce retain their spirits within them, and are drawing nigh to their very last gasp? Can it be doubted but that this anxiety must amount to indifference? not to say, that it is their very least care, or no care at all? You do not act thus in your temporal concerns. Have you to bestow a daughter in honourable wedlock? you take the first opportunity. Have you to obtain some proud distinction for your family? you take the first opportunity. Have you to enlarge your estate? you take the first opportunity. Have you to bring some lawsuit to a close? you take the first opportunity. Have you to prove your title to a property? you take the first opportunity. And why all this hurry? Can you not defer the settlement of such matters to your deathbed? Unquestionably you can ; but you refuse to do this ; for, you say, matters like these require a clear head, leisure time, fixed attention, and prudent arrangement: whereas some have found a single moment quite enough time to save their souls in. Ah! Christians, how can you possibly utter such folly as this? Oh, what detestable words! what out-

rageous nonsense! what a reply for a Christian to make! But grant what you say: you cannot deny me this, that it is, at the least, extremely hazardous to defer the Salvation of the soul to the last moment, and that such a course is not alike successful in all cases: where it succeeds in one, it fails in a hundred. It is not impossible for a man in his last moments to repent. The truth of this proposition is allowed by that famous Doctor, Scotus: but he adds, "Yet this is extremely difficult on the part of man, and on the part of GOD. It is difficult on the part of man, because he is become more hardened in his sin: and it is also difficult on the part of GOD, because He is become more roused in His indignation." What token, in the meanwhile, of your anxiety is this, to prefer the risk of your Eternal Salvation to risking the marriage of your daughter, or the aggrandizement of your family, or of the interests of your farm, your lawsuit, or your property? This would be to set aside that most sure rule of Eucherius, "Salvation, as being our principal concern, ought to demand our principal care and attention."

Such was not the lesson taught us by the prudent Jacob. (Gen. xxxiii.) Listen to it; for it is most excellent. Jacob was in the act of returning with all his family to Canaan, there to settle down again after his long self-banishment twenty years ago, when he fled from the violent and implacable wrath of Esau, his eldest brother. When he was approaching his journey's end, behold this very brother advancing against him with a troop of four hundred brave men in his rear. Poor Jacob at once surmised that Esau, still harbouring in his mind the ancient grievance, was now coming to take vengeance on him; a vengeance tardy indeed, but so much the more grievous and severe, as it would now no longer fall on himself alone, who was the offender, but on his beloved wives and his dear innocent children. At such a crisis, what did he do? He immediately distributed his family into separate bands, after the fashion of a little regiment of soldiers. In front he placed the two handmaids, Billah, and Zilpah, with the four children he had by them: Leah with her seven children he placed next: and hindermost he placed his beautiful Rachel with the lovely child

Joseph, her single blooming offspring. Now, I ask, what did he intend by this particular arrangement? Did he mean to meet the attack? to close in the battle? Or rather to sustain the shock of Esau by virtue of some more gentle and constraining power? For what could a helpless band of women and children avail against a set of ruffians, the very sight of whom was enough to frighten them to death? Well did Jacob know that all resistance on his part was utterly hopeless. Therefore, if he must die, he will, at least, take thought for the best, and by no means expose to an equal danger persons not equally dear to him. His handmaids he esteemed the least; accordingly he put them in front, to stand the first shock. Leah he esteemed more than his handmaids; accordingly, he took more pains for her safety. Rachel he loved still more than Leah; accordingly, he laboured still more for her preservation. "He put the handmaids foremost," writes Oleaster, a famous commentator; "so that the less objects of his love might have to endure first his brother's anger; hereby teaching us that we ought to adventure what we love least, in order to preserve by such means what we love most."

Strengthened by such authority, how shall I speak of you, my brethren, when I observe that, whatsoever the risk be, your soul is the very thing, you first expose to danger: just as if to stand in front, to be on the extreme edge of the battle, was its proper place? It is the soul, that in your estimation occupies the position of the handmaid; it is the soul, that must venture on the forlorn hope, in order that you may preserve your credit, may preserve your property, may preserve your profane amusements; in order that your children, in order that your parents, in order that your friends, in order that your impure female connections, in order that the very horses in your stable and dogs in your kennel may not suffer any damage. Oh, what folly! Oh, what madness! Oh, what brutish stupidity! *I am full of the fury of the Lord.* Let me find some outlet to my feelings. *I am full of the fury of the Lord; I am weary with holding in.* (Jer. vi. 11.) . . .

5. Nevertheless, there is more still to be said. Jacob, it is true, placed his handmaids the first in danger; yet it does

not follow from this that he cared so little for them, as to do this willingly: he only did it, when the danger was unlooked for and quite inevitable: for it was not Jacob, who advanced against Esau, but Esau, who advanced against Jacob; and hence all escape was out of the question. But you treat your souls far worse than the Patriarch did his handmaids, while you not only put them foremost against such perils, as you meet contrary to your will, but actually yourselves thrust them into the very teeth of danger. Just as if you had a liking for what does them an injury, you expose them in societies, where the greatest temptations to sin abound, where evil spirits are, so to speak, not lying in ambush, but with bare arms and in open fight warring against souls to drag them captives into perdition. I say no more about anxious concern for your souls: is this, I ask, paying them even common attention?

6. Forlorn mother of the young pilgrim Tobias! She had intrusted him to the care of an Angel, whom she fully believed to be none other, than some man of distinguished benevolence and extraordinary wisdom. Notwithstanding, in her passionate fondness for her son, she soon repented of this step; and, deeming him to be anything but safe from some terrible disaster on his journey, she was "very sorry," she sighed, she wept, she groaned; "Woe, woe is me, my son, why did we send thee to go to a strange country, the light of our eyes, the staff of our old age, the comfort of our life, the hope of our posterity? We, having all things together in thee, ought not to have let thee go from us." (Tobit x. 4, 5, Vulg.) Such were the constant lamentations of this wretched creature: nor was it of the least use that her aged husband tried to raise her spirits by assuring her that the man, who was the guide of her beloved son in his journey, was most trustworthy: that she might therefore fully rely and rest upon him. "Hold thy peace and be not troubled about it: our son is safe: that man, with whom we sent him, is very trusty." All this was utterly unavailing: it yielded her no comfort whatever. Every day, like one almost frantic, she left her house, traversed the different quarters of the city, visited all the gates, if by chance they would bring back her

son. Sometimes she took her station on an elevated piece of ground in the suburbs, and thence looked all round in the fond hope of being able to recognise him and to welcome him home. But, when this failed, she renewed her complaints, redoubled her expressions of sorrow, and in the evening returned home completely disconsolate. "Ah! most certainly," she would exclaim, "my son is in some great danger. It may be that at this very moment he is dashed over some precipice, and even now is lying at the bottom of it crying aloud to his mother to come and help him. Peradventure he is mangled by some ferocious beast, and is now upbraiding his mother, as the cause of his death."

My dearest Sirs, every one of us ought to guard his soul with such an intense feeling of jealousy, as not even to venture to intrust it to an Angel, unless quite convinced of his being an Angel, having well examined his outward gorgeous apparel, lest some fraud should lurk within. *Believe not every spirit*, was the advice of S. John, in an affair of so much consequence, but *prove the spirits whether they be of God*. (1 S. John iv. 1.) What then shall I say, when I observe how many there are, who intrust their souls to the very Devil himself who hand them over to him, as their guide, who suffer them to be led blindfolded over terrible rocks and precipices, to be conveyed to those lewd resorts of impurity and licentiousness, which, if I may so speak, border upon Hell? Must I say that these persons have any love for their souls? that they care for them? that they value them? that they treasure up all their happiness in them? Ah! were it so, never would they so desperately consign them into the hands of the devil: no, not even to any man would they commit them in this reckless manner; they would not *believe every spirit*. How then? Had they to procure a companion, their first concern would be that he should be a decided enemy to vice. Had they to attach themselves to a master, their first care would be that he should be a firm friend to virtue. For a spiritual guide, they would prefer the man of deepest learning; for a theological teacher, the man of deepest piety; for an adviser in general, they would cling to the man, who was most thoroughly honest: and by such methods they would always seek to ensure, as far as they possibly could, the safety of the soul. But Alas! how many do the direct contrary to all this, and, if I may apply to them the words of Jeremiah, *give the dearly beloved of their soul into the hand of her enemies* (xii. 7.) For not only have they the greatest liking for those companions, who are most dissolute, and those masters, who are most licentious; but even in matters of conscience, when they have to consult a spiritual guide, they look out for one, who is most likely to speak peace to them in their sins. Do they require a theologian? they choose the least orthodox, that he may favour their view: or a counsellor? they prefer one personally interested, that he may flatter them. Oh, what an awful thing! *They give the dearly beloved of their soul into the hand of her enemies.* And call you this an anxiety to be saved? Alas! it seems rather to be a desperate anxiety to perish, in spite of the assistance, which is offered you; a perverting your helps into hindrances, your supports into stumbling-blocks, and your very antidotes into deadly poison.

Solomon in his Proverbs lamented to find some persons so grossly infatuated, that they could *lay wait for their own blood, and lurk privily for their own lives.* (Prov. i. 18.) Who are these persons? Who are they, but the very miserable men, whom I am now describing—the men, who take pains to ensnare themselves by the delusive hope of being able to quiet their conscience on the warrant of certain persons having no conscience at all. How blinded ye are! If they value so little their own souls, how can you think they will worthily esteem yours? But this, as I said before, is the very thing you are aiming at; to hand over your soul to one, who cares nothing about it, to let it out on a venture, to let it perish, to let it go to utter perdition. By such conduct you confirm anew what is asserted in the Book of Wisdom; you prove man to be no other, than a heartless self-destroyer: "A man killeth through his malice his own soul." (Wisd. xvi. 14, Vulg.) Oh, woe, woe is me! Who will give me eyes to pour forth an impetuous flood of tears, the fit expression of my sorrow, my sorrow at such madness! Now, now it is that *my face should be foul with weeping* (Job xvi. 16;) and that with Jeremiah, *my eyes should run down with tears, and my eyelids gush out with waters* (ix. 18.) What impression does this convey to your minds, my hearers? Have you ever seriously paused to consider what is the tremendous import of those words—for ever Blessed, or for ever tormented? What is meant by an Eternity of peace, or an Eternity of pain? What is meant by a Paradise, where one rejoices everlastingly, or a Hell, where one groans everlastingly? Speak, speak, my brethren; have you ever in good earnest applied your minds to this inquiry? If you have not, go, I say with Isaiah; go quickly, and close fast your chamber door: *Come, my people, enter thou into thy chambers, and shut thy doors about thee* (xxvi. 20,) no longer talk of other men's doings, but *about thee;* shut out the distracting objects of time and sense, and submit yourselves to some severe self-scrutiny . . . It is your own exclusive personal weal or woe, that here lies at stake. And if, which GOD forbid, any of you should sink into the depths of Hell, who will be pitiful enough, or who will be strong enough, to raise you out of it? Absalom, when unhappily banished from his country, had one in favour with David to intercede, though it was done with some sinister motive, for his return home. (2 Sam. xiv.) Joseph, when confined in his gloomy prison, had Pharaoh's butler, who had indeed for a season forgotten him, to recover his liberty for him. Jeremiah, cast by wicked men into the muddy bottom of a dungeon, and there left to die of cold, hunger, stench, and filth, had an Ebedmelech who in kind pity let him down a cord, by clinging to which he raised himself up. But whom have you got to help you out of "the depth of the belly of Hell?" (Ecclus. li. 5.) Where is the extended cord, which shall reach from Heaven to the vast profundity below? Where is the strong arm, mighty to raise you up? Hear attentively what Job declares, *He that goeth down to the grave shall come up no more, he shall return no more to his house* (vii. 9, 10.) Think of this. There is no possibility of your return. Have you well considered it? I would say to you then in much sadness with Ecclesiasticus, "My son, glorify thy soul, and give it honour, according to the dignity thereof" (x. 28.) . . . . For to apply to you the reproof of Salvian; "Nothing so bad, nothing so inhuman, nothing so impious can be said of you, as this—It is impossible by any means to make you love your own selves." That you do not love your opponents, I can understand you; that you do not love your enemies, I can make some allowance for you; but that you have no love for your own selves, this I cannot tolerate. "Who will justify him" (I speak with the wise man) "that sinneth against his own soul?" (Ecclus. x. 29.) Oh, if you are so backward to learn from other sources its paramount value, at least consider how the devil carefully watches for every favourable opportunity of stealing it from you, as I told you at first; how artfully in various ways he attempts to deceive you, to coax you, to seduce you, and to obtain the entire dominion over you. He it is, who leads you to prefer every other consideration to this one, which you ought in reason to prefer to every other. Wherefore only tell me (I speak again in the words of the same great Prelate) "What madness is it for you to despise these souls, which the devil values so highly?" Were he Lord of the Universe, be assured, he would be most glad to give you all he has, in exchange for your soul. *All these things will I give thee, if thou wilt fall down and worship me.* (S. Matth. iv. 9.) And will you gladly let him have your souls for a price so contemptible? Will you barter them for a fleeting pleasure? for a fading beauty? for some paltry advantage of this world? For the sake of a mere nothing will you basely cast yourselves into the jaws of this devouring monster? Never let it be said of you, my hearers, that you ever so fatally wronged your soul: never put it to shame and disgrace by such conduct; but begin this very day to commune with your own hearts, to form a proper estimate of your own real worth, and, as Moses said in Deuteronomy, to *take good heed unto your souls.* (Deut. iv. 15, Vulg.)

THE SECOND PART.

7. I have no wish to deny that men's grievous neglect of their Salvation might admit of some excuse, were Salvation, after all, an easy matter. But is it so, my hearers? Is it so, I ask? Sad for you, should you think this: rather, woe unto you, if in a business of such importance you embrace so grave an error! Very far from its being, as you suppose, an

easy matter, it is one, attended with so great risk and uncertainty, that the most eminent Saints with all the pains they have bestowed upon it have lived in fear because of it; they have been horror-struck at the prospect of the appalling judgment of that LORD, who, somehow or other, is formidable even to those, who always compass Him about in the form of an encircling crown : *God is very greatly to be feared . . . . of all them that are round about Him.* (Ps. lxxxix. 8.)

Poor disconsolate Jerome! What did he leave undone, if by any means he might procure some faint assurance to his soul in this great business? In what tangled forests, in what gloomy caves, did he go and bury himself! What a sharp conflict he maintained, even to his old age, against the lusts of his flesh! And yet, in what terms did he describe his state? " Defiled with the pollutions of sin, I toil night and day in fear of having to pay the uttermost farthing." A holy Gregory, a holy Bernard—in what groans and bitter sighs did they not give vent to their feelings! And a holy Augustine —how he shook within him, when he said, " I dread the everlasting fire! I dread the everlasting fire!" All the love, which glowed so warmly in his heart towards GOD, was still unable to deliver him from this fear. But come, come with me, to that frightful grotto of hermits, which, on account of the bitter pains, endured by all its inmates, obtained the name of " the penitent's prison," when it might have been more truly entitled "the convert's Hell." Oh, what severe austerities, what dreadful self-inflicted torments of soul and body were practised among them! what absence of all peace and comfort, what a variety of sufferings was there! . . . .

8. Now considering the great holiness, in which these people passed their days, who would not suppose that they were assured of their Salvation? or, at least, that they came in course of time to regard it, as more probable than otherwise; so that their hope would exceed their apprehensions? And yet, listen to an account of them, which, whenever it recurs to my thoughts, fills me with the deepest horror. So far were these wretched beings from obtaining anything, like assurance, that, on the contrary, when any of their number lay dying on his bed of ashes, his beloved place of repose, the

brethren all vied with each other in crowding around him in the saddest mood; and then with a trembling voice they asked him; "How is it with you, dear brother? how do you feel? what have you to tell us? what is now your hope? or what do you expect? Have you at last obtained what you sought for with so many tears? Or, are you still kept in a state of fear? What is now before you? a kingdom, or slavery? a sceptre, or a chain? Do you seem to hear a sweet sound whispering within you, *Thy sins are forgiven thee?* (S. Luke v. 20.) Or, on the other hand, is it a terrific voice, that you hear, crying aloud, *Bind him hand and foot, and cast him into outer darkness?* (S. Matth. xxii. 13.) What! Oh, what, dear brother, can you say? Oh! we intreat thee, tell us the true state of your soul; so that by knowing your condition we may be enabled to form some conjecture what will be our own!" What answer, suppose ye, did the dying men give to such most doleful inquiries? It is true, that some of them, calmly raising their eyes to heaven, blessed GOD and said; *Praised be the Lord, who hath not given us over for a prey unto their teeth!* (Ps. cxxiv. 6.) But alas! how many of them answered differently—that they were still in suspense. *Perhaps my soul will have to pass through a stream insupportable* (Ps. cxxiii. 5, Vulg.); as if they should say, "We hope, we hope to pass it; but the torrent is swollen; but the water is troubled, and all the way over, even to the opposite side, there is imminent risk of being drowned." There were, moreover, which is more remarkable, there were many of their number, who, heaving a deep groan of anguish, uttered "Alas! alas!"— and said no more. These, when urged to express themselves more clearly, subjoined, "Woe to the soul, that has not perfectly and inviolably kept all the laws of its profession! Woe, woe to that miserable soul; because the time is now come for it to know what its portion must be in another world." I am well aware, my dear Sirs, that a narrative, such as this, must to many persons savour of the fabulous; and we may well ascribe it to the wish of men that it were so: but there is no need of our flattering ourselves. The narrative is all too true. The facts are related to us by John Climacus, that most renowned Abbot of the monastery of Mount Sinai,[1] who was present on the spot, who heard and saw what happened with his own ears and with his own eyes.

9. But, if this be true, from whence comes it, that *we* should be the only people to regard Salvation as something so easy and so certain, demanding of us no sort of anxiety, even as if we had it already in our hands? "From whom," I will sorrowfully ask with S. Bernard, "from whom have we learnt thus to disguise the truth from ourselves? Whence this so fatal lukewarmness? Whence this so accursed self-security?" I can assign it to no other cause than an utter want of all reflection, such as blinds our eyes, and does not allow us, as the wise man says, to observe the precipices before our feet. *The way of the wicked is as darkness; they know not at what they stumble.* (Prov. iv. 19.) . . . Thou knowest, my GOD, how ardently I desire the welfare of this people, this illustrious people, called by Thy Name. How happy should I be, could I give my very life and blood for their sakes, as Thou hast given Thine for me! But, since this cannot be, I promise Thee that I will at least not fail to tell them the Truth. Only do Thou grant, that they may receive it with the same ready good will, as that, with which it is now spoken. I will preach to their ears: do Thou in the mean time speak to the heart. I will inform their understandings: do Thou in the mean time inflame their wills. It is Thine with the gentle force of Thy love to draw unto Thyself the wandering sinner. What more can I do, than hold forth the light, the beacon to the benighted mariner? It remains with Thee to breathe forth that holy propitious gale, which shall waft him to the desired haven safe and sound.

[1] Well may the scene of that system of self-imposed bodily austerities, which here so generally failed to "give a man peace at the last," be placed at *Mount Sinai*, "which is in bondage with her children," (Gal. iv. 24, 25.) For what else virtually was it than a return to the Law, in the vain attempt to work out one's own salvation on the ground of personal merit? We have "not so learned CHRIST;" though we quite admit the necessity in every Christian of a holy filial fear, and cannot but see the danger, among Protestants, in the opposite extreme, of a false unhallowed assurance, a carnal neglect of all mortification and strictness of living. As a caution, then, the passage before us has, after much consideration, been retained. *My flesh trembleth for fear of Thee; and I am afraid of Thy judgments.* (Ps. cxix. 120.)

SERMON VIII.

A DISSUASIVE FROM THE FEAR OF MAN.

S. MATTH. XV. 22.

"AND BEHOLD, A WOMAN OF CANAAN CAME OUT OF THE SAME COASTS AND CRIED UNTO HIM, SAYING, HAVE MERCY ON ME, O LORD, THOU SON OF DAVID."

1. MILON of Crotona, one of the most athletic men ancient times can boast of, was accustomed to exhibit his strength in many wonderful ways, and, among others, in the following. He took an apple, and clenching it in his fist defied any one, who could, to snatch it from him. But who could? None ever succeeded, excepting a weak simple damsel, to whom he was attached. For, while he exerted his strength against all others, to her alone he surrendered, and yielded the prize. I am aware that there are very few incidents of this kind, which can be made available in the pulpit to the edification of the hearers: yet tell me; does it not appear to you something very remarkable that a particular favour, such as the united entreaties of the twelve Apostles could not extort from CHRIST, vehemently as they persevered in saying to Him, *Send her away, for she crieth after us,* should at last have been obtained by this woman of Canaan? Nor did she simply obtain it; she wrested it from Him by violence. *O woman, great is thy faith: be it unto thee even as thou*

wilt! We must surely allow some rare merit to a woman, who was able to do such great things.

But in what did this merit consist? Was it in her faith? No doubt, it was. It is, however, barely probable that her faith should have exceeded that of the Apostles, whose petitions, we know, were generally granted. My belief then is, that what imparted a peculiar power to this woman's intercession was a certain holy effrontery in her, which indeed sprang from her faith. Only observe, how she behaved on this occasion. As she was a heathen, it required a singular fortitude to rise superior to the opinions of the world, when she went to CHRIST. Hence she did not seek any secluded spot for an interview with Him; but she applied to Him in public: nor did her exalted rank prevent her, in the true grandeur of her soul, from falling at His feet and worshipping Him at broad day-light in a crowded thoroughfare; nor did she pay the least regard to what people might say. When rejected by Him with disdain, she perseveres; when dismissed from His presence, she presses on; nor is she discouraged by those cutting expressions, with which CHRIST thought fit to test her humility; when He flouted her by His comparison of a dog; *It is not meet to take the children's bread and to cast it to dogs.* Was it not then right that the utmost favour should be extended to such an excellent person? But I am anxious that you should all learn from her noble example to get the better of that silly fear, which sometimes deters you from following CHRIST. Why think so much, what will people say of me? Why forfeit so much, on account of a little ridicule and ill-treatment? Let them say just what they like; it is no reason whatever for our bating one jot of our good resolutions. Happy will it be for you, should I succeed this morning in impressing this useful lesson on your minds: for, in that case, I am sure, many among you, who are now almost, would become altogether good, and many, who are already good, would become Saints. Let us then, without further preface, come close to the matter and make a beginning.

2. Think not, however, my hearers, that I am such a stranger to the feelings of our common nature, as not to sympathise

with you in your keen sense of all such censures upon your conduct. It raises one's indignation to observe, that, no sooner do any persons of whatsoever station in life resolve for the first time to appear in a more simple dress, or to be more guarded in their conversation, or to retire more from worldly society, than a thousand evil tongues are immediately let loose in raillery against them . . . . *He, that is upright in the way, is an abomination unto the wicked.* (Prov. xxix. 27.) This is certain; it was never questioned. Salvian goes further, when he gives us the reason. For, where men's objects of pursuit are so widely different, an alienation must necessarily follow in their mutual feeling towards each other. How indeed can you expect anything but hatred from the wicked, while your whole life is nothing but a continued reflection upon theirs? With your devotion you put to shame their irreverence: and so your charity reproves their harshness; your modesty, their wantonness; your temperance, their sensuality : hence it arises that, just as they love themselves, they are bound to hate you. "A difference in men's likes and dislikes is the chief cause of discord," writes the holy Bishop: "for it is hardly, if at all possible, that a person can love in another what he is disinclined to himself; therefore they have a strong ground to hate you, when they see how everything about you opposes and thwarts themselves." The poor creatures trace in you, as in a mirror, all their own deformity. What wonder then, if they take offence at you, if they hold you in contempt, and lash out against you? They behave, like camels, who cannot bear to see themselves reflected in the clear stream, and accordingly trample the water with their feet, so as to trouble and make it turbid; so great a hardship does it seem to them to be thus compelled to gaze on their own ugliness. In spite of all this, don't be alarmed at your state, my hearers: for the very knowledge you have of its being irremediable will very materially help you to the cure of it.

3. It being quite impossible then that any of the righteous should ever please the wicked, you at once perceive that your position is not singular: you are not the first to suffer in this noble cause; nor will you be the last. And the reflection

that you have so many glorious companions to cheer you on should afford you no small comfort. Look towards Egypt; there you will see a Joseph, cast into prison through the enmity of the ungodly. Turn your eyes to Jerusalem; there you will see a Jeremiah, buried alive in a deep dungeon. Direct them to Susa; there you will gaze upon a Mordecai, at the foot of a scaffold. Look around in Babylon; there you will find a Daniel, cast to the lions. Fix your attention on Bethulia; there you will contemplate an Achior, bound to a stake. Once more turn your eyes to Babylon; there you will fall in with a Susannah, condemned to be stoned to death. And now, with all their malignant obloquy, when did the wicked ever harm you to any such extent? If, however, you lay so much stress on those censorious speeches, which, I allow, smite you sore, but do not fetch blood, will not the single case of the Magdalene,[1] not to mention other devoted women, give you special comfort? I am aware that you have often listened to her story; but I don't know whether you have duly considered it. This fervent devotee had heard that JESUS was in the house of Simon; thither she immediately hastened with a fragrant box of ointment, which, in token of her dutiful attachment, she poured out on His head. And, behold, just as if at the same time she had poured an equal quantity of poison on the tongues of the guests, seated at Simon's table, many began to whisper, to cry aloud, to rage in their fury against her; *To what purpose is this waste?* (S. Matth. xxvi. 7, 8.) See what a loss! What a lavish waste is here! Such an expensive ointment! How many poor families might have been supported by the money, which the alabaster box alone, if sold, would have raised! *And they murmured against her* (S. Mark xiv. 5,) almost, as if they would have torn her to pieces with their teeth. Here was,

---

[1] It has not been thought fit to correct here the common erroneous notion, grounded chiefly on a mere legend, that this woman (S. Matth. xxvi. 7; S. Mark xiv. 3; S. John xii. 3,) was Mary Magdalene. This is nowhere asserted in Scripture; and, though there was a difference of opinion among the Fathers, touching the identity of the female, whose praise is in the Gospel, yet none of them considered her to have been the Magdalene. The error in question is ably combated and exposed by Bishop Heber. See his *Life*, by his widow, ch. xiv.

forsooth, a mighty matter! In times past she had been at a vast expense in the purchase of ointments and perfumes for the gratification of her personal vanity. Full well more than *three hundred pence* had she spent in articles of dress and finery, on her jewels, on her braided hair, on her rich presents, on her costly banquets, on her profane worldly amusements! But, think you, that any person whatever had ever murmured at *this* expenditure? or ever on *this* account branded her to her face with the character of a spendthrift? Or rather, what multitudes were led to court and to flatter her, and to applaud her conduct, being ready almost, as she passed in the streets, to fall down and worship her. Well, from one of these same vanities she makes a trifling offering to CHRIST; and instantly a general attack is raised against her in all manner of injurious and vilifying observations. She is accused of squandering away the property of her family, of throwing about money in every direction, like a person imbecile, incapable of managing her own affairs. *To what purpose is this waste? to what purpose is this waste?*

You may infer from her history that a similar opposition has been the usual portion of those, who, like yourselves, have openly renounced the world, in their wish to follow CHRIST. *All, who will live godly in Christ Jesus, shall suffer persecution* (2 Tim. iii. 12) says the Apostle: *all, all*. It is worthy of remark, however, that he does not say who *live*, but who *will live:* for it sometimes happens that, in progress of time good Christians enjoy a state of tranquillity; they outgrow opposition and silence the spiteful tongue; but, at the commencement of their career, on their first decision to yield themselves to GOD's service, when they *will*, or *wish*, to *live godly in Christ Jesus*, then nothing can save them from ill usage of this description. *All, all*, says the Apostle; yea, some among them will have still to endure prolonged suffering, resembling in this respect the children of Israel, who not only at their first departure from Egypt had the many people of the land to contend against, but afterwards suffered from the Amorites, the Amalekites, and many others, and finally saw settled in their vicinity, within the walls of Jerusalem itself, as Origen supposes, the Jebusites, whose very name indicated their office; for in our language it means the oppressors. . . . . Let this then be your consolation, that you have many to share with you in your sufferings for righteousness' sake: hence you may regard those evil speeches, which are so apt to disturb you in your duty, as falling upon you not so much in your mere personal capacity, but because you are spiritual; but because you are enlightened; but because you are a follower of Christ: they fall upon Him, rather than upon yourselves.

4. But I am disposed to go a step further and to tell you, that, even if you could command the approbation and esteem of the world for your piety, you ought nevertheless to prefer having its dislike and opposition. Does this seem a strange paradox? Attend, as you have done hitherto; for I feel confident that I can demonstrate its truth. Suppose then that, instead of hating and speaking evil of you, the wicked were to love and commend you: suppose that not one of them should ever open his mouth against you; but that one and all should caress and applaud you. Who in this case would be the obliged person? Would you be obliged to God; or, would God be obliged to you? Surely it appears that you would be obliged to God, when you derive so much advantage from serving Him, when, because of Him, every one sings your praise. But if on His account you are called upon to bear unnumbered calumnies and vexatious outrages, God, if I may so speak, is placed under an obligation to you. An obligation! Yes, I repeat it, an obligation. Nor take this on my credit; for the expression is not mine, but borrowed from S. Chrysostom. "If we are loved for the sake of God, we are indebted to Him for the honour conferred upon us; but if in His cause we are hated, He is become our debtor." And what can a man ever more desire or more hope for, than to have God indebted to him? Holy Doctor, if you give me a promise to this effect, then, as Ignatius dared the fury of the wild beasts against him, so I, for my part also, am prepared to instigate the tongues of men to do their worst against me! Henceforth let the evil-minded indulge their utmost spite; let them bark; let them mangle; let them rend me in pieces; what else can they do, than make God

my debtor? I shall now by their means be enabled to pray to GOD with increasing confidence; I shall now be enabled to dismiss from my mind every fear of being repelled from His Presence; and all, because He is in my debt. *I am, as one mocked of his neighbour,* Job observed, in confirmation of what I am now saying: and what reward shall the man have, who is derided or ridiculed, as I am? See his reward; *He calleth upon God and He answereth him* (Job xii. 4, Vulg.) And seemeth this in your eyes a trifling reward? So far from it, it is one so immensely great, that we should do wisely to procure it at the cost of the whole universe, not to say, at the cost of such a poor, hollow, worldly prosperity, as that, which we renounce in exchange for GOD's service. Nor is it surprising, that GOD should regard Himself thus indebted to the man, who endures so much hardship out of love to Him: for He sees in this an authentic proof, that the man does not serve Him from a fluctuating motive of self-interest, but from a rooted principle of true affection. This demonstrates to Him the reality of our religion, the sincerity of our conscience, the soundness of our faith, when He sees us incurring bitter reproach for those very things, which ought to have gained for us the highest commendation. It was for this reason, that S. Cyprian so often addressed his persecuted brethren to this effect. "The full power of faith is then put forth, when we come in contact with the reproach and evil talk of the world; and when we fortify ourselves with the strength of our religious principles against the mad clamours of the populace; exposing and rebutting all the profane insults they heap upon us, in their wish to damage the cause of CHRIST."

Do you know, my brethren, what constituted the peculiar merit of the Patriarch Abraham in his most famous sacrifice? Some say, that it was the obedience, with which he bowed to a most severe commandment, without once remonstrating: others say, that it was the readiness, with which he discharged a most painful duty, without once delaying: others say, that it was his faith, with which he steadfastly believed the conflicting promises, without once wavering. In this they have all given a sound opinion. But, if you will trust the solution of the question to that most learned Prelate Zeno, he will astonish you with his reply. He will tell you that the merit of Abraham arose from the intrepidity, with which he dared the expression of public opinion. And who among you does not at once see that after this heroic act, instead of his former high character as a righteous man, he was likely to be accounted a barbarian? At the news of his most impious deed every tongue would rise up against him. They would call him a tiger in the shape of a human being, an executioner under the title of a parent. And that very constancy, that earned him so much praise, would tend to his deeper infamy and disgrace. "Mark," they would exclaim, "with what a steady grasp he seizes the knife! Wretch! Did he even shed a single tear? Did he even heave a sigh? Did he even turn away his face, when he gave the fatal stroke? Not at all: on the contrary, he himself with his own hands bound his sweet innocent child: he himself fastened him on the altar; he himself bandaged his eyes; he himself bared his neck to the blow; he himself, unfeeling wretch that he was, severed his head from the body. Here was a father, able, of himself alone, to do the work of many executioners!" And, observe, it would have been no use to Abraham to plead before men, in his defence, the Command of GOD. No, brethren, no: for how could he have convinced any, especially those heathen, who were utter strangers to the principle of faith, that his resolute act was the appointment of GOD, and not rather the frantic offspring of his own brain? They would all have met this plea by saying, that GOD has no appetite for human victims, and that, when Abraham dreamed of a voice from Heaven, he was in fact only listening to the suggestions of Hell. Now, that, in spite of all these malicious cavils, he should so readily have set about this heart-rending sacrifice, and have so faithfully gone through it, *this*, says Zeno, constituted his incomparable merit. He had no fear of the distorted opinion of the world; he had no fear of being condemned for an infamous act of parricide; but he rather rejoiced that GOD had, by means of this command, allowed him such a method to approve his devotedness to Him.

And this is the distinguished merit you should aspire to,

my beloved brethren; that in those very things, for which men ought most warmly to commend you, you should incur their most bitter censure. Do you attend the Sacrament from religious principle? You must bear its being said that you attend it from hypocrisy. Do you stay quietly at home from a feeling of self-diffidence? You must bear its being reported that it is from dissatisfaction with the world. Do you avoid convivial meetings from the love of temperance? You must bear its being believed that you do it to save your money. Do you forgive your enemy for conscience' sake? You must bear its being believed that you act from cowardice. Do you decline worldly honours from humility? You must bear its being thought that this arises from feebleness of character. I seem to be making very high demands: but no other way is left me. *For gold is tried in the fire, and acceptable men in the furnace of adversity* (Ecclus. ii. 5.)

Poor Job! What, think you, gave him the most acute and cruel pain in all his afflictions? Perhaps you have never yet considered this point. It arose from his observing that the spectacle of his body, covered with the foul uncleanness of leprosy, led some to imagine that he had brought this disease upon himself by his indulgence in those early vicious habits, from which he had always kept aloof. This was Satan's enmity against him, as the most learned commentators, with the approval of Pineda, have explained it; to infect his whole body with a kind of disorder, resembling that, which commonly falls to the lot of the sensualist—with *sore boils.* (Job ii. 7.) Accordingly, the poor sufferer was compelled to listen to such invectives, as these, "Ah! lewd, wanton, abandoned profligate! *His bones are full of the sin of his youth!* (xx. 11.) Richly does he deserve it!" Meanwhile Job, leaving them to believe all this of him, had still to persevere in praising GOD with those lips, which alone, of all his members, Satan had left untouched, in the hope that thereby he might be led to employ them in *cursing God:* so Job tells us. *I am escaped with the skin of my teeth* (xix. 20.) Oh, how painful must calumnies, involving so great injustice, have been to the soul of this holy man! Nor was he the only person, who suffered from a like cause. Moses submitted to indescribable toil and fatigue in the government of six hundred thousand persons, who quite bowed down his shoulders with their weight. He had to listen to their complaints; he had to settle their quarrels; and yet, when he hoped to hear himself most highly commended, he had to submit to the observation of a rustic, that he was a fool for his pains; *Thou wilt surely wear thyself away with thy foolish toil.* (Exod. xviii. 18, Vulg.) What shall I say of Hannah, the renowned wife of Elkanah? Instead of being admired for her devotion, when with so much fervour she continued in prayer at the gate of the Temple, she was openly reproached, as drunken. (1 Sam. i. 13.) What shall I say of Vashti, the renowned wife of Ahasuerus? Instead of being commended, as chaste, when with so great modesty she refused to display her personal charms before the assembled guests, she was openly branded, as refractory. (Esther i.) And old Tobias—was he not frequently compelled to hear it remarked by his dearest friends that he deserved his affliction of loss of sight, because of his mighty fondness for going about the streets at night in search of dead bodies to bury? (Tobit ii.) Behold then the distinguished merit, to which you also, in your several stations of life, should aspire. Oh, what a privilege! Oh, what honour is this! To suffer shame, as these persons did, because of your love to that, which is beyond everything else the most commendable, because of your love to virtue. And, know you not well, that *if ye are reproached for the Name of Christ, happy are ye.* (1 S. Pet. iv. 14.) This, this is real happiness, unless CHRIST Himself with His own mouth has deceived us; for He said in S. Matthew, *Blessed are ye, when men shall revile you!* and He said in S. Luke, *Blessed are ye, when men shall hate you!* If there is no truth in this particular promise of Blessedness, then there is none in any other Article whatsoever of our faith; since they all proceed from the same JESUS CHRIST, who is the Infallible Truth.

5. Not to dwell upon this, tell me now, my hearers, for what length of time will you have to persevere in suffering these things? Understand you not, that the Day will come, which will transform all these defamers of your Christian uprightness into so many admirers of your consistency? And in

that Day what will be your raptures of joy, when in the sight of the whole universe, assembled for the last Judgment "you shall stand in great boldness before the face of such as have afflicted you" (Wisd. v. 1); and without fear shall reproach those, who once, to their own sorrow, reproached you! When I wish to represent to my mind, what your triumph will then be, do you know how I set about it? I represent to myself Noah shut up in the Ark. You will understand my reason. If ever a man was despised upon the earth for his goodness, it was Noah. He dwelt in the midst of a set of unbelievers, of impure, profligate, self-willed men: and, since his universal goodness contrasted with their vicious lives, you may conceive how grossly they must have ill-treated him: so S. Chrysostom observes, "As, in opposition to their ways, he cultivated every virtue, it seems likely that he must have drawn upon himself every kind of ridicule and scorn." But the fine time for them was, when God, tired out with the wickedness of mankind, resolved on their destruction, and accordingly commanded Noah to build a sort of moveable house to be his place of refuge from the general desolation. Ah! that was the time, I allow, which gave his mockers a glorious handle for making merry at his expense! When Noah first announced to them the purpose of God and the approaching calamity, it is quite possible he may have instilled into certain minds some sense of fear. But, when such persons observed that a year transpired, that two years transpired, that three years transpired, that very near upon a hundred years transpired, and yet the threatened deluge was not yet come, while, all this time, Noah was toiling more and more vigorously at his work, Oh, how must they have flocked around him and his Ark with their jokes, taunting him at full cry, as being in his second childhood and a false prophet! And then, afterwards, while the sky was shining clear over their heads, as they saw him entering the Ark, leading an enormous troop of different animals, which passed in a splendid procession, going two and two before him, how must their mockery have increased, and fresh venom have been added to their insults! The better sort among them must have said, "Observe, for the very life of you, the wisdom of old age. See what it is, when you might be enjoying pure air and a clear sky, to go and sentence yourself to a gloomy prison and a perpetual night! What a fancy for a person to take, when he is become weary of his life—to build with his own hands the place of his sepulture! And then, not having patience to wait for the hour of his death, to hurry on in advance and bury himself alive! We are quite aware that he will be able to enjoy in his Ark the charming society of wolves and bears, of wild boars and foxes; but what sort of chains will he get, to bind and secure the savage beasts and to prevent their tearing him in pieces? What an arrant fool he must be! The man is afraid, lest the water should overwhelm him; and he has no fear at all, lest the tigers should throttle him, or the leopards strangle him to death!" After some such fashion, as this, they all probably taunted Noah at the critical time, when he was just stepping into the Ark. To such a pitch were their minds still blinded and lifted up with pride. But when, seven days after, on the gradual letting loose of the cataracts of heaven, the rains began to come down, the water-floods to swell, the torrents to roar, the rivers to rise, the seas to run wild, and the plains all around to be inundated—the valleys no longer appearing, and the very mountains astonished by seeing their lofty crags overtopped by waters, such as they had never known—Oh, how wonderfully did the scene then suddenly shift before their eyes! The Ark of the righteous man gallantly floated over the new formed ocean: it was no longer a prison of disgrace, but a chariot of honour. Amidst the rattling of the clouds, which thundered unto the battle, and amidst the howling of the winds, which roared unto destruction, amidst the cries of the fugitives, the screams of the drowning, the groans of the dying, the Ark alone retained its calmness, when fear was on every side: alone it stood secure, when all around was going to ruin.

I can well understand how Noah, safe sheltered within his Ark, must have been disposed rather to compassionate the miseries of the ungodly, than with any vindictive feeling to rejoice at them. Far from him must have been any desire to appear at the window with the view of insulting his old mockers, even by looking at them, and much less by inveighing against them. But suffer me now to perform this office for him. Only suppose that I am gazing from some extraordinary eminence upon this shipwreck of the world; and let me cry aloud—" Where are ye now, where are ye now, ye audacious spirits, who could once find pleasure in ridiculing the simple faith of a holy man? Raise for a moment your drowning heads above the water, and look about you. Do you recognize yonder 'the piece of wood,' which now rides so victoriously over your heads; how it fears no shipwreck, and defies death itself? Where are now your splendid buildings; produce them as a match to this. Where are now your palaces and lofty towers? Can it be possible that Noah finds more safety within his four partitions of fragile wood, than you do within your many barriers of stout walls? Do you recollect all the sport you made of him, because, in the devotedness of his heart to God, he despised your pomps, and abhorred your pride, and kept aloof from your dissipation? You then calumniated him, as one, who in a desperate fit of melancholy, had immured himself in the strait confines of a floating prison. Now, now is the time for you to laugh at him, if you can: now is your time to ridicule his conduct, while death stares you in the face and the deluge is in your throats! O ye most wretched mockers of the righteous! A prey to corruption, even before life is extinct, your bodies already float upon the waters: the sport of a thousand conflicting whirlwinds, dashing you at their rude pleasure here and there, you must despair of ever reaching a desert shore, where you may quietly rest your bones—the privilege of the shipwrecked in their worst distress. Noah only, in the midst of the tremendous tempest, is saved all anxiety about securing a haven; for he carries a haven with him. Go where he will, he is accompanied with the means of deliverance; and, while you must sink down, like lead, to the bottom, having nothing to support you, to him it is given to steer undaunted over the surging wave."

But what am I saying? Whither do I suffer my feelings to transport me? These terms of reproof are indeed well merited; but they are addressed to a people, who can no longer be in a state to hear them, still less to profit by them. Let us rather discuss the subject in friendly conference among ourselves. This catastrophe of the deluge—was it not awful? Did it not render the lot of Noah, the man mocked, far more enviable than that of his abandoned mockers? And precisely such will be your lot, if you continue unmoved amidst the contradictions of sinners. They laugh now at you, because you refuse to join in their licentious revels; they are every day calling you by some reproachful name, and wounding your feelings. They say that, having the notion that you are so soon to die, you imprison yourself in your secret chamber, instead of inhaling the fine fresh air; and that you seek privacy and seclusion on the Festival-days, instead of roaming about the streets and country, and following in the path of lawless dissipation. But Oh, how soon will this merriment of theirs cease, when at the last great Deluge, not of water, but of fire, they will see death before them, and no refuge whatever nigh! Right glad would they then be to get a place in your Ark, so well styled in the Book of Wisdom, "a piece of wood of small value" (x. 4) : cheer up then : the tables will soon be turned, the scene soon shifted; and, as from the heights of heaven you behold them sinking deep into the abyss, you will "stand in great boldness before the face of them that afflicted thee." (Wisd. v. 1.) And are not these, let me ask, blessed considerations, enough to make you scorn all the vain barking of those Cerberuses, who can indeed excite a clamour at you, but cannot hurt you? Yes, yes; let them bark at you now to their heart's content; let them misrepresent you; let them vilify you. In that Day, when their insolence shall at length be confounded, we shall see who has the best of it.

6. O Day to be desired! O Day dear indeed! When wilt thou come to pour a flood of transparent light on those truths, which I so dimly shadow forth? Cheer up, my Christian friends. Life is short. If for a little space we must be the butt of some malignant tongues, why should this disquiet us? Greater will be our glory hereafter. Angels will applaud us! Archangels will applaud us! Why then lay so much stress on what a few paltry creatures of dust and

ashes now say to annoy you? Hear how GOD speaks to us on this matter in Isaiah; *Fear ye not the reproach of men, neither be ye afraid of their revilings: for the moth shall eat them up, like a garment; and the worm shall eat them, like wool. But My Righteousness shall be for ever.* (Isa. li. 7, 8.) Oh, how happy will you be in the constant remembrance of a declaration so important! And what are men, even the most lordly among them? Are they not all perishable, all of clay, all of ashes? And can it ever be that you should regard them more, than you do GOD Himself? Oh, what a reproach! What a disgrace! What a shame is this! Only consider, my hearers, how many among you may be really well inclined to do what is right, to be frequent at the Holy Communion, to fast, to deny yourselves, to read pious books, to reconcile enemies, to promote religion, who nevertheless decline actually to do these things? And why? From the fear of certain tongues, which in a very short time will be rotting in the earth. Consider still more seriously, how many, from the fear of these same tongues, will not unfrequently commit a thousand enormities, from which otherwise they would have kept aloof. A companion meets you: "Why all this going to Church? Let's have a game together. Where are the cards? Quick, go and fetch them."—And you cannot bring yourself to answer, "No." He invites you to the midnight assembly; you respond, "We'll go:" he invites you to the convivial party, to the feast, to the dance, to the merry making; ay, and to the lowest haunts of ill-fame and profligacy—and you have not even then the courage to refuse. You fear a smile; you fear a name; and, because you are afraid to tell him, "he may go there by himself," you allow this your accursed companion to carry you off to the very brink of hell. Ah, Christians, is not this a most signal piece of stupidity, to attach such importance to a creature, who is only dust and ashes, like yourself?

Plutarch records the case of some persons, who, being invited to sup at their neighbour's houses, where they had strong reason to suspect some treacherous design against them, nevertheless went there; only that by going they might not appear uncivil: and he tells us that Diones was accordingly killed by Calippus, Antipater by Demetrius, and a certain Hercules, a silly youth, by Polipersus. But are you not giving way to a worse kind of silliness? You are aware that the companion, who invites you to that notorious place of bad resort, intends to leave you there in the hands of the devil: and, knowing this, you follow him; only from the fear you have of being laughed at, as clownish and impracticable. Why not decline and at once reject his proposals? Why not prefer imitating the many noble souls, who have taught you by their examples to assert your independence? Senofanes, though a Gentile, on hearing that, in consequence of his having refused to play at cards, he was stigmatised, as a coward, by one of his compeers of the name of Lasus, with admirable spirit replied, that "in regard to things morally wrong, he confessed himself to be of all cowards the greatest." And Oh, ye Christians, have you no heart to make the same kind of protest in matters far more nefarious, far more sordid, far more abominable? Oh, once for all, make a decided profession. *I will pay my vows unto the Lord in the sight of all His people.* (Ps. cxvi. 16.) *In the midst of the congregation I will praise Thee.* (Ps. xxii. 22.) *I will praise Him among the multitude.* (Ps. cix. 30.) It is your duty to declare frankly among the multitude, as David did, that you are determined to frame your life by that Law, which you profess. Happy will you be, if you can carry back to your homes this morning any feeling of this holy boldness! How many ladies among you will then immediately fling away those gaudy ornaments, which, as sensible persons, they must know to be highly dangerous to their souls from the vanity they foster, and the scandal they occasion; though at present they cannot bring themselves to dress more simply, lest they should be eclipsed by their neighbours! How many citizens will become more devoted to GOD! How many honourable men more circumspect! This is that holy boldness, which S. Paul so much esteemed, when he declared, *I am not ashamed of the Gospel of Christ,* (Rom. i. 16,) and this it is, that I desire for you. Do not be ashamed, when at Church, reverently to bend both your knees in prayer to GOD: for, had not this been an important duty, it would not have been so expressly recorded in

Scripture that Solomon prayed in the temple *kneeling on his knees*. (1 Kings viii. 54.) Do not be ashamed to attend public Worship with all becoming decency of behaviour, to keep silence, while people near you are talking, to be intent on prayer, while they are laughing. Declare unto GOD with a noble elevation of mind, *In Thee, O Lord, have I put my trust: I will not be ashamed.* (Ps. xxv. 1.) What, my beloved LORD, can cause me shame? *I put my trust in Thee.* Let men deride; let them despise me; let them cast me out: I am content, if I can only please Thee. *Though they curse, yet bless Thou!* (Ps. cix. 27.) Oh, the Heavenly consolation, comprehended in these few words, *Though they curse, yet Bless Thou!* They will say, I am good for nothing: *yet Bless Thou.* They will say, that I am ill-conditioned: *yet Bless Thou.* They will say, that I am unmannerly:[1] *yet Bless Thou.* They will say, that I pretend to be better than I really am: *yet Bless Thou.* In a word, *Though they curse, yet Bless Thou.* By means, like these, fortify your minds, my Christian brethren, in doing good, and settle them on that infallible maxim of Francis of Assisi, "The praise of men is of small consequence to us, if GOD finds fault; and men's finding fault matters little, if GOD praises."

THE SECOND PART.

7. We have encouraged the good to despise the evil-speaking of the wicked, and so to imitate the courageous example of the Canaanitish woman, who disregarded the comments of the world, when she sought CHRIST in the public streets. I cannot now restrain my feelings from turning to the case of these same evil speakers. I cannot refrain my ardent zeal from showing them the enormity of their guilt and their extreme spiritual danger, whilst they deliberately apply themselves in this manner to oppose goodness in other men. And who would ever believe that the chief hindrance, which a Christian meets in the pursuit of virtue, arises from Christians? But let such come hither, and listen, and then answer

---

[1] The Preacher might here have intended to allude to some personal reflections, that had been made against himself; as S. Paul, in some of his Epistles, particularly 2 Cor. v. 13; x. 10.

me. You persecute so violently that righteous man with every kind of obloquy, because you wish to bring him in the end to give up his religion. Is not this your aim? Be it then even so. To please you, let that young female relinquish her modest retiring habits of life. To please you, let that young man relinquish his devout exercises of prayer. Let them both accompany you to the theatre, share in your gaieties, plunge into your delights, and sling your guitar about their necks. Let them in their wayward pursuit of pleasure cull a nosegay from every garden, and scatter broadcast, wherever they go, the seeds of iniquity. In all this what have you done? You think to yourself that you have secured on easy terms a great advantage; and I tell you that by this means you may have incurred an incomparable loss. For weigh this well in your mind. If that unhappy female, who was induced by your importunity to forsake the paths of religion and to venture on the broad way of destruction, should finally through your fault be lost for ever—why, alas! she drags you in her company to destruction: you also are eternally lost; there is no possible escape for you. I feel a chill of horror strike through me, when I reflect how any person can ever tranquilly lay his head on his pillow, while he may have reason to suspect that through his instrumentality a soul is gone to Hell. One single soul, ruined by his means—what anguish, what heart-breaking should it cause him! And Oh, could we hear the groans of that soul, its mournings, its ravings, its execrations, as they are echoed from the abyss below! Would it ever cease imploring vengeance on the head of its betrayer, of its murderer? No; it would raise its desperate howlings to the throne of GOD, demanding the blood, demanding the death, demanding the damnation of the author of its misery.

The HOLY SPIRIT bears witness to the fact that a cry for vengeance constantly arises from the Sacred tombs, where repose the ashes of those righteous men, who found the death of their bodies at the hands of wicked persecutors. And how often do we hear in Church the solemn denunciation, *Oh, let the vengeance of Thy servants' blood that is shed be openly showed in our sight!* (Ps. lxxix. 11.) Yet that death of the Martyrs, howsoever painful, was the beginning of their Eternal happiness: and we may say, leaving out of the question the sin against GOD, that they were more indebted to the swords of the cruel executioners, who killed them, than to the breasts of those loving nurses, who gave them milk. S. Augustine took occasion to say that "never did the respect, shown us by evil men, profit us so much, as did their enmity." But what then may we conceive of those poor sufferers, who regard you, not as having inflicted on them the temporal death of the body, but the Everlasting death of the Soul? Can we conceive them ceasing one single moment from crying aloud in Hell? "Avenge me, Avenge me!" will be the cry of that wretched young man, "because, when I had formed the good habit of regular daily devotions, this person by the sport he made of it diverted me from my purpose, and thereby caused me to die in a state of sin." "Avenge me, Avenge me!" will be the cry of that miserable young woman, "because, when I had adopted the rule of seeking retirement for meditation and prayer, this person by the names he gave me withdrew me from my purpose, and thereby was the cause of my living, like others, a life of vanity." "Avenge me, Avenge me!" will be the cry of that unhappy man, "because, when I had from my early days an inward heavenly call to the Ministry, this person by the opposition he threw in my way estranged me from my purpose, and thereby was the cause of my losing my way to Paradise." And if these lost souls shall in such a manner clamour against us, what shall we do to stop their mouths? Are they then so many Cerberuses, who may be quieted with a honeyed cake, or softened by a lovely song? Not so, not so; saith the SPIRIT of GOD. You cannot possibly bribe them to be silent. *He will not spare in the day of vengeance: he will not regard any ransom, neither will he rest content though thou givest many gifts.* (Prov. vi. 34, 35.) Not only are these poor sufferers unwilling, they are unable to receive any favour: they are capable of no other feeling, but of hatred; no other pleasure, but of revenge. Can we suppose them to be ever pacified, until they see the persons, who were the cause of their sins, made to be the partakers of their punishment? Or can GOD, stunned, if I may so speak, by such yellings and howlings, ever consent to admit us into heaven? Is He not compelled to give us our due portion—flames for flames, torments for torments, death for death? *He that is glad at calamities shall not be unpunished.* (Prov. xvii. 5.) This we must believe. Consequently, if the person, who is only *glad* at the destruction of a soul, shall not be unpunished; what shall be done to him, who was the very cause of that soul's destruction? Alas! believe me, this thought pierces my soul through and through with intense alarm. Nor can I understand how any person, allowing such a thought to have its proper effect upon him, can enjoy any tranquillity by night or by day; or be able to banish from his dreams that horrid spectre of a damned soul, like unto a most hideous Fury, clothed in flames, girded with smoke, and deadly pale with poison, coming to lash him with a scourge of vipers.

And are we really then willing to run this hazard? This very evening, my dear brethren, comply with the entreaty of your most affectionately attached, but unworthy, servant, whose only real wish is, that you may be happy for ever. This very evening, when you examine yourself, as I suppose you do before lying down to rest, pause and reflect, seriously and diligently search out your consciences. Does the religion of my neighbours offend me? Do I dislike any person, because he is good? Do I persecute any person, because he is modestly behaved? Do I make a jest of any person, because he is moral?—If your conscience should acquit you in these particulars, thank GOD for it: but if you discover yourselves to be guilty, fear, Oh, earnestly fear, lest you should have despatched some person to Hell, who shall there prove your enemy, who shall there cry aloud, "Death, death," against you, who shall there scream, "Vengeance, vengeance," against your soul!

SERMON X.

THE SOUL'S FLIGHT FROM EARTH TO HEAVEN.

S. MATTH. XVII. 4.

"LORD, IT IS GOOD FOR US TO BE HERE."

1. To heaven, to heaven, my most dear religious brethren, to heaven, to heaven, I say. Is there one among you, who is not longing to soar above to glory? Why should we take more thought about this valley of tears? Wherever we bend our steps in this world, we hear nothing but sighs and groans; we see nothing but wickedness and misery. The rich man complains of the poor, and the poor man of the rich; the servant of his master, the master of his servant; and there is not a person to be found, who is thoroughly contented with his lot. Rachel is very fair; true: but she mourns, because she is not a mother, as Leah is. Leah is a mother; but she takes it to heart, because she is not fair, as Rachel is. Naaman possesses great riches; but what do they profit him, so long as he is covered with a loathsome leprosy? Augustus is powerful; but he has no son to succeed him: Tiberius is feared; but he is friendless. Not even the little good we have here can be possessed with tranquillity. The power of Princes is endangered by rebels taking up arms; the happiness of favourites by courtiers plotting opposition; the success of literary authors by antagonists producing their answers; the security of rich men by thieves designing plunder;

the pleasure of lovers by rivals fomenting quarrels. All is jealousy, all is strife, all is risk, all is anxiety, all is vexation of spirit. And are we anxious still to abide longer in a scene of so much misery? Seneca long time since observed, that nature practised upon us a most artful deception, when she contrived that man should be born without understanding: because, had it been otherwise, no one would have consented to come into this world. Hear his words: "Nothing is so uncertain, nothing so treacherous, as human life: no person, I am confident, would accept it, had he been conscious at the time it was given him." And we have known all this, ay, and have had actual experience of the world; and yet we can bear to remain here?—Oh, to heaven! to heaven! my most religious brethren, to heaven! to heaven! If we cannot in our present state go there with our bodies, let us ascend with our spirits: if we cannot abide there in person, let us abide there in thought. But how shall we possibly contrive to climb up so high? How shall we manage it? Be not anxious about this. If need be, I will borrow a chariot, not from Medea nor from Triptolemus (for we have no concern with their heathen fables,) but the chariot of Elijah. Nor let the idea alarm you, that it is *a chariot of fire and horses of fire.* (2 Kings ii. 11.) It is fire, which is luminous and ardent, but at the same time harmless: fire, however, it is still; and this intimates it to be no common desire, that can secure us a place in heaven, but that only, which is warm and fervent. And such truly will be your desire, when bearing you aloft on the clouds I shall this morning exhibit to you the first entrance of a soul into Glory. Not only shall I light up your minds with joy and cause you to exult with triumph, like Peter, when he beheld before him a faint glimpse from Mount Tabor; but perhaps I may even charm you to such a degree, as to constrain you to exclaim with Paul, "Away with these chains, tear asunder these fetters; for I can bear them no longer: *Who shall deliver me from the body of this death?*" (Rom. vii. 24.) Give me your attention; and you shall see the success, which I anticipate, not from the power of my speech, but from the sublimity of my subject.

2. Imagine then to yourselves, that the hour is arrived,

when your recovery from sickness being happily despaired of by your physicians, you must exchange earth for Paradise. You take your final leave of all, who surround your bed: "Farewell, parents; farewell, friends; don't be uneasy on my account: Paradise awaits me! *We will go into the house of the Lord.*" (Ps. cxxii. 1.) And now let your spirit with a vault mount the prophetic chariot, all in readiness for you, while I bear you company. Loosen we the driving reins; cheer we on the steeds; and quick let us soar above. Oh, what a wondrous journey you have before you, to be accomplished in less than a single hour! That very journey it is, which David longed to make, when calming his present grief with the sweet hope of future felicity he communed with GOD in these words, *I will behold Thy heavens, even the work of Thy fingers, the moon and the stars, which Thou hast ordained.* (Ps. viii. 4, Vulg.) First, you will have to traverse the air, and to contemplate one after another, its different regions: the lower region being warm from the reflection of the rays, which are beneath it; the upper region being very hot from the near vicinity of the fire, which is above it; the middle region being exceedingly cold, inasmuch, as being opposed on every side by contrary heat, it guards more sternly its own natural frigidity by dint of a most wonderful resisting power. In these regions you will view that vast area, which furnishes open battle-field to the winds; and you will become acquainted with the secret causes of their raging against, and contending with, each other; and from whence it arises, that substances, so exceedingly thin and subtle, should possess a force sufficient to destroy forests, to overthrow buildings, and even to shake the earth. You will discover this to be the womb, that gives birth, from such a diversity of causes, to the rainbows, which tint the clouds; to the dews, which nurse the flowers; to the rains, which water the fields; to the snows, which whiten the mountain tops; to the hail, which devastates the harvest land. It will then be no longer in the power of any person to taunt you with the question asked of Job; *Hast thou entered into the treasures of the snow? or, hast thou seen the treasures of the hail?* (Job xxxviii. 22.) Then you will understand the object of those fiery exhalations, which, under the title of comets, struck fear into the hearts of mighty kings; those sportive fireworks, those flying dragons, those falling stars, and those bands, like unto armed men, seen occasionally to skirmish in the air. Penetrating into those enormous foundries of nature, where she is ever at work fabricating new thunderbolts and new lightnings, you will henceforth be spared the trouble of investigating, whether thunders be aught else, than fire widely expanded; or lightnings aught else, than fire closely contracted. You will at once perceive through what potent arm it is, that darted "as from a well drawn bow, they fly to the mark," to use the fine expression of Wisdom (v. 21 :) and you will ascertain with a simple glance of your eye whether thunders are a huge brand of fire, suddenly extinguished by the cold air, as Anaxagoras dreamed they were; or rather, as Aristotle considered, a vapour, caused violently to explode by the condensation of the clouds. Nor must you suppose that these phenomena will occasion you any alarm. Already are you above the reach of tempests and whirlwinds, and beyond all apprehension of losing your vines by reason of the hail, or your house from the lightning, or your land from the inundation. Let those tremble at the storm, who are still on the earth under your feet. You will not only mount on high above the region of the air, but beyond it you will traverse the sphere of fire, which is there in a state of calm repose, as in its native home, and not raging, as it does below, in its state of exile; and then you will find that you have performed a journey of 126,630 miles, and that without any sense of fatigue. Reaching this first stage in the heavens you will fix your admiring gaze upon the Moon.[1]

3. And here, you will exclaim, is that body, which once seemed to me be so diminutive, and which now appears so

---

[1] The Preacher directs his flight from the earth to the highest Heaven, according to the notions of the ancient Ptolemaic system of astronomy: and it is interesting to observe that Dante in his "Paradiso" represents himself, as conducted by Beatrice through the same successive stages of the celestial ascent. What our own Milton puts into the mouth of "the affable Archangel" may be read in connection with this astronomical sermon, and as pointing out the chief differences between the Ptolemaic and Copernican systems. (B. iii. 481, and viii. 118. See also Tasso, Ger. Lib. Canto ix. 60, 61.)

boundless in its dimensions. Behold that splendid luminary, the object of so much laborious inquiry among men of talent below, who felt hurt at the scanty knowledge they possessed of a planet nearest to their earth. Now I perceive the nature of those spots, which critics have noticed with so much pleasure. Now I understand how it is that the Moon has her eclipses, that she wanes, and is at full, and passes through all those changes, in return for which, while she designs in them the benefit of mankind, she gains no other reward than the reproach of inconstancy. How silly were those philosophers, who fancied this to be another world, distributed, like ours, into plains, mountains, seas, deserts, and habitable land. The poor creatures never enjoyed our privilege of mounting up so high, so as to correct their mistake. Oh, what would not any one give to be able to comprehend, as I now do, the hidden mysteries of those influences, which are from thence unceasingly derived to the earth, and to know whether the Moon is that impetus, that pushes the sea backward and forward every day, with the ebb and flow of the tides, and also with some corresponding sympathy generates silver in the mines, and not rather gold, as does the sun : or iron, as does Mars ; or tin, as does Jupiter ; or lead, as does Saturn; or brass, as does Venus; or quicksilver, as does Mercury? for these were, respectively, the supposed parents of these several metals. You will say something like this, and almost thrown into an ecstasy of wonder you will deem this region to be your Heaven : but, Sirs, let us drive on, let us drive on; for we must yet ascend considerably higher.

4. Having left behind us the first heaven of the Moon, you will pass on to that of Mercury; and from it to that of Venus; nor probably will you stop to observe them with any attention from your curiosity to reach the Solar region, after an ascent which you will have accomplished of full four millions of miles; for such, at least, is the distance of the Sun from our earth, according to the calculations of our mathematicians. Yes! there it is, that you will be astounded indeed! You will see a luminous body a hundred and sixty-six times larger than all our globe; and yet every part of it "full of

the glory of the LORD" (Ecclus. xlii. 16,) all lovely, all radiant, all adorned; and therefore it is called in holy Scripture a Giant, from its immensity; and a Bridegroom, from its great beauty. (Ps. xix. 6, 7.) You will behold the sun in the fourth sphere; that so, like a just and impartial Monarch, who makes his residence in the centre of his dominions, it may equally diffuse its potent influence around, and may illumine the earth in such a manner, that by too great nearness it may not resolve everything to dust, nor by too great distance leave everything to die of cold. You will see how the Sun is the heart of the earth, distributing from its central position a perpetual supply of life to the herbs, to the flowers, to the corn, to the trees, to the animals; that it maintains the stars, that it regulates the nights and days, that it measures out the year, that it divides its seasons; and again, as well befits a benign Monarch, that it is far from being inactive, as some one fancied, but is always indefatigably at work for our benefit; always restless, every moment on the move; yea rather running its course with such impetuosity, *whirling about continually* (Eccl. i. 6,) that in the compass of an hour it performs a journey of a million and a hundred and sixty thousand miles over a track, quick of transit in proportion to its high elevation. With such a spectacle before you, where, you will ask, is that pitiable man, Eudoxus, who, if he might have been permitted only once to see the Sun so very near, and been able from this station to measure its dimensions and to watch its movements, was willing to be roasted alive in its consuming flames? See how I here enjoy an equal pleasure, with no reason to apprehend a like danger. Stationing yourselves here, with a view to its close observation, Oh, how indignant will you feel at those men of old time, the Democrituses, the Metrodoruses, the Anaxagorases, of whom the first declared of the Sun, that it was a mere red-hot iron, and the two last that it was a rough clod of earth, gilded over; as if they all cherished some envious design of detracting from the glory of its Creator. And Oh, the Greatness of GOD! again you will be forced instantly to exclaim. What must Thou be in all Thy living beauty, when Thou appearest to be such in this Thy lifeless image! Every hour, that detains me from seeing Thee, appears to be a hundred years! *When shall I come to appear before the Presence of God?* (Ps. xlii. 3.) Speed we on, speed we on. Let us despatch these other heavens, that remain, with a bound, rather than a step; let us get to the Empyrean, as quick as we can. Let us reach that Blessed spot, where, as my beloved David told me, *The Glory of the Lord shall appear.* (Ps. cii. 16.)

5. Thither you will come; but in the way you cannot but bestow a glance on Mars first, then on Jupiter, and afterwards on Saturn; for when you have admired the vast bulk, and the influence, and the revolutions of these planets, you will reach the Starry heaven, called the Firmament, not so much, as S. Augustin thinks, from its immoveableness, as from its solidity. On setting your feet on so beauteous a spot, I know that you will at once inquire, whether this be not Paradise? No, my brethren, it is not. Paradise is still much further on. The Empyrean is more distant from the back of the Firmament, than the back of the Firmament is far from the earth: and yet these last are separated from each other by a space of a hundred and sixty millions of miles, according to the lowest computation of scientific men. But what will you say, when you are in the bosom of this heaven, containing, as it does, those assembled stars, which, in the words of Ecclesiasticus, "never faint in their watches" (xliii. 10)? This is the very place, to which Greece in her pride laid claim, as her own colony, where she degraded every star by associating it with some act of depravity, while to each she assigned its peculiar hero. Here, in her crazy dreams, she fixed the residence of her Herculeses, her Perseuses, her Cepheuses, her Booteses, her Andromedas, her Ariadnes, and all that other wretched herd of names known to the astrologers. Yea, (be astonished at their presumption!) they introduced into a place, so delectable as this, not only eagles and swans, but bears and dragons; as if hoping thereby to scare away all mortals from heaven, thus to get plenty of associates in the depths below. Oh, how greatly will you rejoice, when you behold those orbs of celestial gold, those crystals of enduring substance, those lights, that never fail! Then think, as you call to mind the difference subsisting between the beauties above and those

below, how naturally you will look down to the earth for a moment, to compare it with Heaven. But Oh, the descent! Oh, the distance! Oh, the depth! Yes, thus it shall be, as Isaiah said, *Thine eyes shall behold the land, that is very far off* (xxxiii. 17.) And where, you will quickly ask, where is the country, in which I once lived? Where is my house? Where is my dear native land? Florence, what is become of thee? Italy, where art thou? Europe, show thyself; for I cannot descry thee. In all that depth below me I can trace no more than a single point. Oh, how dense a darkness must now enshroud the inhabitants of the earth, as contrasted with this light, I now behold, this clear serene, I now enjoy! And was it possible, that any person could ever advise me to risk my inheritance of heaven for a paltry handful of earth? O fools, fools that ye are, who labour so hard to enlarge your property and possessions. That, for which you venture on the seas; that, for which you engage in war; that, for which you rule over kingdoms, is a mere *punctum*. (Seneca.) The entire sphere of your greatness is comprised within a narrow slip of earth; and even that slip is invaded by seas and rivers, and encroached upon by mountains and deserts. There you carry on your contentions with each other; there you confine your ambition; there you desire your happiness; there you imprison your souls, as if they were quite incapable of these great things above. Raise your thoughts awhile to contemplate how glorious that destiny is, which awaits you here; *Lift up your eyes on high, and behold!* (Isa. xl. 26.) Know you not, that the upper vault of this region comprehends a circuit of a thousand and seventeen millions, five hundred and sixty-two thousand, and five hundred miles? *Have ye not known? Have ye not heard?* (Isa. xl. 21.) All this is yours. *He that overcometh shall inherit all things.* (Rev. xxi. 7.) Yours is all this delightful champagne; yours are those spheres; yours are those stars, the smallest of which, let me tell you, would contain your present earth twenty times.

6. If I mistake not, you will be uttering some such exclamations as these, while you ascend; just as a man, labouring under any strong emotion of mind, goes about giving vent to his feelings, even when aware that none is nigh to hear him;

you will do the same, till beyond the starry heaven you traverse the ninth and the tenth sphere, simply called by many the Crystalline heaven. And touching that so much disputed point, what is the real substance of these vast heavens, whether they are fluid, like the air: or, as that learned friend of Job would have them (xxxvii. 18,) solid, *as a molten looking-glass*, this you will ascertain. Reaching this spot, you will be in that sphere, which is the primary cause of motion to all the lower ones: and how great will be your satisfaction, in becoming acquainted with the system, the proportions, and the laws of so stupendous a movement! There you will learn what it was, that formerly led the Egyptians, the Chaldeans, and some of the Greeks, into error, when they considered the heavens, as possessing in themselves an intelligent mind, like ours, that guided their movements: and you will pity such men as Origen, who, under a like false hypothesis, went so far as to endow the stars with a capacity for virtue and vice, for defect and perfection. You will see whether this movement arises from the will of GOD alone, as Albert the Great thought; or whether by the external agency of the Angels, as T. Aquinas, a pupil greater than his master, considered. You will know whether the prime mover be one or many; and with inexpressible delight you will make your minds clear, as to the source of that exquisite harmony and music of the heavenly spheres, which the Pythagoreans heard; although the Peripatetics would not believe them, as proudly disdaining to concede to others a privilege not granted to themselves.

7. Not that any such melodious syrens, as Plato dreamed of, supposing that you could hear them singing over your heads, would, I am sure, be able, with all their flatteries, ever to prevail upon you to linger one moment in your journey. Better songs are in store for you, better harmonies, better entertainments, better delights. Cheer up. We are already come in sight of Paradise. Oh, let us press forward. *Let us hasten to enter into that rest.* (Heb. iv. 11, Vulg.) Not now, as acting the part of your most faithful Achates, would I exclaim, " Italy! Italy!"—Behold the Empyrean! Behold the Empyrean! once the theme of your mournful sighs *by the waters of Babylon.* (Ps. cxxxvii. 1.) Behold the Empyrean,

the beloved country of the living, the delicious repose of the afflicted, the desired haven of the shipwrecked! *Behold the Tabernacle of God is with men!* (Rev. xxi. 3.) Behold it! behold it! Does it not appear to you transcendently beautiful? All, all, that you have admired in the other heavens, as lovely, as brilliant, as joyous, all, at the sight of the Empyrean, must fade into darkness, as a glow-worm at the appearance of the Sun. And why, think you, have I this morning so minutely described to you their several beauties, except that you should infer from the character of its suburbs what the city itself must be? I beseech you to apply your minds willingly to this consideration; nor let any among you charge me with having thus far wasted your time in descriptions to no purpose. No, Sirs, I have not wasted your time, but used it to the best advantage. For I argue in this way. If those parts of the world be so richly and so nobly decorated, which the Blessed regard, as being only underground caverns, deserted and despised, what will those inner chambers be, which are destined to be their mansions for ever? What will those courts then be, where they will assemble for conference? What those gardens, whither they will retire for recreation? If the lowest pavement be thus curiously fashioned, how then will the arches above and the vaulted roofs appear? If the flooring be so magnificent, what will the gorgeous furniture, the arras, and the tapestry? Does it not seem to you that GOD ought to reserve mansions of surpassing beauty for the entertainment of His beloved ones,—of a Peter, crucified for Him, of a Paul, beheaded for Him, and of those martyrs, an immense company, who *loved not their lives unto the death?* (Rev. xii. 11.) If such is the house He keeps open here, in this earth, for the general entertainment even of His enemies, of the Neroes, of the Diocletians, of the Deciuses, of the Caracallas, we may at least draw this inference from Eucherius, "How magnificently will things Eternal appear, when even things, that are soon to perish, shine so brightly?"

8. You will therefore see that Majestic City with its ineffable proportions raised above the most purified, the most splendid, the most sublime sphere of the universe. There are no miles, which can ever reach the vast span of its

circumference, as Jeremiah says; *If the heaven above can be measured.* (Jer. xxxi. 37.) There are no crystals, which can ever come near the transparency of its walls; there are no jewels, which can compete with the brilliancy of its polished stones. S. John, who had but a rough outline of the city, sketched on his map, described it, as *lying four-square.* (Rev. xxi. 16.) If you contemplate the workmanship, it seems to eclipse the materials; if you contemplate the materials, they appear to outshine the workmanship. Yes; this is indeed a city, altogether lovely, *the perfection of beauty.* (Lam. ii. 15.) You will see its twelve most enormous gates, formed symmetrically of twelve most precious pearls. Oh, what delicate tracery! Oh, what a noble elevation! Oh, what an imposing aspect is here! *How goodly are thy tents, O Jacob; and thy tabernacles, O Israel!* (Numb. xxiv. 5.) One sees clearly at first sight that *this is none other but the House of God.* (Gen. xxviii. 17.) With joy then let us descend from the chariot, that has brought us here. Let us knock; let us make our arrival known: *Lift up your heads, O ye gates!* (Ps. xxiv: 7.) Yet why should we take this trouble? Of themselves will the gates of Paradise fly open to receive us: and speedily will a company of Angels advance to meet us with the sweet festal accord of their instruments, and the melodious welcome of their voices, sounding aloud in our ears the well-known salutation, *Enter thou into the joy of thy Lord.* (S. Matth. xxv. 21.) They seem, by the import of these few words, at once to disclose to us the greatness of our future happiness, as being a happiness Infinite and Incomprehensible: thereby, as S. Anselm remarked, they intimate, that this joy, being, like a boundless ocean, too vast to be contained *in us,* we must needs plunge and be immersed *in it.*

9. But I shall do well, my hearers, to leave you at this spot, as I find you now in such good company, with so many Angels to take charge of you. What you will afterwards see and do, while with them, in Paradise, I cannot tell. I have accomplished a task, not at all inconsiderable, in bringing you to its confines. What follows is too far removed from human apprehension; *For eye hath not seen, nor ear heard, neither have entered into the heart of man the things which God*

hath prepared for them that love Him. (1 Cor. ii. 9.) And what can you hear from a poor wretched man, like myself, so very little instructed in the things of heaven? Must I tell you, that you will enter there upon an entirely new country, from which every shadow of sorrow is dispersed for ever? that there will be no night, to depress your spirits with its gloom? no heat, to incommode you with its violence? no cold, to oppress you with its severity? that there your sight will at once find every desired object of beauty; your hearing, every charming sound, it can long for; your smell, every odour, it delights in; your taste, whatsoever it judges to be most delicious; your touch, all that it accounts most smooth and delicate? that there your body will, for brilliancy, become more lustrous than the sun; and for activity, more nimble than the current air; and for tenuity, more penetrating than the flaming fire; and for impassibility, more durable than the diamond? that there all the different ages of man's life will combine in the formation of one perfect age out of them all; the season of childhood with its simplicity, of youth with its vivacity, of manhood with its strength, of old age with its sanctity? that there you will find yourselves suddenly endowed with the knowledge of the languages of all nations, to serve you in speaking; of the histories of all times, to serve you in conference; of the charms of every grace, to serve you in conversation; of the variety of all voices, to serve you in singing; the inventions of all hands, to serve you in working; the theories of all minds, to serve you in the attainment of wisdom? I could indeed tell you as much as this, and even more; but what would my information amount to? Nothing, absolutely nothing. If the joys of Paradise did not far surpass all these, in what sense could S. Paul have pronounced them *unspeakable words, which it is not lawful for a man to utter?* (2 Cor. xii. 4) while, as for the particulars set before you, every preacher speaks of them, every painter delineates them, every pen describes them; so that, instead of being things secret, they are generally and familiarly known.

I will nevertheless tell you what in a dream I imagined to myself would befall you on your first reception by the Angels.

They will quickly conduct you, by a path all inlaid with gold, to the Throne of GOD; only pausing in the way to point out to you those *many mansions*, one after another, with the hope of which CHRIST sustained the drooping hearts of His Apostles. But they will wisely give you to understand, that this distinction of neighbourhood by no means implies any discordance among the neighbours; because here, by an interchange of charity, each individual regards the good of the whole body, as being his own; and all regard the good of the individual in the same light. Numbers do not here cause confusion, nor does pre-eminence engender pride, nor does inferiority provoke competition, nor does inequality sever friendship: and this we owe to the blessed fact that in every case, where Grace subdues nature, it is morally impossible that any one of the brethren should at all covet any inheritance, greater or smaller, than what he sees assigned to him by the FATHER: for there all is concord, all is fellowship, all is peace. So it was revealed to Isaiah, *My people shall sit in the fair beauty of peace* (xxxii. 18, Vulg.;) peace between man and GOD, peace between subordinate and superior, peace between flesh and the spirit, peace between appetite and reason. In this manner, peradventure, the Angels, appointed to be your noble ushers, will discourse with you by the way: and presently, to confirm what they say, you will behold all the Blessed, on the tidings of your arrival, emulating each other in their haste to meet you; in companies, too, more thronged and joyous, than those, which once in the Jerusalem below ran to greet David, the stripling shepherd, after his famous victory. And what will be the transports of your soul, when you may perhaps recognise among them one of your most attached friends or one of your most beloved relatives, who died before you? Oh, how will you extend your arms to embrace them in the joy of your hearts! Oh, with what kisses and demonstrations of unfeigned love will you recover for ever their dear society, the loss of which, though for so short a time, cost you so many tears! "O my tenderly loved husband," will the widow exclaim; "O my dearest mother," will the son cry out; "is it really true that I see you again?" "And are you too here, my most attached friend?" will another say.

"Oh, how far more beautiful art thou now, that I recover thee, than thou wast, when I lost thee! Do you remember the way we used to talk together on the earth about what would become of us in Eternity? Lo, here we both are, without a fear of any more separation. *So shall we ever be with the Lord.*" (1 Thess. iv. 17.)

Nor, believe me, will your rapture be less, when you shall further recognise among the Saints those, who once stood the highest in your esteem.... For, if many considered, that the sight of a Titus Livy would amply repay them their long journey from a distant land, undertaken for this object, how will you be affected, when you recognise in heaven a Peter, the first of the Apostles; a Paul, the teacher of the Gentiles; a Jerome, an Augustine, a Chrysostom; and when you will be able, in reference to all such highly celebrated worthies of the Church, to use the words of Job, "*I have heard of thee by the hearing of the ear.*" (Job xlii. 5.) I once with the greatest delight to myself heard of your virtue, your eminence, and your glory; *but now mine eye seeth thee:* henceforth I shall no longer hear of thee; I have thee present before me." You will, therefore, I conceive, be disposed to cast yourselves at their feet in humble respect and reverence; but, not consenting to this, they will gently take you by the hand, and remind you, that you are no more now their pupils, but their fellow-citizens and associates; you are no longer, as before, *strangers and foreigners,* but *fellow-citizens with the saints, and,* what conveys a far higher idea, *of the household of God.* (Eph. ii. 19.)

10. Thus magnificently escorted you will draw nearer to the vestibule of the Supreme Divinity;.. when on a sudden your mind will be strengthened by a light of supereminent brilliancy; and in that light, in an abyss of splendours, in a circuit of Majesty, in a centre of Glory, you will "see GOD:" *you will see Him as He is.* (1 S. John iii. 2.) And what doth this mean, my Christian brethren, *you will see God?* Who will exalt my intellect, who will purify my lips, so that I may in some poor faint measure explain what you will then behold? You will behold that Being, who, being Blessed in Himself alone, was to Himself an Eternity, before any created

intelligence knew Him; not therefore less happy, because He was thus alone in His happiness; nor therefore less glorious, because He concealed His glory; that Being, who imparts existence to all, and receives it from none; who gives life to all, and takes it from none; who communicates strength to all; and who derives it from none; that Being, who at the same moment of time, is the farthest off from us, and yet the nearest to us; who is never comprehended in any one locality, albeit He abides everywhere; who is never distanced by any one age, albeit He is in every age. Suppose not, on seeing Him, that you see any of those objects, that you see apart from Him. These are created, and He is Uncreated: these are material, and He is a most simple Essence: these are dependent, and He is Absolute: these are limited, and He is Infinite: these are perishable, and He is Immortal: these are defective, and He is Perfect. And yet all, which you see apart from Him, you must suppose yourselves at once to see, on your seeing Him. You will thus see Him, as alone He works in all the creatures without weariness; and how they all subsist in Him, as to their excellency, none, as to their substance. In Him you will see whatsoever delights you in the sun, whatsoever revives you in the stars, whatsoever charms you in the rainbow, whatsoever enraptures you in the flowers, whatsoever refreshes you in the fountains, whatsoever braces you in the atmosphere, whatsoever nourishes you in food, whatsoever enchants you in harmony. But which of these things will you ever see, as identified with Himself? Not the harmony, nor the food, nor the fountains, nor the flowers, nor the rainbow, nor the stars, nor the sun. You will see in Him the perfections of all; but you will not see in Him the very being and existence of any one: and therefore you will not see in Him any defect. In Him you will see the brilliancy of whiteness, but not sullied with a stain; in Him beauty, but not liable to blemish; in Him power, but not obscured by a rival; in Him knowledge, but not dependent on a teacher; in Him goodness, but not amenable to passion; in Him substance, but not attended with accident; in Him life, but not subject to death. What shall I more say? You will *see God.* O ye immeasurably

Blessed, you will *see Him as He is!* Oh, who can tell what will be the transports of your soul at your first sight of Him! what bursts of affection! what ardour of love! what raptures! what ecstasies! what ravishing joys! . . . And who at that time will retain the faintest recollection of what he suffered on the earth for the sake of GOD? Do you think that the remembrance of your self-discipline, your penitential acts of self-denial, will ever then occur to your mind? Rather hear how the Blessed in heaven speak with one accord, *We have joy for the days in which Thou hast humbled us, for the years in which we have seen adversity.* (Ps. xc. 15, Vulg.) They speak not of their having *suffered* their former adversity: they speak of having *seen* it; *we have seen adversity:* because they know that even the very fiercest tortures of persecution and of martyrdom were a dream, when compared with the solid joys, that followed after.

11. Your only wish, I think, is to hear now from me how you are likely to feel, to act, and to express yourselves, under the influence of this Beatific Vision: but don't ask me this: for I am ignorant about it. I very well know what I intend to say for myself, should such a Blessed time be ever my portion, should I ever see myself admitted to the possession of all this glory, and find myself really and truly embracing those feet, and gazing upon that countenance, and *coming even to His seat.* (Job xxiii. 3.) I wish to declare to my GOD, how very exceeding great His kindness has been in willing the salvation of a puny creature, so worthless as myself; that I rather deserve to be consumed in the midst of a thousand flames, than to enjoy all this Blessedness; that I well know all to be the effect of His Grace; that even from Eternity I was predestinated to it, and that I owe nothing to any merit of my own. *He brought me forth, because He had a favour unto me.* (Ps. xviii. 19.) But I would moreover add, that it is this very thing, which so increases my happiness; and that it would not be so dear to me in my ascribing it to my own works, as it now is in my enjoying it solely on the ground of His loving-kindness. These are the motives, which will constrain me to love Him for ever: and this love will be all my joy. . . But, wretched man! What am I dreaming about?

How am I bewildered by thoughts so elevated, and by ravishments of soul so sublime! Can it then really be true, that I am destined to the enjoyment of so great happiness? that this my spirit, that these my members, that these my very bones, shall thus rejoice? *Mine eyes, shall they see the King in His Beauty?* (Isa. xxxiii. 17.) When, Oh, when will the time be? When, ye oppressive chains, that hold me bound, as your prisoner, when will ye break asunder? When shall I soar in freedom to gaze upon my GOD, as fire ascends to its sphere, and the arrow flies to its mark? O life, thou art too protracted! O death, thou art too far removed! To me to live is death, and to die will be life. *Who shall deliver me from the body of this death?* (Rom. vii. 24.) Ye mountains, valleys, plains, woods, gardens, I care no more to look upon you. What can I possibly find of beautiful upon the earth, in comparison of that, which is reserved for me in heaven? Ye princes, you are quite welcome to have your dominions; ye soldiers, keep your renown; ye learned, your wisdom; ye misers, your treasures: I envy you none of these things. Paradise, Paradise is mine! *One day in the courts of the Lord is better than a thousand.* (Ps. lxxxiv. 10.) One single moment of that Blessedness, which I there hope to enjoy—I say not in the inner, but even in the outer courts—one such single moment will yield me more bliss, than all of you put together have enjoyed from the beginning to the end of the world. Oh, the happy triumph! *The time appointed, the solemn Feast Day.* (Ps. lxxxi. 3.) . . . I will end, as I commenced. Let the man, who prefers it, keep the earth for his possession. If any one among you longs to be truly happy, let him aspire to heaven, and resolve to get there. To Heaven! to Heaven! *Seek those things which are above. Set your affections on things above, not on things on the earth.* (Col. iii. 1, 2.)

THE SECOND PART.

12. I have thus far exhibited to your view the first entrance of a soul into Glory, having employed for this purpose such lively imagery, as was suggested to me in my preparatory meditation on the subject. I see, however, but too clearly,

how much the copy falls short of the original. Ezekiel indeed delineated on a common brick tile the earthly Jerusalem (iv. 1;) but fool am I, who have ventured beyond him, and portrayed to you the Jerusalem from Heaven ... I know well that I have told you but the smallest part of the happiness enjoyed by the Saints above: but come, let us imagine that this smallest part was to be their all. Do you not think that even this would be worth the purchase at any cost whatsoever? I hope to convince you of this by one single argument of S. Chrysostom. Were I then to make this simple promise to all the aged, here present, that I would remove every wrinkle from their foreheads, every grey hair from their heads, and every infirmity, with which their necks are bowed down; that I would happily restore them to a most blooming condition of youth, and in that condition secure to them a thousand years in the uninterrupted possession of health, strength, and beauty, what would you not be willing to give me? ... Do we not see how willing people are to suffer to any extent, if they can thereby prolong their lives for a single year? Do they not go so far, as to pay an exorbitant price to one, who performs on them some most painful surgical operation, or torments them with some most nauseous medicine? ... There can then be no doubt that, did you hope to procure from me that flourishing state of health, I spake of, you would not think it difficult to do all I might require of you. With such a promise in your sight you would live like Saints, says S. Chrysostom. "There is nothing, that it would not prevail upon you to do or to suffer." Now, tell me, if I had promised you no other blessing in Paradise, but only this one, the blessing of youth, ever genial, ever immortal, ever unchangeable, (yes, the promise is quite certain—*Thy youth shall be renewed as the eagle's*, Ps. ciii. 5, Vulg.,) this alone should be enough to inflame your mind with a most ardent longing for Paradise, and would have the effect of making you regard for its sake no fatigue as irksome, and no pain as severe. And yet, Oh, how much more have I promised you over and above this? I have promised you the view of such glorious heavens, the dominion over such a universe, the fellowship of such spirits, the variety of such delights, the knowledge of such sciences, the ornament of such graces, and, above all, the unclouded Vision of GOD, which in itself alone is able to fill and satisfy all your heart. *God shall be all in all.* (1 Cor. xv. 28.) And is it then possible that the thing you would so willingly do for a far less object, the same you decline doing for an object so infinitely more excellent?

13. But why do I say, is it possible? It is a fact, my brethren, it is a fact. The good things of this world, which with Ecclesiasticus we may call "lies, that are seen," (Ecclus. xxxiv. 2, Vulg.,) these are what we really value, what we covet, what we purchase at any high price put upon them; but not so the good things of Paradise. Quite the contrary. It seems to me that on every emergency the very thing we are most ready to part with is Paradise. Is it a question of losing either Paradise or our money? Let Paradise go. Is it a question of either giving up Paradise, or some scandalous connection? Let Paradise be given up. Is it a question of either surrendering Paradise, or our worldly honour? Let Paradise be surrendered. And pray, my hearers, what can all this mean? If a merchant leaving the port in high spirits should be assailed, when at sea, with a furious hurricane, I know that his first thought would be to save, as far as he possibly could, all his goods and wares, which he so highly values. But, when the violence of the storm, the rolling of the vessel, the lashing of the billows, the cries of the sailors, and the imminent danger of death oblige him to throw them overboard, how does he then manage? Does he first of all lay his hands upon his most costly merchandise? By no means. What then? With a fallen countenance and trembling hand he begins with those objects, which are to him of the smallest value. He seizes a chest of linen, and he throws it over. Then, should the tempest gain strength, he seizes another chest of silk, and he throws it over. Then, should the waves continue boisterous, he takes another chest of spices, and he throws it over. And now he has only one small precious casket of jewels left him: and how does it go to his very heart to be obliged to throw it over! In the meanwhile the sea rages and roars, as if demanding of him the sacrifice; and he refuses, as loath to make it: and there-

fore he carefully puts away and conceals his casket. But should this be discovered by the sailors, who are quite resolved to lighten the burden of the vessel by all the means, however unreasonable, in their power, then he grasps his casket in his hands, presses it close to his bosom, and waters it with his tears. Once or twice does he extend his arms over the side of the ship, making an effort to throw it into the sea; but as often, repenting of his purpose, he draws it back again into the ship: and he seems, at that critical moment, inclined rather to lose his own life, in company with his jewels, than to live any longer without them. My brethren, under no imaginable circumstances, with whatever degree of impetuosity the storms may dash against us, can we ever be driven to the necessity of throwing over our Paradise; because Paradise is far too precious for any such thing. *All the things that may be desired are not to be compared to it.* (Prov. viii. 11.) It is worth more than riches; it is worth more than pleasure; it is worth more than honour; it is worth more than reputation; it is worth more than our life. And thence S. Augustine took occasion to say, "Though it may be acquired, it can never be valued." Such being the fact, how is it the very first thing, which some of you throw over, is Paradise? We make sure of our reputation, of our property, of our revenge, of our friends, of our kinsfolk, of our amusements now at once: there will be time enough afterwards for us to make sure of Paradise. We will confess our sins afterwards; we will turn to GOD afterwards; and, when we have thrown over Paradise, there may yet be a time afterwards for our managing to fish it up again. Oh, blindness! Oh, infatuation! Oh, senseless stupidity! O Paradise, that thou shouldst ever be disowned, slighted, trodden under foot by men! And is it possible that so many should every day be found, who have *set their eyes to bow down to the ground?* (Ps. xvii. 11, Vulg.) So it is; so it is. They have *set* them; they are resolved: like grovelling beasts, they have no wish to raise at any time their eyes from the earth, so jealous are they of it. They are always thinking of the earth; they are always speaking of the earth; they are always toiling for the earth. And do we wish to be like them? Oh, let it not be so. Let Paradise have our hearts. Let all here present determine to decline accepting whatsoever the earth has to offer us; and, lifting up at last our eyes to heaven, let us say, *Glorious things*, yes assuredly, *glorious things are written of thee, thou City of God!* (Ps. lxxxvii. 3.)

But how am I grieved that I should have been so slow to learn these *glorious things that are written of thee?* If, however, I once so basely preferred the earth, it was not for thy demerit; it only arose from this, that I knew thee not. But now who shall ever prevail to shut thee out from my heart? *Shall tribulation?* (Rom. viii. 35)—not so; for thou shalt change it for me into the sweetest contentments. *Shall distress?*—not so; for thou shalt transform it for me into the most perfect peace. *Shall hunger?*—not so; for thou shalt satisfy it for me with a most luscious nectar. *Shall nakedness?*—not so; for thou shalt cover it for me with Royal apparel. *Shall peril?*—not so; for thou shalt turn it for me into immoveable security. *Shall persecution?*—not so; for thou shalt recompense it to me with a glorious triumph. *Shall the sword?*—No, no; not even the sword shall ever cut me away from thee, my beautiful Celestial country! not even the sword, I say; for thou shalt convert its steel into gold, its point into rays of light, its circling edge into a crown of rejoicing.

SERMON XI.

INABILITY TO REPENT THE EFFECT OF DEFERRING REPENTANCE.

S. JOHN VIII. 21.

"YE SHALL SEEK ME, AND YE SHALL DIE IN YOUR SINS."

1. IT is usual, when an offence has been committed between two persons, and a peace is to be negociated, that the offender, who has done the wrong, and not the person offended, should be the first to seek reconciliation. To this effect the Divine Scriptures remind us how Benhadad, King of Syria, when he sought reconciliation with Ahab, King of Israel, whom he had provoked by raising war against him, was the first to move in this affair between them. He commanded his servants to put sackcloth on their loins and ropes on their heads, and in that condition immediately to go and cast themselves at the feet of the enraged monarch (1 Kings xx. 31, 32,) and with tears in their eyes to implore peace in their master's name. I perceive, however, my hearers, that your present method of proceeding is very unlike this. Speak the truth. Which is the offending party? Are you offended by GOD? or, is GOD offended by you? Nothing is more certain than that it is you, who have frequently and, it may be, openly committed many outrages against Him. You have offended Him by your thoughts; you have offended Him by your words; you have offended Him by your actions: and therefore reason requires

that the treaty of peace should originate with you. Nevertheless, I see that GOD has taken the first step by sending to you us, His most unworthy Ministers, just as if He had been the offender, and you the injured person.

But, after all, I am most anxious to know whether this peace is really concluded between you. When I consider the devotion, the fervour, the contrition, displayed by you during this season of Lent, I gladly think that it must be concluded; but, since we shall always find some so intractable in their tempers, as to neglect the present favourable season of coming to terms with GOD, on the plea of their yet having plenty of time, left for this purpose, when they are about to die, CHRIST bids me plainly assure all such, that they deceive themselves, and that, if they decline accepting the peace He now asks of them, He will decline granting peace to them, when they will have to ask it of Him. *Ye shall seek Me, and ye shall die in your sins.* And Oh, ye hard-hearted sinners, is not the menacing tone of this denunciation enough to awaken, to terrify, to subdue you? *Ye shall die in your sins!* Do you understand the words, *Ye shall die in your sins?* What use then is there in your telling me that you need be in no such haste to return unto the LORD, because you very well know that, in regard to Salvation, it matters not so much how you live, as how you die. Oh, your deluded minds! Oh, what blind counsels! Oh, what infatuated resolves! How can you possibly reckon upon your dying well, if this should be denied you by that very Being, on whom it entirely depends, and who most plainly and expressly protests that *you shall die in your sins?* But, lest you should believe that I am designing this time to force your assent by dint of clamour, I crave your calm attention: for I am resolved to meet you here, not so much at a sermon, as at a conference. I wish to have an open discussion with you on a subject no less weighty than this of your conversion, and that we should very carefully examine it together. Should it appear to you prudent to defer your conversion even to the last moments of your life, as perhaps you intend doing, I have no desire whatever to compel you to it immediately: but, should you yourself clearly see your error, how can you then be in any wise offended at me, for respectfully exhorting, or rather intreating you, to correct that error, that you may escape the miserable end of every sinner, who is deluded by it? Hear me therefore attentively.

2. But, before we go further, let me ask, who among you, with the means before him of at once avoiding some imminent bodily danger, would at the same time with his eyes open continue in it? Where is the prisoner, when able to strike off his chains, who would delay his escape? Where is the sick person, when able to get rid of his malignant disorder, who would defer his recovery? Where is the shipwrecked sailor, when able to reach the harbour in safety, who prefers still sporting with the billows? And is there any one of you, who, being able now to secure the salvation of his soul, will carelessly wait for another season? Did you ever apply your mind to consider the exceeding stupidity of Pharaoh, when he hardened his heart against the famous plagues of Egypt? Moses said to him, "Take good care; for, if thou refusest to let my people go, thou shalt suffer for it. I will not subsidize a mighty army of soldiers to destroy thee. I will not invoke the lightnings from above, nor bring the lions from their forests, nor the bears from their caves. What then? For thy deeper disgrace, I will raise against thee armies of frogs from their slimy pools. These weak puny creatures shall defend my cause against thee. They shall besiege thy houses; they shall take possession of thy saloons; they shall hunt thee out of thy chambers." Pharaoh laughed at the threatenings; but ere long his laughter was turned into mourning. From every pond, from every river, from every fountain burst forth, at a signal given by Moses, a countless host of clamorous frogs. These, like soldiers, who press on to the sack of a city, spread themselves in every direction. They made themselves masters of the chief positions, they obstructed the thoroughfares, they forced their way into the houses; and triumphantly advancing to the Royal palace they attacked Pharaoh on his very throne. Did he run to some place of shelter? They forcibly, as it were, unearthed him out of it. Did he recline at his banqueting table? They compelled him to get up. Did he lie down to rest? They obliged him in

a fit of rage to spring from his couch. Only conceive, what must have been his state of mind, on seeing himself at the mercy of these desperate assaults? He called for Moses; and, as if bowed down with sorrow under a sense of his misconduct, " 'Tis enough," he said to him, " I give in. Entreat the LORD your GOD to take away this plague from me; and I will then grant your request; *I will let the people go, that they may do sacrifice unto the Lord.*" (Ex. viii. 8.) Moses, his mind being set on the repentance and not on the destruction of this wicked man, replied: " Well : I agree. Tell me, *when* do you wish that I should pray for your deliverance? You shall immediately be heard: *Set me a time; when shall I entreat for thee and for thy servants, and for thy people, to destroy the frogs from thee and thy houses?*" (viii. 9, Vulg.) Pharaoh, on hearing this, paused to reflect on the matter; and thus replied, " *To-morrow, to-morrow* I wish you to entreat the LORD for me :" and accordingly it so came to pass. Now is there one among you, my brethren, who can listen to this narrative, and not be astonished at the stupidity of Pharaoh? What a madman! He finds himself hemmed in and persecuted on every side by these dreadful enemies, whom he cannot escape; and yet, when an immediate deliverance is offered him, he interposes a delay, and would have a little more time: *And he said, To-morrow*. . . . And " Why not to-day ?" exclaims the most eloquent S. Ambrose. " When placed in such jeopardy that he ought to have asked him to pray directly and not delay a moment, he answers *To-morrow:* poor, idle, easy man, fated to pay the penalty of his procrastination with the destruction of Egypt!" I am convinced that there is not one among you, who will not smile at such absurd conduct on his part, or be disposed to pity him. But if the man, who shows so little anxiety for his bodily preservation, is to be regarded as a fool, how are we to speak of you ?—of you, I say, who, though exposed to the risk, not of a temporal but an eternal loss, who, though always invisibly besieged, not by poor puny frogs but ferocious devils, contending with each other in their eagerness to tear your wretched souls out of you, who, though knowing you are rebels against GOD, exiles from Paradise, and sentenced to hell, yet cannot, in despite of all this, make up your minds immediately to fly from such imminent danger? Have not you also within your reach tender-hearted men, who like Moses, are ever nigh at hand with the offer of deliverance? *Set me a time.* The Priests are constantly ready to help and direct you, to provide you with the sure means of escape and deliverance, if the sinner will only apply to them. Why then do you so long delay? Can any of you say in reply, *To-morrow?* Yes, indeed, ye stubborn men, this is your too common speech, "Put it off." I converse with this person, and say to him, "Sir, you are keeping up highly improper connections: bad women, like leeches, have preyed upon your bodily health and your property: your soul is still left to you: don't you wish at last to secure its salvation? *Set me a time!* When do you wish to abandon these connections, to wipe away these stains from your conscience, and to recover God's favour?"—"*To-morrow:* that's the time;" these unclean livers will answer me: "I am still in health. When I am near dying, I will repent." I converse with another person, and remonstrate with him: "Sir, you are cherishing vindictive feelings of hatred in your heart. Your angry passions, like furies, have disordered both your youth and manhood. Old age is still before you. Don't you wish, after all, to end your days in peace? *Set me a time.* When will you cease from strife, propose a reconciliation, and agree upon some friendly terms?"—"*To-morrow;* that's the time;" these self-avengers will answer me: "I am still in the vigour of my strength. When I am near dying, I will forgive." Oh, what is this you say, blinded blinded men, that ye are? *To-morrow!* Well, have your own way. Give the rein to your lusts. Indulge them to the fullest extent: but, in this case, you must first manage to make your escape from a flood of questions, with which I now intend to overwhelm you.

3. For, tell me, since you reckon upon accomplishing such great things on your dying bed, have you yet discovered for a certainty what particular disease is to carry you off! No doubt you have pictured to yourselves that your last decline will be that of the swan, all calm, genial, and delightful; your spirits more on the alert, your thoughts more alive at that hour than ever. Oh! how grievously are you deluded! What

doctor then have you found so skilful, as to assure you of this? *Man knoweth not his time*, saith the Preacher (Eccl. ix. 12.) May not your last sickness be rather some fever, which will suddenly deprive you of your senses, and throw you into a fainting fit, a delirium, or a frenzy? May it not be some lethargy, which will quite stupefy your faculties? May it not be a convulsive seizure? May it not be a swoon? May it not be a violent stroke of apoplexy? Or, if none of these, may it not be a pain in your head, so excruciating, as not to allow you to think for a moment on anything you wish? Believe me, you have no security whatever, however strong your constitution may be, against sinking under one of such attacks. So far from it, if we are to credit Hippocrates, the stronger sort of people are more liable to strange diseases, than are the more advanced in years: for it happens with the humours of the body, as it does with the strings of a musical instrument, which the more they are tightened and sharpened the greater risk they run of a more violent rupture. But I return to my question. Are you prudent in cherishing this hope of being converted in your last sickness, when you do not even know what your last sickness may be? We will suppose it to be such, as will leave you in sufficient possession of your senses. Behold you now in still greater danger; because you will hardly believe that such a sickness, as this, can ever terminate fatally. You will then rather flatter yourself; you will go your own way; you will act, like the lazy traveller, who, on falling in with the mountain torrent near its source, cannot make up his mind at once to pass over it, but talks about getting over a little lower down; he then follows its course so far down, that at last, when he would pass, he finds there is no means of crossing. But, even should you have the rare good fortune of retaining your strength to the last, how and in what particular manner do you intend to employ it for your salvation? You intend, you say, to make a true confession of your sins: but what gives you courage to expect that at a season so precarious, and, what is worse, so full of distraction and terror, as are the last moments of a man's life, you will be able to prepare yourself for such a confession by a close examination of your conscience, and by a full and accurate remembrance of your sins against GOD, together with all their minute circumstances and aggravations?

4. "Perhaps not," you will say; "but what does it signify? If this should not be possible, don't we all know that certain signs, when a man is dying, are sufficient? A bend of the neck, a pressure of the hand, a striking of the breast, these, even when we are incapable of uttering a single word, are still left us, as means of making our peace with GOD." Ah, Christians, can I hear such things spoken without turning frantic, and astounding you with my yells and groanings? Wretched man! What is it you say? Why, what a madman's speech is this? Who has robbed you of your senses, and so utterly divested you of all common humanity, that you evince less anxiety in arguing a case, thus affecting yourselves, than if it related, I say not to a stranger, but to an enemy? Is a confession, made on a death-bed by signs, sufficient to make your peace with GOD? It certainly is, you say; nay more, you say you may by this means get absolved from any sin whatever and at the hands of any Priest whomsoever. . . . Is it then really come to this, that, in your general ignorance and neglect of the sacred doctrines of our religion, you have yet managed to get some knowledge of those only, which by being perverted in their meaning will help to involve you in perdition? Observe well. This confession you are speaking of is a last resource. And who does not know that all last resources and remedies are very uncertain in their effect; and that, in consequence of this, we should only use them from absolute compulsion, and never from our own choice? Can you then believe that the absolutions, however many they be, received by a dying man, have the effect of immediately obliterating all his past transgressions? "Yes, I can; if the man truly repents, if he has a right intention of mind, if he comes prepared with all those inward dispositions, which are requisite to a good confession." But, pray, who is to insure you all these requisites? Have you not long accustomed yourselves to drink in iniquity with a relish, comparable to that of Lysimachus, who in his burning thirst gulped down a cup of water, which cost him an entire kingdom? Are you not wont to speak of your sins, as acts of gallantry

and fashion, to feel a self-complacency in them, and to boast of them in the company of men like yourselves? And how can you ever hope all of a sudden to change your temper and your style of talk, and to shudder at that, as being the greatest evil, which you now prize, as being the greatest good?

Who are they, whom you hope to convert to your opinion? Inexperienced children, I suppose, who know nothing of what true repentance is. But, let me tell you, you must make a convert to your opinion of a Jerome, who laughs at every kind of death-bed repentance, and says to this effect, "What sort of repentance must that be, which a man resorts to, only because he sees he has no longer to live?" You must persuade an Augustine, who calls it insufficient. You must persuade a Bernard, who calls it presumptuous. You must persuade an Isidore, who calls it doubtful. You must persuade a Cesarius, a Hugo, an Ambrose, a Gregory, a Chrysostom, a Thomas Aquinas, and other such men, who all of them treat your opinion with undisguised ridicule and contempt. What more can we say? S. Cyprian, the great Bishop of Carthage, went so far as publicly to enact that no Priest of whatever rank in his diocese should presume to administer the ordinance of reconciliation to any sinners, who, having despised it during their lives, should ask for it on their death: he pronounced that the repentance of such persons was no repentance at all. "We have decided that persons should be excluded from all hope of receiving the Holy Communion and the benefit of absolution, when they first apply for it in a time of sickness and of danger; because it is not repentance for their sins, but the alarm of approaching death, which compels them to urge the request." I know very well that this saint of God erred in his decision; because it is just possible that a sinner of this description even on his death-bed may heartily repent: but, at the same time, when a holy man of so much learning, of so much wisdom, and of so much experience came to the conclusion that the thing was not possible, surely we must, at the least, take it to be not quite so easy, as you think. Do not however make a mistake here; because it is just possible that at the very last you may repent of your sins. But how repent?

Can you tell me this? Why, repent, as Antiochus did, who lamented that he had ever persecuted the Jews, because on this account he had to be eaten up of worms; as Cain did, who bitterly bewailed his treachery towards his brother, because on this account he had to be a vagabond in the woods; as Hagar did, who regretted that she had behaved ill to her mistress, because on this account she had to be turned out of doors; as Saul did, who felt very sorry that he spared the Amalekites, because on this account he had to lose his kingdom; as Shimei did, who retracted his reproachful words against David, because on this account he had to fear his being put to death. Just so say I of you. There will be nothing so wonderful in your being sorry for your many offences committed against GOD; but this will arise from the abject fear you have of death, from hell being open to your eyes, from damnation being close at hand; so that, were such punishments removed to a distance, you would cease to be concerned for the sins, which exposed you to them.

5. Independent of this, think you, that Lucifer, who has enjoyed so long and so complete a tenure of your souls up to that last moment, will quietly allow himself to be thus robbed of them? And for such a trifle? It rather will be his time to put forth all his rage. "There be spirits," writes Ecclesiasticus, "that are created for vengeance, which in their fury lay on sore strokes" (xxxix. 28.) You cannot but know that, when a battle is near its close, the whole power of the army is brought into the field: no soldier is left to stay in his quarters; every troop and company, the whole reserve is ordered out. And why? Precisely because that is the last decisive hour of the battle. All now is at stake. Should defeat then ensue, adieu to all further hopes of victory: should victory then ensue, adieu to all further fears of defeat. Therefore at such a crisis every nerve is strained to the utmost. Now conceive to yourselves something very like this happening at our death. The hellish one knows that everything depends upon this moment. And Oh, his fury at this moment! How much more savage will he be! Won't you believe this on my credit? Believe it then on the word of the LORD in the Apocalypse: *The devil is come down to you*

having great wrath. Behold him, for he comes against you in a most terrible fury; behold him, behold him, *having great wrath! having great wrath!* And whence arises his extraordinary rage? *Because he knoweth he hath but a short time.* (Rev. xii. 12.) If he takes you then, there is no further danger of his losing you. Prepare therefore at this crisis to have him ordering out all his Furies together, as in the field of battle; to have him unchained, and let loose near your dying bed, engaging you in the most deadly conflict, to which his wrath can possibly excite him. . . . And will not these evil spirits have the best of it, when it will be seen that the accusations they bring against you are all perfectly true—so many hypocritical prayers, so many profane Communions, so many obscene jests, so many daring calumnies, and, as I was on the point of saying, such habitual depravity? Will they find it a difficult matter to make you believe that it is all over with you, that hope is utterly excluded in your case, that your salvation is quite impossible? More than this. You have long accustomed yourselves to speak with great boldness on matters of religion: how very easily then may the spirit of infidelity seize upon you, filling your minds with doubts on some mystery of the faith? More than this. You have long accustomed yourselves with sad irreverence to profane the Name of God: how readily then may the spirit of impiety seize upon you, causing you willingly to assent to some blasphemous indignity against God? More, still more. But why need I take any further trouble? Explain to me, and I shall be satisfied; explain to me only a single one of these difficulties, which I have been able in a few minutes to urge upon you in this most important inquiry. Stand on your defence: parry and ward off the blow, should you think there is a chance of your evading me. What will you say? That you rely on the help of your Christian brethren? But how will you dare look face to face on those persons, whose name you have so often despised? That you rely on the protection of the Almighty? But how will you have courage to apply to Him, whose worship you have so little observed? That you rely on the power of that heavenly Grace, which at other times has given you strength to effect your deliverance? But do you not see that this is quite a fallacy? God has given you strength at other times: therefore He will continue to give you strength now. I deny it, I deny it. The conclusion does not follow: and, if you wish me to make this clear to you, listen to me.

Is there one among you, who has ever felt disposed to sympathise with Samson in his melancholy history? Not one, I should think; because by his own rashness he brought his disgrace upon himself. The case is remarkable. He was lying in the arms of such a harlot, as Delilah. Bribed by the Philistines, she endeavoured to discover the secret of his great strength. "Tell me, Samson, how is it that no power on earth is too strong for you? Suppose a man wished to overcome you, what should he do?" "It would be very easy," replied Samson. "If I were bound *with seven green withs, that were never dried, then shall I be weak, and be as another man.*" (Jud. xvi. 7.) The wicked woman sought to know no more. She gets these withs from the Philistines, she contrives her plot, she forms her ambuscade, and, having bound her wretched paramour, "They are at thee, Samson," she exclaims; *the Philistines be upon thee!* Samson gives a shake with his arm: and *he brake the withs, as a thread of tow.* Delilah feels ashamed at being so mocked in the presence of her countrymen. "Ah! treacherous man," she says to him, "is it in this way that you mock me? How can I ever believe you love me, if you won't let me into your secrets, if you hide your heart from me?" Samson listens the second time, and tells her that he must be bound with new ropes. Delilah binds him accordingly, and repeats her former cry, *the Philistines be upon thee, Samson!* He with a mere shift of his body extricates himself from the strong bandages, as if they were made of a spider's web. The woman, becoming more enraged, renews her attempts, first by way of reproof, and then of inquiry: and he in like manner answers again, telling her that he must be nailed to the floor of the room by the hairs of his head. Delilah nails him accordingly, and cries aloud, as before, *the Philistines be upon thee, Samson!* He with a mere lift of his head draws the nail from the floor, as one would a rush from the sand. . . .

See to what straits this guilty female had reduced him! Three times she had handed him over to his enemies; three times she had brought him to the very brink of destruction: and yet he still cleaves to her. Nay, he does worse; he becomes blinded and infatuated to such a degree, as at length to reveal to her the true cause of his superhuman strength—that it was placed in his hair. This was all she wanted. She recalls the Philistines; she lays her ambuscade afresh; she lulls her miserable paramour to sleep on her lap; she has the razor brought; she makes a man shave off the locks of his head; and then she awakes him, and casting him off from her arms throws him into those of his enemies, exclaiming, like one overjoyed, *the Philistines be upon thee, Samson!* Samson awakes out of his sleep; and, thinking that he could effect his escape after the same manner he had done before, says with a feeling of inward complacency, *I will go out, as at other times before, and shake myself.* But it was no longer the time; for the LORD already *had departed from him.* Thereupon he was bound, blinded, and ignominiously dragged away, as a prisoner, with nothing but his life left him.

Search, my hearers, the Scriptures through, from the beginning to the end, you will scarcely find an example more calculated to illustrate the folly of sinners. But let us consider it well, in reference to our subject. What was it, which completed the ruin of unhappy Samson? Was it only his love to Delilah? No, Sirs: it was that false presumption of his, which led him to brave future risks, because he had fortunately escaped preceding ones. *I will go out, as at other times before, and shake myself.* This was the fallacy, that betrayed him; and these are the fallacies, which betray sinners throughout the world by their not perceiving that the day will come, when *the Lord will depart from them.* Take the case of a young man, charged with the commission of some capital offence: he finds it going hard with him: hasten, and give him some comfort. "O Father, let GOD by His gracious help only get me out of this sad affair, what a change you will see in me! Never again will I be found in those haunts of dissipation, which have reduced me to my present distress. I'll never touch a card again. I won't even look at the dice."

The man does get off. At first his behaviour is guarded; afterwards he begins by gentle degrees to draw near to his former associates. What harm, he thinks, can come of it? "Can I ever again be involved in the same trouble? And, even if I should, did I not on a former occasion contrive to escape? *I will go out, as at other times before, and shake myself.* Come; let's resume our play." Take the case of an old man, found implicated in some fraudulent money transaction. He falls sick: hear how he expresses himself. "O Father, if GOD would only be so gracious to me, as to restore my health, what a different man I shall be! I will never embark again in those usurious speculations, which now weigh so heavy on my conscience: never again will I oppress the widow: never again will I defraud the hireling." The man does recover. At first he is very circumspect; afterwards he also begins by gentle degrees to get ensnared in the same old bird-lime. What harm, he thinks, can come of it? "Can I ever again be brought into my former difficulties? And, if I should, will it be for the first time? *I will go out, as at other times before, and shake myself.* Come; let's return to our usury." Is it then so? *I will go out, as at other times before, and shake myself.* It is false, it is false. You are unable to do this: for *the Lord will depart from you.* To infer, that, because GOD has helped them in times past, He will therefore help them for the future, without observing how He first hides and withdraws Himself, then forsakes them altogether, is a mode of reasoning, which deceives many; and therefore, Christians, look well to your own state, nor suppose the mercy of GOD to be so great, as never to allow Him to abandon you in the hour of your death to the power of the devils, as it did Samson to the clutches of the Philistines .... You say, that GOD will protect you at the last, because He is merciful; and I in return, say to you that, because He is merciful, He will not protect you. Are you surprised at hearing this? Does it sound new to you? Does it appear strange? I will place it before you in a clear light, and then conclude.

7. If GOD be merciful, as unquestionably He is, then, to act consistently with this character, ought He to have in His view the private salvation of yourselves only, or rather, much

more, the general salvation of the whole human race? The general salvation: this is clear. But how many, who were previously well acquainted with your disorderly and reckless life, when they come to observe that your death, notwithstanding, was as prosperous, as that of a righteous man, would be encouraged by such a precedent to frame their own lives accordingly! On seeing this, how many weak brethren would be secretly offended! What a snare might it prove even to good men! How would the wicked presume upon it! And how many souls would thereby lose heaven for one single soul, which should gain it!

The mercy of GOD therefore is concerned, even perhaps more than His justice, to provide that, as a general rule, the bad liver should meet with a bad end: otherwise, who can doubt, but that the whole world would soon be peopled with wickedness, the Churches deserted, the Clergy dishonoured, and that, in the eyes of the ignorant vulgar, shame and ridicule would be attached to the names of an Hilarion, a Macarius, a Saba, an Arsenius, and their fellow-saints, men foolish enough to pay so dearly for what most Christians, however faithless and wicked, were in the habit of getting almost for nothing? Observe, I said, most Christians: for I am ready to allow that some few persons, of invariably most abandoned lives, have died happily. I grant this. But what does it prove? Jonah, when cast into the sea, what time the tempest raged at its height, found a whale to receive him into its belly, who after three days vomited him up on the shore alive and well. (Jonah ii. 10.) Will you take occasion from this, when your life is endangered in a storm, to say to the sailors, "Quick, cast me into the sea?" Or, would you not rather stand firm, and keep your ground, as long as there was a plank left for you to cling to? Joseph found a prison to be the path leading him to the first distinctions of Egypt. Will you take occasion from this to court renown by putting your feet into the stocks? Mordecai found calumny the means of raising him to the highest honours of Persia. Will you take occasion from this to advance yourself by making people hate you? And, if it be permitted me to mix profane with Sacred history, I might adduce what Pliny relates respecting a man named Falerius. He was afflicted with an obstinate cancer, and had spent all his fortune to no purpose in trying to get it cured: quite despairing of his recovery, he then plunged into the thickest of a battle, where an arrow struck him on the part affected, opened a wound for him, and extracted every particle of its venomous matter: in this way he recovered. What then? Will you take occasion from this, should you ever suffer from a like disorder, to go about making inquiries for some scene of uproar or fighting in your city, that you might risk your life in the quarrel? The thing is absurd: and why? Because a few rare instances should never furnish the rule of conduct to a wise man. Don't be surprised then, if sometimes a wicked man is converted on his death-bed; because this happens extraordinarily, and because God would never absolutely cut us off from all hope: and so, in this point of view, would distinguish us from the finally condemned. On what ground, however, do you rest your pretensions of being so highly favoured? Have you received any extraordinary promise to this effect? or any special revelation? Or, does your present design, that, I mean, of repenting, when you come to die, give you courage to hope for such a result, just as if by this design you were showing a respect towards God, instead of doing Him an insult? Speak out now, once for all, and speak distinctly: explain to me, what you mean by this speech of yours, "Before I die, I will repent?" It is nothing else than mocking God in fine language. It is virtually saying to Him, "Lord, I promise to leave off offending Thee, when I have no longer the power or the time to do so. I will sacrifice my will to Thine, when I can no longer do, as I like. I will mourn over my outrages against Thee, but only, when I shall be unable to increase them. I will yield to the stern necessity of confessing that I have done wrong in rebelling against Thee, when the chain is about my neck and the halter about my throat. While I am my own master, I will have my own way; and I am determined on no account to leave my sins, until my sins leave me." Behold here the true interpretation of this accursed design you have of never repenting, till you come to die: and does it then appear to you that God will feel Himself highly indebted to you for this mark of respect, which may be more correctly called a downright insult? Most certainly He will not. If so then, throw down your rebellious arms and allow that you are vanquished.

The Second Part.

8. . . . .

9. Listen now to a dreadful and horrible story. A nobleman of an illustrious family, but of bad moral character, was deeply enamoured of a young female of Moorish origin, whom for his wicked purposes he had for many years living with him under his roof. He disregarded both the severe warnings of the Priests and the sportive remarks of his friends; and, in order at once to get rid of every troublesome interference of this kind, he was in the habit of sternly and indignantly rejecting every reason, offered him, why he should dismiss her, by saying "*I cannot:*" he said this, as if he would have men believe that his own corrupt free choice was a kind of natural necessity imposed upon him. While he thus continued unwilling to break off this bad connection, it so happened that death came to do it for him. The unhappy man in the flower of his age fell sick. He gives himself over and takes to his bed: and, as he was now pronounced in danger, a certain Priest, well known to me, comes to prepare him for his last struggle. He enters the sick room, he approaches the bed, he accosts him, and in the most prudent manner gently proffers his spiritual aid. "I am glad to find, Sir, that in your case there is more ground for hope than for alarm. You are still young; you have a strong constitution, and you don't look so very unwell; numbers too have recovered from this sort of disorder: nevertheless, I am bound to say, that many have sunk under it: and, however pleasant it is to one's feelings to rank you among the former, still, what harm will there be in your preparing yourself, as if you belonged to the latter?" "Tell me, then," anxiously replied the sick man, "tell me, what is it my duty now to do? for I am ready to obey you. From what I feel I am quite aware of the greatness of my danger, which is

more than you suspect; and, though I may have led a bad life, notwithstanding this, I desire beyond anything else to die well." It is quite incredible how the good Priest felt encouraged on hearing these words: he would at once have pointed out the necessity of his breaking off the bad connection: especially as, to his sorrow and disgust, he saw the female in the room at the time: for the nobleman had always some excuse or other for having her constantly about him. But prudence suggested the expediency of paving the way for this more difficult sacrifice by first requiring of him something more easy. Accordingly, he addresses him thus. "Very well, Sir; since, by God's blessing, I find you so religiously disposed, I will speak with that freedom, which both the sanctity of my profession and my zeal for your happiness dictate to me. All the medical men have given you over: only a short time is now left to you for settling your conscience and making your peace with God."—"On this very account," the nobleman answers, "let us be quicker about it. What must I do?"—"Are you," the Priest then demands, "in debt to any person, whose claims must be satisfied?"—"I was in debt; but it's all settled already."—"Are you now possessed of the property of any person, to whom it ought to be restored?"—"I was; but I have restored it."—"It is possible that you may have borne ill-will towards some one: if so, do you now lay it aside?"—"I do lay it aside."—"Do you forgive your enemies?"—"I do forgive them."—"And you ask pardon of those, whom you have offended?"—"I do ask their pardon."—"Well; is it now your desire to receive, for the last time, like a good Christian, the Holy Communion; as a means of strengthening your soul against the assaults of the devil and the terrors of hell?"—"Most willingly will I receive it, if you will have the kindness, father, to administer it to me."—"But are you aware that this cannot possibly be done, unless you first dismiss this young woman?"—"Oh! as to that, father, *I cannot, I cannot.*"—"Alas! what is this you say, I cannot? Why cannot you? My dear Sir, this is what you ought, what you must do, if you wish to be saved."—"I tell you, I cannot."—"But don't you see, that in a very short time you will be compelled to part with her? Surely there is no such great difficulty in your resolving to do that of your own free will, which at all events you must soon be obliged to do from necessity."—" I cannot, Father, I cannot." —" How? Cannot you grant this favour to a GOD, once Crucified for you, and who now asks it of you? For you He was mangled on the Cross; for you He was besmeared with Blood; for you He was obedient unto Death. Does not this thought soften your heart and make you relent?"— " I cannot, I cannot; I once more tell you."—" But consider; you will be deprived of the Holy Communion."—" I cannot."—" But you will suffer the loss of Heaven!"—" I cannot."—" But you will be banished into Hell!"—" I cannot."—" Is it possible that these should be the only words I can get from you? Unhappy man! Hear me: is it not far better for you to lose this woman only, than together with her to lose your reputation, body, soul, Life, Eternity, CHRIST, and Paradise; and then, as dying excommunicate, to have the vile burial of a brute beast?" Heaving a bitter groan the poor wretch then returned to his former reply—"*I cannot, I cannot,*" and, collecting for a last effort his little remaining strength, he on a sudden grasped the bad woman by her arm, and with a loud voice and a highly impassioned expression of countenance broke out in these words, which, I solemnly protest, are the very words he used, neither more nor less—" She has been my glory in my life; she is now my glory at my death; and she shall be my glory for ever!" Having said this, he forcibly pressed her to his bosom and embraced her; and so, what with the vehemency of his action, the agitation of his mind, and the violence of his disease, he desperately breathed his last in her polluted arms.

Have you listened, my Christians, to this true story? See, in it, the last straits, to which sinners are brought: they are obliged to cry out, "*I cannot, I cannot.*" And why so? Why, if they had the will, did they want the power? We cannot deny them the power; because a sufficient grace is never withholden from any one on his asking for it. But, in a case like this, in the case of a man of such confirmed bad habits, something more than a sufficient grace is required. It must be that grace, which was called by S.

Augustine "triumphing grace;" that, which entirely subdues and casts down the stubbornness and rebellious opposition of men; in a word, it must be effectual Grace. But this is so high a favour, that God is not bound to give it to any person. He is not bound by the law of Providence; nor is He bound by the Law of the Gospel. He can deny it to whom He will deny it. And is it not just, that He should deny it to those, who, often as they might have had it, never once cared about it? *They said unto God, Depart from us, for we desire not the knowledge of Thy ways.* (Job xxi. 14.) Go now, in proof of what I say, and speak to a certain class of men, who will immediately answer you; "I cannot, I cannot." "If I now dismiss that woman from my house, I make myself the gossip of the neighbourhood."—"Restore that property." "If I do it, I am ruined."—"Restore that injured reputation." "If I do it, I shall risk my own credit."—"For God's sake, be reconciled to your enemy." "I cannot; can I bear to have the man, who has so grievously wronged me, now all of a sudden looking boldly in my face?" And so it is, with this wonderful "*I cannot*" people think to evade their duty. Ah, ye deceivers, Ah ye, who suffer yourselves to be deceived, God forbid that you should ever have to say in truth what you now openly adduce, as a pretext! S. Augustine tells you, "The most just recompense of sin is, when the man, who would not do right, when he could, on his being willing to do it, is unable." No, my Christians; now is the time for you to work out your salvation; now take pains: now improve the grace God gives you while the season of grace lasts. *We are replenished with Thy goodness, O Lord, in the morning.* (Ps. xc. 14, Vulg.) Therefore delay not the time, till the *evening.* And let this further consideration prevail with you; that they, who are converted in the evening, shall *suffer hunger, as dogs.* (Ps. lix. 6, Vulg.) And why? Simply because the poor creatures arrive, when it is too late: they arrive, when the supper is over and the table cleared.

SERMON XII.

ON SHAMELESSNESS IN SINNING.

S. MATTH. XXIII. 5.

"ALL THEIR WORKS THEY DO FOR TO BE SEEN OF MEN."

1. ONE of the most envied men of all antiquity was a certain Gyges. By the virtue of a magical ring on his finger, he had the power of making himself invisible. Hence he could commit any sort of crime without a blush on his countenance, or the least fear of detection in his mind. This man, I assert, was to be most envied: because, as all sinners court secresy, they would have given the world to possess the privilege of casting a dark shade around them at all times and whithersoever they went. If this Gyges, being tempted by such a security, violated a queen with her consent, murdered a king off his guard, and raised himself from his former poor condition of a shepherd, as Plato relates, to be the ruler of Lydia, I can well fancy that other people also, more wicked than he, would never have suffered chastity to remain uncorrupted, nor a Royal treasure in safety, nor any rival in peace. All of them without any restraint would have freely gratified their bad propensities: and thus the whole world would have been polluted with the sins of impurity, violence, and bloodshed. Notwithstanding all I have said, supposing a ring, like this of Gyges, was now publicly exposed for sale among a

Christian people, few in my opinion would show any great anxiety to purchase it, though they might have it at half price, or almost for nothing. And why so? Is it because Christians at the present day have no wish to commit any sin? or rather is it, because they know the absurdity of attempting to conceal from their fellow-men what they cannot at the same time conceal from GOD? Would to heaven, my hearers, that such were the true reason! The reason is this—(I pray you, be not offended at my presuming frequently to speak to you with so much freedom)—because now-a-days Christians are not afraid to commit their sins openly, even in broad daylight; and, so far from any anxiety to conceal them, they contrariwise pride themselves on this very account. They talk about them in society; sing about them with their guitars; parade them at the theatres; and, as the Apostle says, make what should overwhelm them with shame, a matter of boasting. *They glory in their shame.* (Phil. iii. 19.) But whither does my overheated zeal transport me, so that I forget the Gospel, from which my text is taken? CHRIST at this time was reproving the Pharisees, because, when they occasionally performed some good works, they ostentatiously desired to be seen, to be noticed, and to be praised of men. They had no inclination modestly to hide their virtues, as the sea hides its jewels and the earth its gold. *They do all their works for to be seen of men.* But I was somehow rather disposed to think lightly of their sin. Certainly no such Pharisees are to be found in our times. Could I find any, and did CHRIST graciously allow me, I should not only make some excuse for them, but even hold them up before a certain barefaced people among ourselves, as worthy examples to follow. We have, indeed, far outstripped the Pharisees. For, if a feeling of pride induced men in those times to conceal the bad, and boast of any good in them, the contrary now holds with us. We are induced to conceal what is good, and to boast of what is bad. "Christians," says S. Ambrose, "now think it a fine thing to be wicked, and, when they fall into sin, regard it, as something, that does them credit." You will not therefore wonder at my having withdrawn my thoughts from the Pharisees to fix them nearer home, only suffer me, I pray you, in this discourse, to vent my grief and indignation against all such shameless offenders.

2. No sooner, however, do I enter upon my subject, than the holy prophet David takes the words from my mouth, and, as though deeming me not half alive to the cause in hand, nor zealous, as I should be, against so great a sin, cries out in my stead, *Why boastest thou thyself in thy wickedness, who art so mighty in iniquity?* (Ps. lii. 1, Vulg.) He seems to me in these few words to express very deep meaning. For, on serious consideration, is there any greater blindness to be found than that of *boasting ourselves in our wickedness?* Search carefully throughout the various occupations of mankind, where will you find a man, who was proud of his having committed an error? Herodes Atticus, the Athenian, the first orator of his day, as he was making a speech in the presence of the Emperor Marcus Antoninus, was suddenly seized with loss of memory; he wandered in his thoughts; he became speechless, quite unable to recover the thread of his argument: he descended quickly from the rostrum. Do you believe that he considered this to redound to his honour? Quite the reverse: he felt so ashamed of it, that he fell sick, and, losing all relish for food and resigning himself to despondency, was very near dying. Did Labienus consider it any honour to himself, that he had published those works, which were openly condemned by the Senate? Quite the reverse: he resented it so deeply, that he endeavoured to shelter himself in a catacomb. Did Sophocles think it any honour to himself, that he had produced on the stage a tragedy, which failed in obtaining the unanimous applause of the people? Quite the reverse: he was so affected by a sense of shame, that he went and inflicted on himself severe corporal punishment. And that invincible son of Emilius Scaurus, how did he behave? Did he plume himself on the fact of his having deserted his post in a battle? So far from it, he regarded himself on this very account quite unworthy to appear before his father, and scrupled not to plunge a dagger into his bosom; and so, overwhelmed with shame, he rushed out of the world. It is then only as regards religion that men find in their conduct matter for proud self-compla-

cency? Has such a one succeeded in his well-contrived project of adultery? How he rejoices! Has another succeeded in his well-concerted project of revenge? How he talks about it! If this courtier has attained his end in blackening and traducing the innocent man, who stood in his way, does he not chuckle over it among his intimate friends? If that steward has cunningly managed to swindle the widow lady out of her property, does he not pride himself upon it among his compeers? And shall this then, I again ask with David, be to you a matter of boasting? *Why boastest thou thyself in thy wickedness, who art so mighty in iniquity?* Do not ye profess yourselves to be Christians, to be Catholics? How then can you ever make a boasting of what is so directly at variance with your most noble profession? Unhappy man! What other inference can we draw from such conduct than this, that your state is desperate and incurable, and that consequently it will be a very difficult thing for you to escape everlasting perdition?

3. I am well aware that to despair of the life of any patient, even when the symptoms about him are fatal, savours more of a gloomy physician, than a wise one. The great prelate Leo teaches me that, so long as life remains in the body, we must not despair of a sinner's repentance; but in every instance cherish hope. Nevertheless we have in no case less ground to hope, than in regard to those, who have accustomed themselves to sin wilfully with a high hand against GOD: and all such sinning we know to be a sure sign of a man's being "accustomed to do evil." No one, the first time he sins, sins with a bold face, but rather with a blush. Too strong is that aversion, which nature, not as yet perverted, entertains against sin. It yields indeed to temptation, but it is with fear; it commits sin, but it is with misgiving. Hence it arises that in the first stages of a bad life men avoid the thoroughfare; they court secresy; they suspect the walls; and when they succeed, as Seneca observed, however glad they are to enjoy the fruits of their sin, they conceal the sin itself. Nor must you suppose this only to happen, where people are afraid of their liability to be punished in case of detection. No, Sirs; although we are sure

of escaping both detection and punishment, we shall wish, if novices in wickedness, the thing not to be known. We shall hide it; and, should it be discovered, we shall be overwhelmed with the deepest confusion. This can only be ascribed to that instinctive horror of sin, which belongs to our nature.

4. Was ever a sin committed with such impunity, as that of Cain? I beg your attention to this. No court of law was yet opened in the world to adjudicate in matters of wrong. There could be no fear of prosecutors: judges were not in existence: executioners were unheard of: the very name of punishment was unknown among men. What now had Cain to fear? There was no other family then on the whole earth, as S. Ambrose seemed to think, save that one, which, had it revenged Abel by putting Cain to death, would have been left utterly childless. And supposing, which is the more probable opinion, other families had existed at the time, which of them would not have shown deference to Cain? He was the great progenitor of them all, still in the prime of life, of a strong frame, of a determined character: and yet, notwithstanding all this, when he first conceived this design of murder, what care and precaution did he not employ? I can well imagine the horror of his soul, at this early stage, when envy of his brother's goodness first inspired him with his bloody purpose. Accordingly, Scripture testifies of him that before the commission of the fatal act *his countenance fell* (Gen. iv. 5,)—a concise phrase, intimating that his colour fled, his aspect was troubled, his eyes were sunk in his head, his cheerful expression gone, his whole countenance changed. Oh, how many restless nights was he doomed to suffer! How many broken slumbers! How many horrid dreams! Summoning courage at last to do the deed, think of the contrivances he had to resort to! He feigns toward Abel the utmost attachment and friendship; *Let us go forth abroad* (Gen. iv. 8, Vulg.) He got as far off, as he could, from the house; he sought a distant spot, a secluded meadow: and there uplifting his treacherous arm he smote him on the head. *It came to pass when they were in the field that Cain rose up against his brother and slew him.* And why, let me ask, was he at all this trouble? Whatever place he might fix on, was not Abel

entirely at his mercy? Was he not older than Abel, more courageous, and better armed with opportunities for his purpose? Abel had not the remotest suspicion of any harm intended him; and therefore went about always easy in his mind, always off his guard. Cain, on the other hand, was hatching mischief; and therefore went about always ready, always prepared: in fact, he proceeded with nearly as much caution, as a man would use at the present time, when, for the terror of all evil-doers, we have so many appliances at hand for the detection, the conviction, and the punishment of crime.

And do we not trace here a striking illustration of that horror, which sin occasions, the first time it gets possession of a soul? It does not then dare go abroad with an open countenance: it wears a mask; it dissembles. So anger is masked under cheerfulness, envy under courtesy, hatred under love. We fly, when there is no one to pursue; we hide ourselves, when there is no one to see; we tremble, when there is no one to punish. And that this is really the fact, need I tell you, my hearers, what punishment GOD afterwards inflicted on Cain for a sin of this description? It was not to make the earth swallow him alive, as it did a Korah; nor was it to burn or blast him with lightning. What was it then? It was to leave him, after the commission of his sin, to the effects of that fear he felt in committing it. "For all his offences," writes S. Chrysostom, "he received but one penal torment—that of fear." He had no other punishment, except this fear: and he was indebted to himself for its being the fear of a person, who had only just begun to sin, when the conscience, being not yet hardened, it is beyond belief what tormenting furies it encloses within itself, how it is vexed with disquietude, how it is loaded with shame, how it is torn with suspicion. *Every one that findeth me shall slay me.* (Gen. iv. 14.) Thus surmised the wretched man in the anguish of his soul. *Every one, every one;* as if *every one* was a witness of his crime, as if the very beasts of the forest were bound to resent it, to manifest against him their disgust and their abhorrence. To this effect Chrysostom after a divine manner draws his conclusion; "Such is the way of sinners: they suspect everything: they fear to be in the dark, they shake at the least sound, they suppose every man to be coming against them." Tell me, now, my brethren, if sin shows itself so terrible, when first admitted into the soul, as to raise so fierce a storm in the bosom of Cain, a man, whose breast was probably hard as a rock, and his heart fierce as a lion, what judgment are we to form of the state of those, who are unconscious of any such mental disquietudes? *They committed abomination;* and nevertheless, as GOD adds by the mouth of Jeremiah (viii. 12,) *they were not ashamed.* How shall we speak of certain characters, who not only are unconscious of any uneasiness, but derive thence a sensible pleasure? who not only do not court retirement, but delight to be in company? who not only do not attempt any disguise, but openly show their faces before the world? *who are glad when they have done evil, and rejoice in most wicked things?* (Prov. ii. 14, Vulg.) Is not this a clear sign of the soul's being already accustomed to evil? that it has now silenced the former admonitions of conscience? that it has now overcome early fear and deadened the first sensitive nerve of compunction? As long as we are conscious of any struggle within us, it is not possible for us to go any great lengths in iniquity. That inward worm, which preys upon the conscience—what inconceivable anguish does it cause us! Conceal, as best we may, the virulence of its poison, the countenance, fallen, discoloured, and faded, will betray it: and, when no such symptoms are visible, and when the sinner still wears in safety his former gay and easy manner, we have sad reason to affirm that he is sunk into the very lowest depths of depravity. *The wicked man, when he is gone into the depths of sins, despiseth.* (Prov. xviii. 3, Vulg.)

5. I remark that, in this passage, the HOLY SPIRIT does not define any particular way of despising, but states generally, *he despiseth;* and with reason. For, when a sinner has once overcome that sense of shame, which is the natural attendant of guilt, he despises every other kind of restraint. Give him seasonable advice; he *despiseth* it: place before him terrible warnings; he *despiseth* them: insist upon the wrong he does to GOD; he *despiseth* it: show him his immi-

nent danger of Hell; he *despiseth* it. In a word, he *despiseth* everything, reproofs, entreaties, hopes of reward, fears of punishment, GOD and man: all are alike to him; he *despiseth* them every one. He dares to say, *Who is Lord over us?* Judge therefore, brethren, for yourselves, how little hope can there ever be of the salvation of such wretched men? How can they amend, whose sin has become habitual? How can they bestir themselves, whose conscience is fast asleep? How can they yield, whose heart is hardened? There can be no moral probability of their salvation, when their conversion is thus made so difficult. It is not so difficult with a man, who sins with fear and trembling, or at least with some degree of modesty; according to the opinion of S. Gregory, "As the mind of man sometimes blushes to be seen, in regard to what it fears not to be, it will also sometimes blush to be, in regard to what it would not have seen." He, who is ashamed to appear vicious, probably in the main will be ashamed actually to be so: but how shall he take shame to himself for the fact, who has no shame for the appearance? The last feeling, of which wicked men divest themselves, is this desire of seeming to be good. Hence the miser gives to his grasping covetousness the name of parsimony; as Judas did, when he complained so bitterly of the ointment poured on the head of CHRIST, regarding it as an open wrong done to the poor. The coward designates his mean spirit by the name of cautiousness: the arrogant man his pride by the name of magnanimity: the unfeeling man his severity by the name of justice: and so of the rest. Who ever went greater lengths in iniquity than the treacherous Jezebel? Yet, all abandoned as she was, she did not dare to pollute her hands with the blood of that poor citizen, whose vineyard she had coveted, without first veiling her design under the comely mask of religion. She pretended that Naboth deserved to be punished, because he was a blasphemer: with this view she proclaimed a public fast, she assembled the Senate, she had the matter discussed before it. So far was this haughty queen from blazoning her wickedness in the sight of the world. Thus did an Amnon study to conceal his unnatural lust, under the pretence of being sick. Thus did a Haman study to conceal his savage rancour, under the colour of a public benefit. If then a person goes so far the other way, and sins so boldly, that he unmasks his faults, that he rejoices in them, that he exults over them, we must needs affirm one or other of two things: either, he does not view sin in the light of an immense evil; or, he does not consider disgrace to be a heavy punishment. And, when he has reached this extreme point, what hope remains of his recovery? It is so far excluded. He is so little likely to repent, that we cannot hesitate to assign him his place of punishment with Lucifer.

For I consider, and perhaps with truth, that Lucifer made an exceedingly proud boast of his own beauty, of his own perfections. *Thine heart was lifted up because of thy beauty;* so Ezekiel speaks in addressing him (xxviii. 17.) He boasted of his deep searching intellect, of his most extensive knowledge, of his most exalted rank: he boasted of the jewels, eclipsing all of their kind, with which his person shone resplendent. He boasted of his being the most brilliant image of the Divine Majesty, the most like Him in excellency, the most near Him in glory: so that no other creature stood between Lucifer and GOD. It may be that a pride of this particular kind may admit of some excuse, agreeably to the words of Isaiah; *Thy wisdom and thy knowledge it hath perverted thee* (xlvii. 10.) But, as for those wretched transgressors, who glory in their being clothed with iniquity and covered with shame, who value themselves upon their very offensiveness to a holy GOD, who make the most of the uncleanness and even brutality of their hearts and lives, what extenuation of their guilt can they expect? Will GOD suffer them to be proud of their vices, when He suffered not a Lucifer to be proud of his perfections? So far from it, those alarming punishments, which He has inflicted on the proud-hearted of every class, are expressly recorded, in my opinion, to put these men in still greater fear. For, if the giant Philistine was so dreadfully chastised, because he bragged of his strength; and Absalom, because he plumed himself on his fine hair; and Sennacherib, because he boasted of his army; and Haman, because he was puffed up with his power; and Antiochus, because he exalted himself for his conquests; and

Herod, because he was vain of his eloquence; and Nebuchadnezzar, because he glorified himself in his buildings; and Hezekiah, because he prided himself on his treasures; and a Pharisee, (a still more remarkable case,) because he was flushed with too good an opinion of himself, on account of his fasting, his tithes, so strictly paid, and his alms, so amply scattered;—if all these persons were severally and respectively punished, O heavens! what shall become of you, who are proud?—proud of what? proud of your falsehood, of your dishonesty, of your double-dealing, of your lying and malicious speeches, all which, instead of hiding them, as your shame, you make a boast of, as your credit? Can you expect GOD will show you any patience, while He is such a GOD, as Judith described Him—one, who breaks the horns of the high-minded, who "humbles all, who boast of their virtue?" (vi. 19, Vulg.) Can you expect Him to wait for your repentance, or to forgive your sin? It cannot, cannot be. This impudence of yours is carried much too far; and must therefore kindle, in proportion, the wrath of GOD against you, a wrath, never to be pacified.

6. And who among ourselves is not affected precisely in the same way? If a wrong is done us in private, we feel hurt by it; still, after all, we are more inclined to overlook it. There is no one, who knows it: we hear no one talking about it; and therefore it does not appear so seriously to injure our reputation. But, if the person, who wrongs us, goes and tells it to the public, that he may brag of it, how angry and indignant we feel! We decline the interference of friends, we refuse to accept any satisfaction, we will hear of no excuse. We think nothing short of a revenge, taken by our own hand, can wipe off the stain upon our character. Now suppose a similar case, in regard to GOD. One, who offends Him in private, with a certain degree of modest and respectful fear about him, does not so highly inflame His wrath; the offence not being public. But how aggravated must it prove, when a man proclaims everywhere the very fact of his having offended Him? In so doing he seems to come forward and protest that he regards not His laws, that he fears not His threatenings, that he does not mind His dealings, that he

does not respect His honour, that he does not value His friendship; and, by way of confirming this protest, he appeals to all those persons, in whose presence he described the outrage. It is no wonder then that GOD should so heavily chastise this insolent publicity in sinning. However this may be, one thing is certain, that a private offence, though in itself more grievous, will more easily be pardoned; whereas a public offence, although in itself more venial, will with difficulty escape punishment. This proposition I should not have dared to assert, unless I had the authority for it of S. Chrysostom. His words are express. "Although the sin of a man be heinous, yet, if it be done in secret, it will not be so severely punished as the sin of another, which, though less in itself, is aggravated by its insolent publicity." Did not GOD openly attest the truth of this fact in the case of a man, who was one of the dearest friends He had upon the earth? Look at the case of Moses. He had suffered greater troubles and annoyances in bringing the children of Israel into the promised land, than any, which fall to the lot of a commander at the head of his troops, when besieging a city. . . . Whether the Israelites were at peace or war, Moses was equally made to labour for them. Oh, how deeply mortified then must he have naturally felt, when, just on the brink of the land he so much longed for, he received the intimation of his death! *I have caused thee to see it with thine eyes: but thou shalt not go over thither.* (Deut. xxxiv. 4.) He had spent his strength; but another was to gather the fruit: he had endured the hardship; but another was to carry off the honour.

And now, for what cause did GOD treat Moses with such marked severity? Can any of you tell me this? Was he not a man most correct in his conversation? most subdued in his temper? most devout in his religion? and most zealous for the LORD? He was indeed all this: but simply, because he once spake unadvisedly with his lips, GOD was so bitterly provoked to anger, that it was afterwards impossible to appease Him. You remember the incident. The people were fainting with thirst in the wilderness, and with loud menaces demanded of Moses something to drink. Vexed with their contumacy he lifted up his rod, and crying with a loud voice, *Hear now, ye rebels,* he said; *must we fetch you water out of this rock?* (Numb. xx. 10.) Then suddenly recollecting himself, as conscious of having spoken distrustfully, he sought to correct with his hand the fault of his tongue; and, as he smote the rock with this intent, behold the plenteous stream gushed forth, as if to reproach him for his incredulity. But it was too late. For GOD, unsatisfied with such an amends, suddenly appeared to him with an intimation that, since he had stumbled at the Divine promises through his distrust, he should not have the honour to inherit them. A just punishment this. And yet, to tell you the truth, I am not altogether satisfied in my mind about it. Tell me, was this the first time the good old man had sinned by distrust? Surely before now he had committed equal, if not greater, offences of this kind. It is a recorded fact that, not knowing on one occasion how to feed so vast a multitude, he distrusted the power of GOD Himself to supply the means, and went so far as in a familiar kind of way to take Him to task, treating Him as incompetent, and almost reprimanding Him, as being a mere boaster. Hear his words; whether they were not full of daring. *The people among whom I am are six hundred thousand footmen: and Thou hast said, I will give them flesh that they may eat a whole month. Shall the flocks and herds be slain for them to suffice them? or shall all the fish of the sea be gathered together for them to suffice them?* Still, the LORD gave him a most gentle answer, only referring him to the evidence of a miracle, in proof that His words were not the words of a boaster. *Is the Lord's hand waxed short? Thou shalt see now whether My word shall come to pass unto thee or not.* And then on how many other occasions did he evidence an obstinate spirit against GOD? Did he not resist, when GOD wished to send him on an embassy to Pharaoh? How stubbornly he stood out against accepting the charge of leading his people through the wilderness? Afterwards, did he not many times show his reluctance? Did he not indulge in fits of anger and in complaints? Did he not even ask for death, as an escape from his troubles? *If Thou deal thus with me, kill me, I pray Thee, out of hand: and let me not see my wretchedness* (xi. 15)—as if GOD was now reduced to a strait, and had no other way left to protect or comfort him. And yet on not one of any of these other occasions did God punish him: He rather answered him with invariable kindness, encouraged, and strengthened him. It was only this hasty slip of the tongue, when he talked of fetching water out of the rock, which was so severely chastised. Now why was this? I do not wish you to listen to what I say, because my interpretation here may have no weight with you; listen to that of S. Chrysostom: "Nothing else could rob Moses of the rewards promised him than the single offence he committed at the rock; which, being in its nature less than his other offences, was nevertheless more strictly judged. For his former sins happened in private and under concealment: but this was done publicly and before all the people." Can there be a clearer explanation? The sin by the side of the rock, although it might be less considerable, was committed openly. Those other acts of his incredulity were, it is true, more considerable; but they had hitherto been kept in secret; no one saw them, no one heard of them, no one knew them; and hence God did not resent them in so signal a manner. But of this last the whole multitude was a witness; and therefore, albeit Moses was so far from boasting of it, that he lamented it, it could not, on this very ground of its being so well known to others, go unpunished. My dear Sirs, so long as we sin in doors with the curtains drawn and the doors closed, we do ill, most ill: for God sees us everywhere. *There is no darkness where the workers of iniquity may hide themselves.* (Job xxxiv. 22.) Still, we may entertain in this case some greater hope of pardon. But when we sin in public, let us indeed fear and tremble; because then we shall beyond all doubt have to give a most rigorous account and to exercise a most bitter repentance. *The show of their countenance doth witness against them: they declare their sin; they hide it not. Woe unto their souls!*—Why this woe? *For they have rewarded evil unto themselves.* (Isa. iii. 9.) But gently here awhile. When a person utters a threat, does he not intend a future harm? The prophet therefore should have said, Woe unto them, "because they *shall* reward evil unto themselves;" not they *have* rewarded. Yes, Sirs; but the punishment hanging over the heads of these scandalous sinners is so sure, that it may properly be said to have already lighted upon them.

7. And, in point of fact, what are the sins, which so mightily degrade the Name of CHRIST among the enemies of His religion? Are they the secret sins? By no means. They are the public sins. Yes, my brethren, the public sins. The thing, that brings discredit on our religion is the well-known fact that among Christians the modesty of their females is publicly exposed to sale by certain persons, so that there is scarcely a district in their cities, where a Tamar may not be met with; that the arts of impure love are publicly taught at their theatres; that pictures, calculated to excite lascivious thoughts, are hung up in their public galleries; that books, having the same pernicious tendency, are read in their public schools; that obscene jests are with wanton licentiousness banded about at their midnight revels; that, even in their public Churches, assignations, smiles, and jesting are going on, or at least an uninterrupted talking, with as much impudent coolness, as if it were in a common street; that usury of the basest sort is publicly allowed; regarded, too, not as reflecting disgrace, but as indicating cleverness; that personal enmities, even of a fatal character, are publicly defended; regarded, too, not as causing ignominy, but as denoting courage; that resistance to Ecclesiastical authorities, that contempt of the Clergy, that defamation of their Sacred character, are things of common occurrence; and—(which is worse than all, so that I shudder in mentioning it)—that the most Holy Name of GOD is publicly blasphemed in the hearing of all, in their streets, in their shops, in their private dwellings, in their taverns, in their clubs, just as if it was the name of some infamous wretch; and, all the while, not a single person is to be found in the company, who will faithfully discharge his duty by resenting the insult. These are those sins, which bring the faith of CHRIST into contempt among His gainsayers: *The Name of God is blasphemed among the Gentiles.* (Rom. ii. 24.) So long as they know that sin among Christians is modestly concealed, they have no doubt that virtue among Christians is prized; for nobody would ever conceal what he prizes himself for: but when they know that sin among them

goes abroad with an open forehead, that it is made a matter of self-complacency and of boasting, what would you have them report of us? They must needs be of opinion that with us goodness is at a discount, that wickedness is in high favour, and that it is not only a shame to be a follower of CHRIST, but a credit to be His enemy.

8. Then, too, how often do we carry matters so far, as to cause the sins, done by us in secret, to become public sins by our way of talking about them! It is not enough that our sins of impurity should have their birth in the darkness; we expose them to the light. Let walls conceal them, let doors shut them in, let the night with its thickest security mantle them over, it is not enough. No, Sirs; we must trumpet them forth at our clubs, we must relate them in our coteries, we must sing about them on our guitars; and, in order that every sin we commit may be public, we divulge all that we do in private. And is this, think you, a trifling offence? Is it possible, think you, to have any hope of that person, by whom it cometh that the credit of religion is thus placed in jeopardy, and the friendship of CHRIST is so scandalized? I repeat then, *Woe unto their souls; for they have rewarded evil unto themselves!* These are not offences, that carry with them an easy hope of pardon. Hear how GOD in His anger cried aloud to Jerusalem by the mouth of Jeremiah, *Shall the holy flesh take away from thee the crimes, of which thou boastest?* (xi. 15, Vulg.) As if the LORD should say, "Something more than your sacrifices is now required to pacify My wrath. These, I admit, would suffice, if thou wast ashamed of thy sins, and didst hate, bewail, and lament them. But thou art gone so far, as to *boast* of them: and therefore your case is desperate. Miserable city! Thou owest Me the penalty. To Death! To Death! See the Chaldeans, how on their mounted chargers they dash upon thee to execute My revenge! I care no longer for your sacrifices. I care no longer for your whole burnt offerings. 'Tis your own blood, that I must have. *Shall the holy flesh take away from thee the crimes of which thou boastest?*" So GOD once spake to Jerusalem. Never, if it be His Blessed Will, may He have cause to speak in the same way to any of our cities!

The Second Part.

9. It now remains for us briefly to consider two points, relating to this publicity in sinning, which we have so strongly condemned. The first is, what ought we to do to repair the past injury? and then, what can we do to prevent its recurrence for the future? In regard to the first, our course is obvious. Any person, conscious of having caused some grievous scandal to religion by his misconduct, must now apply himself to do just as much, with a view to do it credit; being now converted to GOD he must have no wish to be like many, who really seem to shrink from the idea of their being seen to perform any good action .... Such base cowardice, in thus concealing the fruits of his repentance, would be quite unpardonable in the man, who had committed his sins in public. *That which you have said in your hearts mourn over in your secret chambers:* these are the words of David. (Ps. iv. 4, Vulg.) I am quite satisfied with them. If your sins have been committed by you within, in your own *hearts*, you are allowed to exercise the various acts of repentance of them in your *secret chamber.* It is not however so, if your sins have been divulged to other people. In that case it is necessary for you to resolve on rising superior to the opinions of the world; so as not to evince a shame in doing good, which you never felt in doing evil. You must henceforth publicly attend all the Ordinances of the Church. Your religion must be visible in the sight of all men. In a word, you must redress the wrongs you have done; and you must contrive to render back to GOD a full equivalent for the open shame and dishonour you have inflicted upon Him. Hear how the Apostle addresses the Romans on this duty; *As ye have exhibited your members servants to uncleanness, even so now exhibit your members servants to righteousness* (vi. 19, Vulg.) Have you marked the expression, *ye have exhibited,* and the corresponding one, *now exhibit?* Secresy in what is to be done is here quite out of the question. You have manifested yourselves, as sinners; you must now manifest yourselves, as true penitents.

10. So much for the reparation of the past injury. And now for the best way of effectually preventing its recurrence for the future. What means can we discover the most safe, the most simple, and the most direct? I will tell you. Persons, invested with any kind of public authority, must advance, patronise, and reward the good; and they must on principle discountenance the bad. Then every one for his own interest, even though his life be wicked, will try to get the credit of being thought good;[1] and therefore he will no longer make a boast of his sins, but will conceal them: and thus the desire of the favour of one man will bring about that end, which the fear of the disfavour of a GOD could not accomplish. Oh, did our rulers in Church and State know at what little cost they might preserve outward decorum in their respective spheres of authority, they would be astonished at the influence they possess! Only let them profess with David, *Mine eyes are upon the faithful in the land, that they may sit with me* (Ps. ci. 6, Vulg.;) that is to say, let it be known, that nothing will have so much weight with them in a man's favour, as his virtue, and that nothing will so much tell against him, as his vice; that they will look, not to party connections, but to personal merit; not to the recommendation of friends, but to the qualifications of the man himself; not to any private feelings of their own, but to a sense of public justice. Only get them to act on this rule, and you will then see how the most aspiring candidate for promotion will try to appear the most honest man. And what I here assert of a public man in his relation to the State, I assert of a private man in the rule of his establishment; I assert of a family man in the ordering of his household. If any such person requires in his dependents a good character, even though he has it not himself, he will

---

[1] Though we may not doubt the practical expediency of such a course of conduct, we must surely object to its moral impropriety. Looking simply to the individual, without respect to public benefits or probable consequences, to urge him to pretend to a goodness, which he knows that he does not possess, is to make him add sin to sin. In other words, the end will not justify the means. This was, however, the mildest form, which the doctrine of *intention*, carried to such lengths by the Spanish Jesuits, could well assume. Segneri was of too pure and upright a mind to be misled by their immoral sophistry. He was a thorough disciple of Loyola, but not of Escobar.

be doing more for the public benefit, than if, when having it in himself, he did not require it in them. And, as a general rule, in every Government small or great, civil or ecclesiastical, were it once known that the good would be preferred and the scandalous rejected, the unblushing boldness of sin at least, if not the actual commission of it, would already in a considerable degree be taken away.

11. But, you will tell me, this seems a more likely way to encourage hypocrisy, than to promote virtue: for so, in order to be thought good, the appearance will suffice; the reality is not necessary: accordingly, on this principle, men of worldly ambition, if they can only hide their vices, will never be at any pains to correct them; and the consequence will be, we shall have in our cities many seemingly good people, but few of them really good. Dismiss such an apprehension. Of all vices, that of hypocrisy is found the most difficult in practice. We may wear a mask for a short time; but we cannot wear it long. The sham of goodness becomes in itself irksome, when divested of all truth. Hence you will find on inquiry that there are far more profligates in the world than hypocrites. These last have all the distasteful part of virtue, and none of its pleasantness. Theophylact observed of them, that, "though they may for a season feign successfully, yet sooner or later they are detected." The occasions of sin are so continual, its allurements are so frequent, its incentives are so strong, its appeals come so close and home to our hearts, that no mere outward human respects can possibly bear up against them all: and, at the best, should we resist minor temptations, we should yield to greater ones. On the other hand, do you know what will happen, on its being known in any Government that the less religious are kept in the background? This will happen. Such persons, by dint of practising a feigned virtue, will conceive a liking for a real one. They will begin on a worldly motive; but afterwards they may come to be led by a Heavenly motive. At all events, they will be a check to those grievous scandals, which arise, when men are not only allowed to be wicked, but are entitled openly to appear so. . . . . Or, is it possible that the love of CHRIST should fail in exacting of us what a respect

for men can obtain? "That, which the fear of man extorts from us, we ought to yield to the love of CHRIST." So spake S. Augustine to the same purport. Did we know that any among our superiors would exclude from his friendship all persons, who did not make an open profession of religion, that he would not admit them to posts of honour, that he would not advance them to any lucrative office, that he would not bestow on them any of the preferments in his gift, we should, one and all, take very good care to make the open profession required: and, when CHRIST deals with us in this same manner, shall He not so far prevail, as to restrain us at least from glaring and outrageous sin? Oh, what a disgraceful, Oh, what a heartrending reflection is this! Has then a temporal ruler more influence over us, than a Heavenly? a human friendship, than a Divine? a fleeting advantage, than an Eternal? CHRIST by the mouth of S. Paul publicly denounces sinful men; *The unrighteous shall not inherit the kingdom of God.* (1 Cor. vi. 9.) Yet how few, in consequence of this, forsake their sins! He condescends to the mention of particular offences, and cries aloud, *Neither fornicators*—and yet what indulgence in the sins of impurity! *neither adulterers*—and yet what unfaithfulness to the marriage tie! *nor effeminate*—and yet what looseness in men's sensual appetites! *nor abusers of themselves with mankind*—and yet what brutishness in men's carnal lusts! *nor thieves*—and yet what fraud in payments! *nor covetous*—and yet what sordidness in gains! *nor revilers*—and yet what excess in evil speaking! *nor extortioners*—and yet what impudence in swindling! If a Prince were to adopt no other measure than this, to take this very text of the Apostle, and, having copied it out with his own hand, to order it to be conspicuously hung up in the most frequented streets and thoroughfares—only with this alteration, that, whereas S. Paul wrote "*Shall not inherit the Kingdom of God,*" *Kingdom of God* should be struck out, and "*my friendship*" inserted in its place; meaning that they should not enjoy his favour, nor his preferments, nor any of his rewards—Oh, what a vast improvement should we soon witness in the public morals, as to all those particular sins, which are here mentioned! . . .

SERMON XIII.

THE CURSE ENTAILED ON ILL-GOTTEN WEALTH.

S. MATTH. XX. 21.

"GRANT THAT THESE MY TWO SONS MAY SIT THE ONE ON THY RIGHT HAND AND THE OTHER ON THE LEFT IN THY KINGDOM."

1. IF there was ever a poor person in humble life, who sought to benefit her family in an honest way, it was unquestionably the blessed mother of James and John. Earnest was her desire to raise her sons from a boat to a throne, from the fisherman's craft to power: hence she would have them placed, as the principal assessors of CHRIST, *one on His right hand, and the other on the left*, now that she thought Him just about to establish His earthly Kingdom in Judea. But she did not forward her designs by those unjustifiable means, which are now commonly resorted to. She did not set about persecuting any of the other Apostles, who might stand in her way and prove her most formidable competitors. She used no artifice, she laid no traps; she had recourse neither to flattery, nor to any kind of bribery, open or concealed, in order to gain the good will of the new Sovereign. What then did she do? After she had for some length of time bound over her sons to the laborious service of CHRIST, after she had sent them to accompany Him in a poor and needy condition, after she had so frequently exposed them, as His disciples, to the ridicule of the people, to the hatred of the Scribes, to the contempt of

the Pharisees: yea, after she had herself left her house and her home, and bidden farewell to all her domestic duties and engagements, in order that she might follow Him whithersoever He went—after all these sacrifices, made for His sake, she did no more than simply appear before Him and cast herself at His feet with this respectful supplication, set forth in the most simple and artless manner, *"Grant that these my two sons may sit one on Thy right hand and the other on the left in Thy kingdom."* So far, however, was CHRIST from entertaining her ambitious request with any mark of His approval, that He rejected it as foolish, and by His answer, *Ye know not what ye ask,* publicly overwhelmed the petitioners with shame. Where now are those persons, who, in their eagerness to advance and enrich their families, are not content with employing such means, as are lawful and innocent, but proceed to falsehood and trickery, to oppression and cruelty, to calumny and sin? Where are they, who, in order to compass their end, dare to deliver false judgment in our courts of law? Where are they, who misconstrue wills and documents of that nature? Where are they, who oppress the hireling, and who defraud the Church of its due? Where are the many, whose constant aim it is to oppress the orphan, to cheat the widow, and to wind their way into minors, that are expecting property, so as to suck and drain them to their very last drop. Let all such characters come this morning to hear me. For I wish them to see in a clear light what evil counsels they are following in such weighty matters. For how stands the case? Does CHRIST in this instance make no allowance for that strong natural affection, which prompted a mother, in other respects so meek and exemplary, to make her request for the aggrandizement of her family? And will He spare a like desire in the man, who would aggrandize his family in spite of Him? Oh, pains ill taken! Oh, solicitude badly employed! You wish then to raise your house by means of usury, of rapacity, of plunder, of oppression, in consequence of the extreme love you bear it. Listen, and you will learn how cruel is a love like yours, if love it can be called.

2. In the first place, how is it possible that you do not see

with your own eyes the utter insufficiency of these artifices to gain your end? If your heirs would behave like Christians, it is quite certain that they will never retain a single farthing of the property you have so wickedly acquired for them. On your death then they must return to their former condition: they must give up their expensive establishments and luxurious mode of living. In a word, to use the language of Job, they must *vomit up again the riches they have swallowed down* (xx. 15.) And what, if they should be unable to reconcile their minds to such a loss? What must happen? Why, GOD Himself will come, and with His own hand drag these possessions out of their very bowels; *God shall cast them out of his belly.* What do I mean to say? I mean this. If they are bent on retaining a particle of what they have no right to, behold, GOD immediately becomes the sworn enemy of your family: and then, tell me, do you think you can leave it, when exposed to so potent an enemy, in any tolerable degree of safety after your death?

I remember to have read of Julius Agricola, a powerful senator of Rome, how, on his incurring late in life the hatred of the Emperor Domitian and being by him deprived of his most extensive estates and most distinguished honours,—yea, poisoned, as some writers tell us,—he prudently concealed his sorrow for these heavy losses; and, being more anxious for his family than for himself, he had recourse, when about to die, to this extraordinary measure. He made his will: and in it he declared, first of all, the Emperor to be his chief heir: he took care to speak of him in the strongest terms of gratitude, such indeed, as might have been rather expected from a slave, raised to the Consulship, than to a Proconsul, carried off by assassination. Persons less discriminating were astounded at such a strange decision; and they viewed the conduct of Agricola, as savouring of the insane folly of a man, who would sooner part with his life, than give up his habit of flattering Princes. But the wiser sort did not regard it in this light: they saw clearly that it was more to the advantage of an honourable family to have a poor inheritance left it, accompanied with the friendship of their King, than a rich one, charged with his enmity. And so it was; the event proved that Agricola had acted in this business with that admirable good sense, which he had always displayed. And, to speak the truth, just tell me; supposing that you were to be placed in a like critical condition, would you not infinitely prefer leaving your family in the possession of a smaller fortune, but having a Prince in its favour, than with a larger fortune, but having a Prince against you? Indeed to leave your family exposed to any considerable enmity, though it were only that of a private individual, would cause you much anxious thought; and my belief is, that you would spare no sum of money, if at any cost you could heal matters before your death. If it be so, how is it that you fear so little to leave to your successor a GOD for an enemy? Do you then look upon GOD, as so weak, as to be incompetent, or so stupid, as not to be concerned to take His just vengeance upon you? Rather hear how He spake to Malachi of the people, who in spite of Him would raise their houses on high, yonder in proud Idumea; "Go on building, go on building; the end will show, which has the stronger arm; they to erect, or I to destroy. *They shall build, but I will throw down.*" (Mal. i. 4.) Even so, LORD, may it ever be!

3. Haste, and make your search in the Divine Scriptures concerning all those families, who have succeeded to the wrath of GOD, together with their ill-gotten wealth; and then return, and tell me, whether illustrious birth, or powerful family connection, or large property, or vast incomes, or even Royal pre-eminence, was in a single case among them of any avail. You will, on the contrary, find this to be the very cause, which moves the Almighty to act in some extraordinary manner. You know the general rule, laid down in the Law, that *the son shall not bear the iniquity of his father* (Ezek. xviii. 20.) GOD, as absolute LORD of all, has, however, sometimes dispensed with His own law. For the sin of the father He has punished not only the sons, but the grandsons and great grandsons; and this even to the fourth generation; inasmuch as the fourth was the last, which any father, getting far advanced in years, could ever hope to behold. And if you inquire for what particular *iniquity* of the fathers GOD was wont to take such extreme vengeance upon the children, you will

find it was solely their ambitious desire to enrich them with ill-gotten possessions. By ill-gotten possessions Achan sought to enrich his children, when, in spite of GOD's prohibition, he stole in Jericho a certain sum of gold, which he secretly found (Josh. vii. :) and hence it was that not he alone, but his whole family with him, was cast into the fire. By ill-gotten possessions Gehazi sought to enrich his children, when, with the help of sly and cunning falsehood, he took from Naaman a part of the presents, which the prophet Elisha had refused (2 Kings v. :) and hence it was that not he alone, but all his descendants with him, were smitten with leprosy. By ill-gotten possessions Saul sought to enrich his children, when in disregard of the warning of Samuel he covetously reserved the spoils of the vanquished Amalekites (1 Sam. xv. :) and hence it was that not he alone, but all his offspring with him, was deprived of the kingdom. By ill-gotten possessions, Ahab sought to enrich his children, when by an open injustice he took from Naboth the vineyard, which he was unable to get from him by lawful means: and hence it was that not he alone, but his whole progeny with him came to a violent end (1 Kings xxi.) And yet this Ahab (a thing almost incredible) left his family on his death propped up with no less than seventy children, all of them, too, males: this fact, combined with the family's being so amply provided for, and having such widely-extended branches and connections, gave a fair promise that it would pass through continued generations and endure for many ages. Notwithstanding this, in less than fifteen years it utterly perished; utterly, utterly, without a single near or distant relative left surviving. *And Jehu slew all that remained of the house of Ahab . . . he left him none remaining* (2 Kings x. 11.) So that you learn from these instances that from this sin of ill-gotten possessions, not only the parents, who commit it, but even the children also, for whose sake it is committed, are brought to suffer; and with them the grandsons, and with them the great-grandsons: it being a most proper thing that man should bear the punishment in that particular, for the sake of which he perpetrated the offence. How then, with a view to aggrandize your family, can you bring yourselves to employ those very methods, which are precisely the very ones to destroy it? Do you think it can promise itself any permanence, whilst it has that same God for its enemy, who in so short a time could sweep away families so populous, yea, so proud, so magnificent, and so mighty? Should you have no doubt nor misgiving in this matter, do then as you like: but if the danger is evident, what folly it is, for the sake of leaving your successors somewhat more comfortable, to leave them so wretchedly insecure!

4. If, my hearers, you had to build a house, I don't suppose that you would set about building it in the cold of winter; no; you would rather wait for the summer, and would gladly choose any season in preference to the one, which is most severe. And why so? Because houses built in the winter are not durable. The frost and the rain have such an effect upon the mortar, that the stonework does not take firm hold and settle. Now what, pray, is it to build your house with another man's money? It is to build it in winter. Hear this stated in Ecclesiasticus, " He that buildeth his house with other men's money, is like one, that gathereth himself stones in winter" (xxi. 8, Vulg.) This is tantamount to building in winter, as all commentators affirm. You are building in the winter, my Christians! You are building in the winter! Stop your work; otherwise your house will soon crack, and shake, and totter, and come down, and all the labour you are bestowing upon it will be utterly lost. *Woe unto him that buildeth his house with unrighteousness and his chambers with wrong:* so exclaimed Jeremiah (xxii. 13;) and Habakkuk to the same effect, *Woe to him, that buildeth a town with blood,* (that is, the blood of the poor,) *and stablisheth a city by iniquity* (ii. 12.) And do you give more credit to your own foolish plans than to the sure warnings of these Prophets? Think of the many, many, many once illustrious families, which we see every day completely ruined on this very account. They entirely lost sight of the fatal end of those torrents, which, because they wish to extend and enrich themselves by the help of other waters, are therefore much sooner exhausted, than the inoffensive rivulet, that thrives on its own resources. Zaccheus said to Christ, *If I have defrauded any man I restore fourfold.* What was our Lord's

reply? *This day is salvation come to this house, forsomuch as he also is a son of Abraham.* (S. Luke xix. 8, 9.) Pause here a moment. Was not this a strange reply? Ought He not rather to have said *to this man,* since Zaccheus himself had committed those thefts and frauds, the ill effects of which he would now immediately repair? It would seem from this that the salvation spoken of was to be his alone. Yes; but the LORD understood this matter better than we do: and He therefore did not say *to this man;* no, *to this house, to this house:* for He clearly perceived that, had Zaccheus failed to make restitution, he would not have been the only person to suffer the punishment of those filthy accumulations of lucre, although he had been the only person to make them.

5. Come, however; let it be, as you desire. We will grant that the enmity of GOD will never do your family the least harm. We will grant that by ill-gotten possessions you may ensure its perpetuity and obtain for it a nobler name, a wider influence, and greater connections. And do you suppose that therefore your plan will succeed? "Oh most miserable of men!" Let me express what I deeply feel in the words of that great prelate Salvian; "O most miserable of men! You take much thought how others may live after you: you take no thought at all how ill you yourselves may die!" And who has ever taught you to value so highly the temporal prosperity of your offspring, as to embolden you to risk on its account the Eternal happiness of your own soul? Oh, most deplorable blindness! Do you then stand so low in your own estimation, as to be quite willing, for the sake of any one else, to cast yourselves into the ever burning flames, there to rave with reprobates and howl with devils? Hitherto I have always been given to understand that every man loved himself beyond every one else: from my childhood that simple aphorism of Terence was imprinted on my memory, "All wish better to themselves than they do to others." Alas! I must now unlearn this celebrated truth: for I perceive there are numbers in the world, who contrive with all their might the advancement of others and the ruin of themselves; who, if only others may abound in the pleasures of time, deliver themselves up to the flames of Eternity. And what greater harm than this could your cruellest enemy do

you? It is true that your enemy might persecute you: but how far? To your bier, to your grave; but not an inch beyond. For "death puts an end to all human enmity," observes the same Salvian in his argument. But you are not content with so little as this. No, no: "You so manage the case against yourselves, that not even after your death you shall evade your enemies." It is not enough that you spend your days upon earth in toil and trouble for the benefit of your heirs, plunging yourselves up to your very neck in every kind of worldly distraction and annoyance; but, over and beyond this, you carry your self-persecution into another world: and, after you have wasted your health and peace of mind for the sake of others, you do not hesitate to suffer the loss of your souls and of Paradise for them. And who of your enemies, however inhuman and inexorable, could inflict on you so sore an injury, as this? See the truth of the words of Habakkuk confirmed in your case; *Woe to him who heapeth together that which is not his own!* O thou fool! thou fool! Knowest thou what thou art doing? *How long also doth he load himself with thick clay?* (Hab. ii. 6, Vulg.) He does not say others, but *himself, himself:* because, while seeking with a love so strangely cruel to benefit others, he ruins himself, lading himself with that same heavy clay, under which he must finally succumb. And you see here by the way, Christians, what GOD Himself calls that gold, which is the idol of your supreme choice and affection: He calls it mud, *thick clay.*

6. It may be, however, that you will find, when in hell, some comfort from knowing how grand and glorious your successors now are. So far from it, it will be this very knowledge, which probably more than anything else will torture your soul—only to reflect that they are so triumphant at your expense, and that you are so miserable from the love you bare them. Wretched indeed will be your condition, should this dismal lot (which GOD forbid!) befall any person among us— the loss of his soul for the sake of enriching his family. How often every day would the ill-fated sufferer gnaw his lips at his own outrageous folly! How often would he curse that day, when he first opened his eyes to see the sun! How would he curse that hour, when he unloosened his tongue to the accents

of speech! Meanwhile, the spirits of darkness would be crowding around him, and would say to him with the most insulting bitterness, "Cheer up; cheer up. We are just come from the earth, and there we have seen, one after another, all the members of your family. They are well, every one of them lusty and strong; they are in the full enjoyment of that patrimony, the acquisition of which brought you down here among us. One of them is now in attendance at the court of such a Prince; another is settled with a certain Lady; another has managed to get into a fine piece of preferment, and will soon aspire to the Prelacy. Why then, poor man, do you so mourn in your heart? Did not you choose for yourself a damnable death, if thereby they might rise higher in the world? You have made their fortune. Therefore be of good cheer. You had no scruple to drain the blood of the poor and to despise the labours of the hireling, in order to leave behind you a rich dower for that daughter of yours: well; she has succeeded in forming the very matrimonial alliance you so much coveted for her: you have grandsons growing up; there is even a hope that great-grandsons are on the way: yet here you are, wretched man, howling, and fretting your soul!" Christian friends, do you think that reflections, such as these, would ever succeed in yielding you the least comfort? I think quite the contrary. They would rather penetrate into you, like arrows, darted forcibly into the very centre of your hearts—*mighty sharp arrows with hot burning coals.* (Ps. cxx. 4.)

Again, you must not reckon upon retaining that affection, you now feel towards your offspring. That affection will then be totally changed into rancour, envy, bitterness, and cruel rage. We read of Agrippina, mother of the Emperor Nero, that, being anxiously bent upon her son's advancement to the sceptre of Rome, she employed every available means she could find to effect her purpose, beyond even what became her sex. The Chaldean soothsayers, whom she consulted on this weighty business, all agreed in telling her, that, should she obtain the sovereignty for him, he in return would cause her death. "What is that to me?" replied the aspiring woman, "Let him kill me: only let him reign. Let Agrippina die, provided that Nero be Emperor!" But, when once she had succeeded in her design, Oh, how altered was her conduct! No sooner did she perceive, though still from a distance, in the cruelties of her son on his coming to the throne, the preparatory signs of her own death, than she immediately began to repent of that, which had been the prime object of her ambition. Behold her (a thing almost incredible) even now undertaking to remove Nero, her own son, from the throne, and to substitute Britannicus, her step-son, who indeed by right of succession was the lawful heir. She went so far, as actually to tell Nero that she was on the point of appealing in her own person to the army, and of prevailing on the soldiers, by dint of her importunate harangues and tears, to resolve on the election of a new Emperor. But threats, like these, more furious than wise, were of little service to the wretched woman: they only inflamed the anger of Nero to such a height, that he first had Britannicus poisoned; and shortly after, under the mask of doing her honour, had his mother confined in a palace. Now, tell me, what is your opinion? Had any one gone to visit Agrippina, while she was raging within her prison-bounds, like a lioness in an inclosure, or a tigress in chains, and had said to her, " My most Serene Highness, what is it, that afflicts you? Were not these your own express and emphatic words, ' Let Agrippina die, provided that Nero be Emperor; let him kill me, only let him reign?' How then is it, that you have now so soon forgotten them? But take comfort: your son already sits triumphant on that throne, which you have procured for him by your wisely directed, not to say, your wicked exertions. He now exacts tribute from foreign provinces. He receives the submission and homage of the army. And his power is even consolidated by the death of the youthful Britannicus, who alone could have disputed his sovereignty. Let not then the imprisonment you are now suffering grieve you; nor let the prospect even of impending death alarm you: all these deplorable events were foreseen and yet chosen by yourself, if on such conditions you might secure the Empire for your beloved Nero." Please to tell me, my hearers, had any one addressed Agrippina after this fashion, do you think that it would have afforded her any consolation? It is far more likely that she would have broken out in a more desperate passion, knowing that there was none, but herself, against whom she could vent her rage. And it is quite clear that no such arguments could tranquillise her mind: for even in her prison she set on foot as many base manœuvres, that she might wrest the Empire from her son, as she had before employed to bestow it on him. Indeed this proceeded to such lengths, that she had to vindicate herself publicly from the charge of high treason: and finally, after she had in vain sought to elude that death, to which she had been doomed, she showed in her last expiring struggle the intensity of the hatred she bare that very person, who had been once the object of her tenderest love. For, when she saw the officer enter her chamber with his drawn sword, ready at once to sever her neck, or thrust it into her bosom, like one in a frenzy of exasperation, she offered him her belly. "And here," she exclaimed, "here it is you must strike!" By this act she meant to express the detestation she felt for herself, or to signify the vengeance she would inflict on her own womb, for its having ever conceived a monster, or, to use a more fatal disastrous name—a Nero!

You will, I am sure, my dear Sirs, pardon me for having set before you at some length for your serious reflection an incident, which, though it be of profane history, may still prove instructive. For it seems to justify me in drawing from it this most certain conclusion. If a mother, who was so intoxicated by her love to her son, as to brave her own death in her attempt to make him Emperor, afterwards, when she felt this death to be drawing nigh, experienced such a complete change in her views and feelings, how will it fare with those miserable men, on their finding themselves doomed in hell to an everlasting fire, not indeed for having made their children Emperors—for this truly would be something considerable—but for having raised them a grade higher in society above their former station? Don't you think that they will rave with a degree of fury exceeding that of the ill-fated Agrippina? But go now this very day; go, speak to one of these avaricious money-makers, of whom we have been speaking, and say to him, "Beware, Sirs, of what you are about: for these securities of yours are illegal; these notes of exchange are counterfeit. You may indeed succeed by your systematic oppression of the poor in raising money for the purchase of a commission in the army, or some preferment, or some title, for your son: but this may afterwards very likely prove the irrecoverable loss of your soul." What answer do you get from such people? They laugh at you; they tell you, if not with their words, at least with their actions, "What is that to me?" "Let him kill me, only let him reign. Let him kill me, only let him reign! Let my soul be lost, if my family be raised." Say you so? Oh wretched men! You know not now what is meant by losing your soul. But, when the hour for you to know it draws near, and when you behold yourselves besieged on every side with all the horrors of penal torture, with all the pains of hell, Oh, what a sudden and complete alteration will there be in the cruel love, you now entertain towards those of your house and kindred!

7. I feel quite assured—(listen well to what I say)—that, should the Almighty allow you a short leave of absence from hell, that you might return to them, you would enter your former house and abode at the darkest hour of the night; and gazing, when there, on the costly furniture and all the splendid refinements and decorations, which your own hands had collected by such wicked means, you would be unable any longer to control the fury of your soul: you would wish with the very flames, attached to your person, to set every thing around you on fire: you would burn those couches so expensively gilded, those damasks of the finest silk, those paintings so full of vanity, those precious well-filled coffers, those superfluous and gaudy dresses. In your rage you would rush to the stables and suffocate the horses: you would destroy with fire the gay equipages; you would proceed to the gardens, to the orchards, to the rural villas; and rushing to those farms and granges, which were bought with your sinful gold, you would instantly wrap them in the devouring element, together with the vines, the trees, the fish-ponds, the choice plantations, and all the stores of corn and forage; seeking in this way, like so many madmen, to discharge the fulness of your anger and remorse against those objects, which were the fruits of your sin.

But may God divert far from every one among you an

omen of such deadly import! May you rather candidly confess, if not to me, at least to Salvian, who makes the inquiry of you—Would it not be the height of folly for any of you to damn himself for the sake of another? "Oh sad and pitiful condition! Thus to procure with your possessions happiness for others, for yourself misery; joys for others, for yourself tears; pleasures for others, for yourself an everlasting fire!" Let your own salvation, your own happiness, your own soul be dear to you. How, Christians, can you rate it at so mean a price, as to hazard its loss for the sake of any relative, any kinsman, any adopted son whatsoever? Love your relations: this is all right; but next to your own souls. Love their temporal prosperity; but love more your own Eternal happiness. Love their earthly advancement; but love much more your own Heavenly glory. In a word, "We object not to your loving your children; only in a degree next after yourselves. So love them, as not seemingly to hate your own souls. For that is an ill-advised foolish love, which is mindful of others, but unmindful of itself." Thus far Salvian.

8. Howbeit, this really is not any love to our families, but rather a hatred towards them, expressing itself in a manner most inhuman and quite devilish. For hear me. Don't you see that, when you leave to your successors any portion of your ill-acquired riches, you thereby expose them to an evident danger of damnation? "All riches, procured by however honest means, are always dangerous, when excessive." Hence the eloquent observation of S. Cyril, "What are carnal riches, but the incentives of lust, the panders of corrupt desire, and the weights of death?" Peter of Blois confirms it by saying that "they are the destruction of virtue and the seed-plot of vice." S. John Chrysostom confirms it; he condemns them in every possible way, styling them "homicidal, bloody, implacable foes, ever maliciously plotting against their possessors." He speaks of them, as being "the winds, that stir up a continual storm; the wild beasts, that never cease to tear the heart; the flames, that constantly are burning up the world." "Hence," he declares, " arise our hatreds, hence our contentions, hence our wars, hence our misunderstandings, hence our evil speeches,

hence our thefts, hence our murders, hence our sacrileges." Therefore it is quite certain, as a general rule, that the more wealth you leave behind you to any of your relations, so much more danger also you leave them: nor do you act more considerately in this, than a man would, did he put into the hands of a little child a sharp-edged knife, simply because its handle happened to be studded with jewels. If this be true of all riches, how much more so of those, which, being the produce of sin, are wont, as it is well observed in Ecclesiastes, to prove the mothers of perdition. *Riches are kept for the owners thereof to their hurt* (v. 13.) How ensnared would be the conscience of your heir on his reflecting that he could not honestly retain a farthing of all, that your ungodly thrift had acquired for him! For him to restore it— this would be a hard task: and yet, if he fails to do so, it becomes his death. Who then does not see the ruin you bring on them by such bequests? And is this love? Is this, I ask, the tenderness of a father? It is rather malevolence: it is rather the rancour of a parricide. *A man's enemies are the men of his own house.* (Micah vii. 6.) Better for them, says S. Chrysostom, had you left them beggars: for, after all, they might from the very lowest state of destitution have been able to derive some good for their souls, as Lazarus derived from his sores so much good for his; but "no good at all can come of unjustly acquired riches." It is not lawful with such riches either to decorate Churches, or to provide for the poor, or to help charitable institutions, or to make any offerings to God. Without sin they can neither be retained, nor can they be spent. Tell me therefore, what person in the whole world is more wretched, than the man, who abounds in this kind of property? And this—this is what you wish at your death to leave, as a patrimony, to those you most love! Oh, cruel love! Oh, outrageous impiety! Oh, barbarous act of a distracted mind!

Antonio, Archbishop of Florence, mentions in his Summa a most atrocious case. One of these ungodly rich men, of whom we are speaking, was fast approaching his latter end; and was therefore exhorted by the Priest to restore those ill-acquired possessions, which were his sin. This, firm, as a rock, he refused to do. He would neither yield to entreaties, nor be wrought upon by menaces. His two sons therefore at last interfered, with a view to persuade him; to whom he replied, "I cannot, my sons, I cannot make any restitution; because, should I recover my health, I shall then be compelled to beg a hard-earned life from door to door: whereas, should I die, then you will have to beg." The sons answered, that, as for themselves, they wished him to dismiss all anxious thought: for they would much sooner have their father saved and themselves left poor, than themselves left rich and their father damned. On this, regarding them with a scowl, "Silence," he said, "ye children; you are void of all common sense. Have you yet to learn how much more pitiful GOD is, than man? If in this I commit sin, GOD, I have some reason to hope, will show me mercy: but, should you ever come to be beggars, what reason have you to hope for any pity from man?" Convinced by such foolish argument, as this, he miserably breathed his last. His dying words produced a strong impression on the minds of the two brothers, who are now heirs to the guiltily acquired property of their father: and so it happened, that one of them, wisely turning the matter over in his mind, decided upon making a full restitution of his moiety; but the other was bent on retaining his share for his own use. A short time elapsed, when this last wicked brother died... and him, in company with his father, did the good brother see appearing to him in a dream. They were both in Hell, chained, like two furious mastiffs, one to the other among a multitude of the reprobate; they were attacking, tearing, mangling each other with the most desperate ferocity; each ascribing to the other his torment and damnation. The father was cursing his son, and the son was cursing his father!

See then, my brother, on the relation of so celebrated an Archbishop, what will be the profit, accruing through all Eternity to fathers from the evil riches they left to their children, and to children from the evil riches they inherited of their fathers! Seemeth it now to you a proper thing, thus, at so costly a price, to purchase the short-lived prosperity of your family? If this be love to one's self, what, I ask, must be hatred? If this be helping one's relations, what must be persecuting them? Therefore, let it be determined, that, if money, when heaped up by improper means, could serve in any wise to raise a man's family, yet that such an elevation would be expedient neither to you, nor to yours. And then, consider, what must be the final result, when, as we have already proved, this is of all ways the very surest to effect your family's ruin? *Woe to him that coveteth an evil covetousness to his house, that he may set his nest on high.* (Hab. ii. 9.) But why so, holy prophet? Why so? *Thou hast consulted shame to thy house.* Do you ponder this in your minds: and I will take a little rest.

The Second Part.

9. Granting then, for all these weighty reasons, that you ought not, in contempt of God, to desire any riches for your family beyond those you at present possess, let me in the remainder of my discourse persuade you henceforth to lay aside all that immoderate anxious care, which, in your wish to provide for your successors, has by a cruel love led you to overlook the claims of your own soul. Oh, begin, just for once, to value what it is your highest interest to value, and to give it a serious place in your thoughts. You are already, it may be, advanced in years; your constitution shows symptoms of breaking: your death therefore is not far off. It cannot be very long, before you will have to stand before the Divine tribunal to give an account of your soul. On the one side Angels are already waiting for you, those faithful witnesses of all your actions; on the other side are devils, your relentless accusers: and you are still devising in your mind how, after your death, your heirs may fare most sumptuously, and be most comfortably housed, and live in all manner of delights. Do these then form your chief solicitude? Are these your most constant thoughts, just as if your state before the Divine tribunal would be more safe, in proportion as you had left your family more wealthy? I am quite aware that a prayer to the Lord for mercy on our souls, in the prospect of that Day, will avail us much, when we have it in our

power to say, "In obedience to Thy command, I have clothed so many, who were naked; I have maintained so many orphans; I have ransomed so many prisoners; I have fed so many hungry mouths; I have succeeded in promoting by so many many ways the glory of Thy Name! But not so, my Lord: I plead not this. Have mercy on me, because I have left my family amply provided for; because my successors will fare sumptuously every day; because they will recline at their ease on the expensive couches, I have provided, and indulge themselves on the fine silk cushions, I have left for their luxurious use: therefore have mercy on me, and save me!" If you think a plea of this kind can be of any service to you, then go on heaping up your money with all this intense anxiety: but, if you see how it will rather tell against you, turn this same anxiety, I beg you, into a better channel, and, instead of thinking so very much about other people, think of yourselves." But, if, nevertheless, you still feel some misgiving respecting your dear children, be fully persuaded that God will constantly have them under His more than paternal care, if you always make His honour your first consideration. Poor Ruth! Did she not betake herself to Bethlehem a young widow in absolute destitution? And yet, because God had her under His care, in that same country, where she was a perfect stranger, she met with a person in great affluence, who took her to be his wife. Poor Esther! Did she not dwell in Susa an orphan girl utterly unknown? And yet, because God had her under His protection, in that same country, where she was a slave, she met with a Prince of mighty power, who raised her to the throne? Trust then and earnestly believe that God will not fail to interest Himself in your welfare also: and, if you wish to have a beautiful pattern to copy after in this matter, set before you the example of the renowned Tobit.

10. He in his grey old age had one only child, a son, who was the hope of his family, the prop of his declining years, and almost a light to his blind eyes. Notwithstanding this, and though he doted on him with an extreme tenderness of affection, he was so far from any desire to enrich him by unlawful means, that, chancing one day to hear a kid bleating in his house, he immediately took alarm and cried out, "Woe

is me! What is it I hear? A kid in my house! Take care, I beseech you, that it be not the property of one of my neighbours, from whom it has escaped. If it be, restore it to its owners: for we must by no means eat nor even touch what belongs to another person. Is it not stolen? Render it to the owners: for it is not lawful to eat anything that is stolen." (Tobit ii. 13.) Nor did it satisfy him to act in this way: all his little savings, after the daily necessary wants of his own poor family were supplied, he charitably distributed among persons, more destitute and afflicted than himself. It might seem to his stripling of a son something almost cruel that his father, now far advanced in age, should so entirely neglect making, if not a handsome, yet a decent provision at least for his maintenance. Wherefore the old man, as if desirous of justifying his conduct in this respect, one day called him, and, after he had given him much useful instruction, acquainted him with the very slender means and the narrow income they possessed. Then with tears in his eyes, "Don't be anxious, my dear son," he added; "I well know how very little it is, that I can leave you: our dwelling is on the smallest scale; our raiment and mode of living are most wretched and contemptible; but know, my son, that we have wealth in abundance, if we are not destitute of a holy fear of the LORD and of a conscientious observance of His Law. Fear not, my son, that we are made poor; for thou hast much wealth, if thou fear GOD" (iv. 21.) Thus spake old Tobit. And think ye not, that, even as he promised, so it came to pass? Not very long after, the young man had the opportunity of forming a most desirable connection in marriage, and of settling in a very honourable and affluent condition of life. Now I wish you to learn a useful lesson from this example, and, when a proper occasion presents itself, that you would reason in private with your young people. "My sons," I would have you say, "you clearly see what is the present state of our family. I too, did I wish it, could amass wealth by that unprincipled industry, which is now resorted to by many in our own city. I, too, could avail myself of counterfeit bills of exchange, of fraudulent investments, of trickery, and double dealing, and forgery, and lawsuits, and a thousand other roguish methods of transacting business. But may

God preserve me from such sin! Never would I seek by these means to benefit you or myself. My dear children, fear God, and never give way to distrust: for you will have a good protector to take care of you. Don't envy your neighbours of your own grade in society, when you see them, by the help of their ill-gotten gains, erecting new houses, so much finer than those they were born in; or spreading their country villas close by your little property, on a scale far surpassing anything they inherited. Don't envy them on this account. 'Set not thine heart upon unjust possessions,' is the good counsel of the preacher (Ecclus. v. 1;) but rather bear in mind that a small patrimony is more to a good man, than a large one is to a sinner. *A small thing that the righteous hath is better than great riches of the ungodly.* (Ps. xxxvii. 16.) Leave them awhile to their own way; leave them to have now the advantage over you. God at some future day will render to every man his righteousness. Only observe His Law, honour and revere Him: then, should He fail to provide for you, come and complain of me. 'Fear not, my son, that we are made poor: for thou hast much wealth, if thou fear God.'"

Let such be the counsels you give to your children, after the pattern set you by good Tobit: and in the meanwhile begin to recollect yourself at your mature time of life, to care more for your soul than for your family, more for your conscience than your worldly business, more for God than Mammon. And, if in times past any among you should have begrimed your hands (which I can scarcely believe) with filthy ill-gotten lucre, shake off with the utmost possible speed the accursed thing. Satisfy the just demands of poor hirelings: pay your due to the support of the Church and its charities: fulfil the trusts, committed to you for pious purposes, and fear to retain in your hands, even for a single moment, that money, which can do nothing else, than cause perdition to yourself, bring ruin to those about you, and as Micah said, make the enmity of God burn implacably against your family. *The treasures of wickedness in the house of the wicked are as a flam*

www.ingramcontent.com/pod-product-compliance
Lightning Source LLC
Chambersburg PA
CBHW031737230426
43669CB00007B/370